RUSSIA THROUGH EUROPEAN EYES

No. 6

General Editor: Dr. A. G. CROSS, University of East Anglia

ENGLAND AND RUSSIA

ENGLAND AND RUSSIA

COMPRISING

THE VOYAGES OF
JOHN TRADESCANT THE ELDER,
SIR HUGH WILLOUGHBY, RICHARD CHANCELLOR,
NELSON, AND OTHERS

TO

THE WHITE SEA

BY

Dr. J. HAMEL

TRANSLATED BY
JOHN STUDDY LEIGH

LONDON AND NEW YORK

First published 1854 by
FRANK CASS AND COMPANY LIMITED

Published 2013 by Routledge
2 Park Square, Milton Park, Abingdon, Oxfordshire OX14 4RN
711 Third Avenue, New York, NY 10017, USA

First issued in paperback 2016

Routledge is an imprint of the Taylor and Francis Group, an informa business

All right reserved No part of this book may be reprinted or reproduced or utilised in any form or by any electronic, mechanical, or other means, now known or hereafter invented, including photocopying and recording, or in any information storage or retrieval system, without permission in writing from the publishers.

Notices
Product or corporate names may be trademarks or registered trademarks, and are used only for identification and explanation without intent to infringe.

ISBN 13: 978-1-138-99345-7 (pbk)
ISBN 13: 978-0-7146-1536-3 (hbk)

TRANSLATOR'S PREFACE.

At a period like the present, when we are involved in a contest with Russia, and when all information bearing on that country is caught up with avidity, to present to the public a translation of Dr. Hamel's valuable work may not be deemed a superfluous task; for, although his historical and descriptive sketches are somewhat loosely scattered through its pages, they possess the advantage of coming from the pen of a Russian who unwittingly discloses to our generation much of the aggressive and barbarous policy by which the rulers of his country were actuated even at the early period to which this Work principally relates.

Moreover now that, notwithstanding the great scarcity of books hitherto published having reference to that vast empire, our information with regard to its present resources is gradually becoming more correct, and we are made aware of their importance, it is curious to observe, in Dr. Hamel's notices, how very insignificant they must have been at that time; for we find that, in spite of Russia's would-be aggrandisement, she was subjected to repeated disasters, owing to her inability to defend herself effectually either against the Poles on the one side, or against the Tartars on the other, whilst at the same period she was oppressing the Fins, Samoiedes, and other tribes, who were destitute of the means and were too few in number to oppose her.

But before proceeding any further with the deductions to which a perusal of the Work itself naturally leads, we will mention what knowledge we possess of the author, and ascertain how he became acquainted with the facts he adduces, and what reliance can be placed on his statements. Unfortunately that knowledge is not very extensive; for we are merely informed that Dr. Hamel came to England in the train of the Emperor Alexander in 1814, and that with so good an introduction, and his already acquired reputation for learning and science, he found no difficulty then and in succeeding years in obtaining access to many of our public establishments, and, more especially with reference to this Work, to the Bodleian Library and the Ashmolean Museum at Oxford. There he diligently applied himself to decipher the MSS. containing accounts of the early naval and commercial intercourse between the two countries, a task in which he was eminently successful, as will be seen by the following pages, where much is brought to light that is interesting, not only from its relation to the voyages of the northern navigators of those days, and, as already mentioned, to the history of Russia, but to that of England herself. So far as regards his sketches of his own country, he was also in a great measure favoured by his position, which enabled him to have recourse to the archives at St. Petersburg and Moscow, for he was (and probably still is) a Privy Councillor, and a Member of the Imperial Academy of Sciences.

One of the most striking points in the whole Work is to be found in the first page, where the author recommends, that in order to commemorate the long duration of amicable intercourse between England and Russia, which at the time he wrote (1846) had existed uninterruptedly for nearly three centuries, there should be a jubilee in 1853, when that period would be completed, and which, owing to a curious coincidence, proved to be the very year in which diplomatic relations ceased between the two countries, followed by the war in which we are at present engaged. Unfortunately, then, Dr. Hamel's amicable idea has been frustrated by events which must have inflicted much pain on a mind imbued with such friendly feelings towards the English.

What will also strike the reader is the elaborate minuteness with which he has sought out and given the genealogy, with all its ramifications, of the families, not only of the leaders, but even of the abettors, of the early voyages of discovery to the North, and more especially that of Sir Hugh Willoughby, the chief of the first expedition which reached Russia from our shores, and who, with the crews of two vessels, perished miserably, being frozen to death, in the winter of 1553-54. To those devoted to studies of this nature, the details he gives will doubtless prove highly interesting, and possibly throw light on circumstances connected with the ancestry of some of our aristocracy which were previously either obscure, or not known to the mass of readers.

In his recapitulation of voyages in the Arctic Ocean, there are likewise several statements which deserve notice, particularly that James Bisbrown, commanding a vessel Hamel does not name, but sailing out of Liverpool in 1765, reached the extraordinary latitude of 83° 40′, and then saw open sea before him towards the north, whilst, at the same time, the weather was mild and genial. Might not this circumstance, corroborated as it has been by our later discoveries, lead us still to hope that Franklin, or, at all events, many of his brave companions, may survive and be restored to us?

As other subjects interesting to the public, and especially to the mercantile community, we may allude to the details Hamel gives of the establishment of English factories in Russia; the nature of the cargoes we at first shipped to that country, and of those we received in return; the mode of bartering, and the value of English and Russian commodities at that early epoch of our commercial intercourse, and the reception given by us to the first Russian ambassadors—all information derived from the beforementioned MSS., which for so long an interval had remained unnoticed, and of which Dr. Hamel has so industriously availed himself.

Of Tradescant, the elder, no mention is made until towards the close of the first section, and to him Hamel justly ascribes the merit of establishing the first museum in England, which now incorrectly goes by the name of the Ashmolean, so called from Ashmole, to whom Tradescant, the younger, bequeathed it, but the contents of which were collected by the former indefatigable naturalist and botanist, whose descriptions will doubtless prove acceptable to the scientific of the present day.

London, 5th June, 1854.

CONTENTS.

CHAPTER I.

Arrival of Sir Hugh Willoughby and Richard Chancellor at the Mouth of the Dwina in 1553 1

CHAPTER II.

Early Russian Voyages—Intercourse between Russia and Western Europe 32

CHAPTER III.

Melancholy end of Sir Hugh Willoughby—Chancellor's Visit to Moscow 86

CHAPTER IV.

Establishment of the Russia Company—Chancellor's Second Expedition 108

CHAPTER V.

Shipwreck and Death of Chancellor—Escape of the Russian Ambassador, Nepeja, and his Arrival in England . . 142

CHAPTER VI.

Voyage of Anthony Jenkinson—Raphael Barberini in Russia, with a Letter of Queen Elizabeth to the Czar Ivan Vassilovitch 158

CONTENTS.

CHAPTER VII.

First Arrival of Russian Merchants in London—Their Reception by Queen Elizabeth—The Czar Ivan Vassilovitch's Proposal of Marriage to the Queen — New Charter Granted to the Russia Company . . . 181

CHAPTER VIII.

Treachery and Punishment of Doctor Bomel — Dissatisfaction of the Czar at the Conduct of the English—Suspension of the Russia Company's Charter—Moscow Burnt by the Tartars—English House in the Varvarka Destroyed—Robert Best and Anthony Jenkinson Dispatched from England with Letters to the Czar . . 201

CHAPTER IX.

Negotiations of Daniel Sylvester—Freedom of Trade Restored to the Russia Company—English Depôt at Rose Island 220

CHAPTER X.

Voyage of Tradescant—Memoir of Tradescant—His Collection of Varieties—Discovery of a MS. by Tradescant, a narrative of his voyage to Archangel 243

CHAPTER XI.

Tradescant's Description of Life in Russia — Forests—Flowers—Dress—Origin of the English Whale Fishery—His Voyage Home 269

CHAPTER XII.

Geographical Discoveries promoted by Members of the Russia Company—Sir Francis Cherry and others . . 299

CHAPTER XIII.

Expeditions of the Russia Company from 1612 — Their Utility in the Advancement of Science . . . 325

CHAPTER XIV.

Companions of Tradescant in his Voyage to Archangel—Sir John Merrick—Sir Thomas Smith — Sir Dudley Digges—Dr. Richard James—Captain David Gilbert—Captain Robert Carr—Jessy de Quester . . . 374

APPENDIX 409

ENGLAND AND RUSSIA;

COMPRISING THE

VOYAGES OF TRADESCANT THE ELDER,

AND OTHERS.

CHAPTER I.

ARRIVAL OF SIR HUGH WILLOUGHBY AND RICHARD CHANCELLOR AT THE MOUTH OF THE DWINA IN 1553.

As it is my purpose to describe the visit made to Archangel in the year 1618 by the great English naturalist, John Tradescant, it may be as well to cast a glance, by way of introduction, on the first arrival of the English at the mouth of the Dwina.

Nearly three hundred years have now elapsed since England there greeted Muscovy. So great have been the benefits to trade, the arts, and industry in general, arising from the friendly relations between England and Russia, which, in 1853, completed the third century of their continuance, that one might have expected to see this period closed, in both countries, with a jubilee to commemorate so remarkable an example of uninterrupted amicable intercourse between nations.

On the 24th of August, in the year 1553, the ship Edward Bonaventure cast anchor on the southern shore of the White Sea, in front of the settlement "Possad" of Nenocksa, not far from the Korelian mouth of the Dwina. Richard Chancellor was chief in command of this vessel, and Stephen Burrough, ever memorable in the history of navigation (as was also his assistant, John Buckland), was sailing-master.

The arrival of this English ship on the Russian coast was merely accidental, for her real destination was China and India. The recent voyages round the globe, which had been attended with remarkable geographical discoveries, had led to the present expedition, so that this landing near Nenocksa was connected with the most important epoch in the history of navigation.

Lisbon, owing to the conquests made by the Portuguese in Western Africa in the last quarter of the fifteenth century, and the acquisition of a part of India after Vasco de Gama's voyage, had become a second Venice. Spain, through the discovery by Columbus of the southern portion of the New World which had fallen to her share, was accumulating countless riches at Cadiz and Seville. These acquisitions, as is well known, England had allowed to escape her, and was now obliged to content herself with the commercial advantages of minor importance, which had fallen to her share through the discovery by Cabot, of the northern portion of the new Continent.

England's maritime trade was thereby comparatively restricted, although many an obstacle to its extension had already been removed. The Hanseatic League sought to maintain its old and odious monopoly, although in 1505 an English corporation of merchant adventurers had likewise been established for trading to the Netherlands, where Antwerp occupied the first place among the commercial towns of Europe. But in 1551 a serious inquiry was instituted into the complaints incessantly made against the Hanseatic League, in consequence of which the Steelyard was at length deprived of its unreasonable privileges. Thus were loosened the strong fetters by which commercial speculation in England had been cramped, and London merchants were tempted to imitate the examples of Portugal and Spain, and seek new paths for commerce on the sea. It was a favourable circumstance that at that time Sebastian Cabot, who belonged to that period of great discoveries, was still living in England, and could opportunely impart the experience which he had acquired in the course of half a century. When only twenty years of age he had already (in 1497) made the memorable voyage in the ship Matthew belonging to his native city of Bristol, during which, on the 24th June, North America was discovered.

His father, Giovanni Cabot or Caboto, was a Venetian, but Sebastian, as already stated, was born at Bristol, in the year 1477; and, when barely four years old, he was taken by his father to Venice, where he remained some time. The Royal Letters Patent issued by Henry the Seventh for the discovery of a North-West passage, through which Europe was made aware of the existence of North America, were made out on the 5th of March, 1496, in the names of Giovanni, and his three sons. Ferdinand the Second, King of Arragon, wrote in 1512 to Lord Willoughby, Baron de Broke, who was then in Arragon with the English troops sent thither in fulfilment of the terms of the alliance against France, to invite Sebastian Cabot to come to him from England. This was done, and Cabot entered into Ferdinand's service, but returned to England after the death of the latter in 1516. To record all that he had performed there up to 1518, and what he had done in Spain, as well as the voyages undertaken by him, would lead us too far from our subject. Nevertheless we may observe, that after his return to England for the last time, in 1548, the Emperor Charles the Fifth requested Edward the Sixth, through Sir Thomas Cheyne, who, as a reward for his valour in the defence of Boulogne, had been named ambassador to Spain, to send Cabot back, as he, the Emperor, much required his services, (Cabot indeed received a pension from him,) whilst he would be of less use to England in the naval expeditions which she was then fitting out. Notwithstanding this invitation, Cabot remained in his own country, where the Court, as well as the speculating mercantile public, knew well how to appreciate his services. He received a pension in the year 1549, and in 1551 a present of money; and an effort was made to turn to account his extensive knowledge of naval affairs.

For a long time he had entertained the opinion, already plainly expressed by Robert Thorne at Bristol in 1527, that India and China, (at that time Cathay, and still called by the Russians Kitai,) might be reached from England by sailing northward round Norway, and finding a strait similar to that of Magellan, in order to compete with Portugal and Spain by this route. This project he imparted to several of the merchant adventurers in London, who, in connection with sundry other persons, formed a company by the allotment of shares, appointed Cabot, the promoter of the scheme, to be Director thereof, and determined on making an experiment. This company received the name of " The Mystery, Company, and Fellowship of Merchant Adventurers for the Discovery of unknown Lands, &c."

In 1552 and 1553 three ships were fitted out in the most careful manner: the Bona Esperanza of 120, the Edward Bonaventure of 160, and the Bona Confidentia of 90 tons; and each vessel had a pinnace and a boat. As Cabot was too old himself to take the command of the expedition, it was confided to another, he, nevertheless, drawing out the plan of operations for the voyage. Sir Hugh Willoughby was appointed chief, and Richard Chancellor second leader.

Here the question naturally suggests itself—Who were these persons, hitherto unknown as Navigators? And how happened it, that the command of so important a maritime undertaking was confided to them?

In the account of the Expedition compiled by Clement Adams, Governor of the King's Pages, from the communications made to him by Chancellor, the only mention made of Sir Hugh Willoughby is, that he was a man of good birth ("vir strenuus non obscuro loco natus"), well-known on account of his military merit, ("ob singularem in re bellicâ industriam"), and distinguished by a stately and imposing exterior ("ob corporis formam; erat enim procerae staturae"). Let us endeavour to obtain a better insight into the history of so interesting a person.

The first recorded ancestor of Sir Hugh Willoughby was, at the end of the thirteenth century, settled at Willoughby upon the Would, on the southern boundary of the county of Nottingham. At that time another Willoughby (it was written then Willegby, Willoweby,) had already, through his marriage with an heiress of the old house of Bec, in the neighbouring county of Lincoln, received the title of Baron d'Eresby, whose family still exists, and since 1828 has been represented by Peter Robert (Drummond) Burrell. From this stem, likewise, sprung two other families with the title of Baron: in 1492 that of Broke, and in 1547 that of Parham, which became extinct in 1779.

Although Sir Hugh's ancestors, the descendants of the Nottinghamshire Willoughby, did not rise quite so suddenly to distinction, still we find them as early as the year 1320 in possession of the estate of Wollaton, four miles west of the town of Nottingham, and soon afterwards holding that of Risley, not far distant, although in Derbyshire. At a later period they came into possession of Middleton, in Warwickshire, as well as of other property.

The name of Sir Hugh's father was Henry. Through his prowess in battle, he had won not only the honour of knighthood, but likewise the title of

Banneret. The first he received after the victory, which, on the 16th of June, 1487, he assisted in gaining, in presence of King Henry the Seventh, over the Dutch and Irish troops which had been assembled in favour of the Pretender Lambert Simnel. This battle was fought in Nottinghamshire, not far from the Wollaton estate, at East Stoke to the south of Newark-upon-Trent. He became a Banneret on the 17th of June, 1497, in consequence of the valiant conduct by which he distinguished himself in the fight on Blackheath Common, near London, where the rebels from Cornwall were defeated. He died on the 7th of May, 1528, and was buried in Wollaton Church. Sir Henry married four times. By his first wife he had two sons, John and Edward: the second and fourth died childless; the third was the mother of Sir Hugh referred to in our narrative.

The eldest son, John, the offspring of Sir Henry's first marriage with Margaret Markham, a daughter of Sir Robert Markham, of Coatham, in Nottinghamshire, was knighted in the year 1533, on the occasion of the coronation of Ann Boleyn, Henry the Eighth's second consort. He married Anne Grey, eldest daughter of Baron Edward Grey, Viscount de Lisle, and died in 1547, leaving no children.

The elder brother of the Viscount de Lisle, Baron John Grey, who was slain in 1460, in the battle of St. Alban's, was the first husband of the beautiful Elizabeth Woodville, whose charms, even when she was a widow, had sufficient power to enthral King Edward the Fourth. She became Queen in 1464, and was the mother of King Edward the Fifth and of Henry the Seventh's queen consort. In consequence of this marriage, the family of the Barons Grey (of Groby) acquired considerable power; but it was also the cause of a bloody war, and of all the great events which took place in 1469 and the following years. The son of this Elizabeth, Thomas Grey, was at first Earl of Huntingdon, and afterwards Marquis of Dorset.

Edward, the younger, brother of John Willoughby, whose line, at John's death, came into possession of the property, married Ann Filliol, eldest daughter of Sir William Filliol, of Woodlands, in Dorsetshire, and co-heiress of his great wealth. The younger sister, Catherine Filliol, was the first wife of Edward Seymour, afterwards (in 1547) Duke of Somerset. Anne Filliol had one son by Edward Willoughby, named Henry. After her first husband's death, she married Lord St. John, one of the sixteen statesmen named by Henry the Eighth, in his will, to form the Regency during the minority of his son Edward.

This Henry Willoughby, named above, took to wife Anne Grey, one of the daughters of Thomas Grey, second Marquis of Dorset. He was the son of the Thomas Grey before mentioned. The brother of this Anne Willoughby contracted a matrimonial alliance still more elevated than had fallen to his lot through his descent, for his second wife, Frances Brandon, was the niece of the reigning king. As she was left the only child and heiress of Charles Brandon, Duke of Suffolk, by his third marriage with Mary Tudor, widow of King Louis the Twelfth, and sister of Henry the Eighth, he (in 1551) obtained the ducal title of Suffolk. The eldest daughter, by Grey's marriage with Frances Brandon, was that memorable lady Jane Grey, whom Roger Ascham, in 1550, when she was thirteen years old, surprised at their country house, at Broadgate, with Plato in her hand, whilst the family were amusing themselves out of doors, and who, three years later (in 1553), was, against her wishes, called for a short time Queen of England, after she had married Lord Guildford Dudley, a son of John Dudley, Duke of Northumberland, who became Duke in 1551, was Earl of Warwick in 1547, Viscount de Lisle in 1542. A sister of the Lord Guildford Dudley, Catherine, married Henry Hastings, third Earl of Huntingdon, but had no children. Her consort was the son of Francis Hastings, second Earl of Huntingdon, and of Catherine Pole, eldest daughter of Henry Pole, Baron de Montacute, grandson of George Plantagenet, Duke of Clarence, and nephew of King Edward the Fourth. Henry Hastings had two remaining sisters, who were considerably younger, Ann and Mary, whom I here name, because Queen Elizabeth proposed to the Czar Ivan Vassilovitch, that he should marry one of these Ladies Hastings (probably Mary, the younger) when he showed an inclination to obtain the Queen's own hand. Henry Willoughby had by Ann Grey, two sons, Thomas and Francis. As for himself, he was slain at Norwich, which town he had entered with the troops assembled to disperse the powerful body of rebels led by Robert Ket, a tanner. The· before-mentioned John Dudley, at that time

Earl of Warwick, was chief in command when the victory was gained.

The young Thomas Willoughby, after his father Henry's death in 1543, came into possession of Wollaton besides other property. He was barely thirteen years old when his great uncle, Sir Hugh Willoughby, undertook the voyage to Cathay, in 1553. He had scarcely married Dorothy Paget, one of the daughters of the accomplished diplomatist, Baron William Paget de Beaudessert, the ancestor of the late Marquis of Anglesey, when he died, in 1558, without issue.

The estate descended to his younger brother Francis, at that time but eleven years old. At a later period, between 1580 and 1588, the latter built the house at Wollaton, which is one of the most beautiful architectural monuments remaining of the Elizabethan age. The architect was Robert Smithson. Thorp, however, appears to have been consulted. The stone was quarried at Ancaster, in Lincolnshire, and it must have been exchanged for pit coal!

Sir Francis Willoughby married Elizabeth Lyttelton, the eldest daughter of Sir John Lyttelton of Frankley, who bore him six daughters.

In addition to other property which Sir John Lyttelton acquired by purchase, was the beautiful country seat of Hagley Park, since mentioned by Pope in his Poems, which still belongs to his descendant, Lord Lyttelton, who resides there.

I find that somewhat later, Francis Willoughby separated from his wife. Thirteen months before his death he contracted a second matrimonial alliance with the widow Dorothy Tamworth (*née* Coleby), who managed to spend a great deal of his wealth, and, after Willoughby's death, became the spouse of Lord Philip Wharton.

Sir Francis died in 1597. His eldest daughter, Bridget, who inherited Wollaton, and a great part of her father's wealth, married Percival Willoughby (who was knighted in 1603) of Bore Place, in Kent. They had one son, Francis.

Thomas Willoughby, uncle both to the first William Willoughby d'Eresby, who, on the 17th of February, 1547, was created Baron of Parham, and to the before-mentioned Charles Brandon, who after the death of the king's daughter, his third wife, took, as his fourth, Catherine Willoughby d'Eresby, was in 1539 appointed, by Henry the Eighth, Lord Chief Justice in the Court of Common Pleas. The above-mentioned Percival, who married Bridget Willoughby, was his great uncle.

Francis Willoughby, who was likewise knighted, married Cassandra Ridgway, the daughter of Thomas Ridgway, Earl of Londonderry. From this marriage sprang Francis Willoughby, well known to lovers of natural history as an ornithologist and ichthyologist. He spent his youth at Trinity College Cambridge, and there became a friend of John Wray (since 1669 spelt Ray), the Linnæus of his time, afterwards so famed as a botanist. The latter was eight years older than he, and superintended his studies, out of gratitude for which Willoughby supplied him with ample resources for the study of nature and for travelling. From 1661 to 1666 they made several tours together as naturalists, both at home and abroad.

They certainly visited together, when they came to London, Tradescant's Museum, as well as the gardens at South Lambeth. Wray tells us (in 1676) that they there saw the stuffed Dodo. Wray found there likewise the Puffin mentioned at page 3 of Tradescant's Catalogue (*Anas Arctica clusii, Mormus arcticus seu Fratercula Arctica* of the moderns), which is also to be met with in the Royal Society's collection (Grew's Museum Regalis Societatis, 1681, p. 72), of a larger size than the specimen described by Willoughby. They travelled abroad, from 1663 until 1666, in Holland, France, Germany, Switzerland, Italy, Sicily, and Malta. Willoughby was likewise in Spain in 1664.

At the formation of the Royal Society in the year 1663, Francis Willoughby was immediately elected a Fellow, but Wray was not admitted to this honour until 1667. Willoughby, whose father died in 1665, resided at Middleton Hall, where he established a Museum of Natural History. In 1668 he married Emma Bernard, the daughter of Sir Henry Bernard. Wray took up his residence with him soon afterwards at Middleton Hall, where they made observations together on the ascent of the sap in trees. In the year 1670 Wray dedicated his "Catalogus Plantarum Angliæ" to his highly-respected friend and Mæcenas, Francis Willoughby. The mother of the latter died in 1676.

A few years subsequently to 1668, Willoughby was preparing to undertake a voyage to America for the purposes of science, but died on the 3rd of July, 1672, after appointing his friend Wray to take charge of the education of his two sons, Francis and Thomas, who were still very young. Wray on this account continued to reside at Middleton Hall. He there wrote, in 1672, as he says, for the use of his pupils, the eldest of whom, however, was barely four years old, his " Nomenclator Classicus of Animals and Plants," and then undertook the revision and publication of the " History of Birds," which Willoughby had left behind him. This Ornithology first came out in Latin in 1676. Willoughby's widow, Emma Bernard, disputed payment of the expenses, which were considerable on account of the seventy-seven copper plates. In the preface Wray dwells upon the excellent qualities of the heart and understanding which distinguished his departed friend and patron. The "Ichthyology" he commenced in 1684, and it appeared in 1686. Here I must incidentally remark that the zoologist wrote his name Willughby; his father, and also his great-grandfather, had written it Wyllughby. The eldest son, Francis Willoughby, had not yet attained the age of seven years, when, in 1676—probably as an acknowledgment of the scientific services of his father (the "Ornithology" had just appeared)—he was created a Baronet. He died in 1688 unmarried.

His brother Thomas inherited the property and title. Wray dedicated to him in 1690 the first edition of his " Synopsis Methodica Stirpium Britannicarum." He exhorted him to follow the example of his excellent father in promoting the study of Natural History. This second baronet, Sir Thomas Willoughby, was, in 1693, elected a Fellow of the Royal Society. He was likewise for several sessions a member of Parliament. In the year 1711 Queen Anne bestowed upon him the title of Baron as Lord Middleton of Middleton. He died in 1729.

The present representative of the family, Digby Willoughby, who succeeded in 1835, is the seventh baron. Besides Wollaton House, which is so interesting in an architectural point of view, he is proprietor also of Middleton Hall.

I now come to Sir Henry Willoughby's third son, Sir Hugh Willoughby, with whom we are more immediately concerned. His mother was Ellen Egerton, daughter and heiress of John Egerton, of Wrinehill, in Cheshire, who married the eldest daughter of Sir John Gresley. Who is not reminded by the name of Egerton, not only of the well-known Lord Chancellor Thomas, Baron of Ellesmere, afterwards Viscount de Brackley, but of Francis, third and last Duke of Bridgewater, who, with Brindley's assistance, laid the foundation of the inland navigation of England, and so essentially contributed by his canal to extend the industry of Manchester?

His Majesty, our most gracious Emperor, on the 21st of December, 1816 (2nd of January 1817, new style), stopped to examine this great and useful work, and went some distance on the Bridgewater Canal and into the Tunnel at Worsley, in order there to see the mode of obtaining pit coal. The excellent writings of Buckland, Whewell, Charles Bell, Roget, Kirby, Kidd, Chambers, and Prout, demonstrative of the might, wisdom, and goodness of God, displayed in the creation, will always bring to our recollection Henry Francis, Earl of Bridgewater, with whom this title died in 1829.* Wrinehall has since come into the possession of the family of Lord Grey de Wilton. The very old house of Gresley still has its representatives at Drakelow in Derbyshire.

By what has been said of Hugh Willoughby's brother, we know that he had good connections at Court. He was one of the persons appointed to receive Ann of Cleves, in 1539-40, when Henry the Eighth sent to Flanders for her. He was also steward of the royal household.

Had Hugh's brother Edward, like the elder, John, left no son, Hugh would have succeeded to the Wollaton, Middleton, and other estates; but as Edward was succeeded by his son Henry, and the latter again by Thomas, Hugh was induced to embrace the military profession. Owing to the position of England at that time, when war was about to be declared against Scotland, and afterwards against France, an opportunity was not wanting for him to acquire fame in the field of honour.

In 1542 an army was sent to Scotland, and soon afterwards Mary Stuart was born. Henry the Eighth wished to secure possession of this Princess for his son Edward, at that time fifteen years old. As this union

* In addition, I may here remark that Lord Francis Leveson Gower, brother of the present (the second) Duke of Sutherland, George Granville, took the name of Egerton in 1833, because he inherited the whole of the great Bridgewater property. He as well as the Duke are great grandsons of Louisa Egerton, daughter of the first Duke of Bridgewater, and the latter, again, was great grandson to the first Earl of Bridgewater, whose wife was a

was agreed to in Scotland in 1543, but immediately afterwards opposed by Cardinal Beatoun, the King of England sent a strong army there in 1544, under the Earl of Hertford, as Commander-in-chief. Hugh Willoughby accompanied this Scottish expedition. John Dudley, at that time Viscount de Lisle and Lord High Admiral of England, subsequently Earl of Warwick and at last Duke of Northumberland, received on board his powerful fleet, of about two hundred sail, anchored at the mouth of the Tyne, below Newcastle, the troops which had marched thither, and landed them in the Firth of Forth, at Granton and Newhaven, not far from Leith. This place, as well as Edinburgh, into which they forced an entrance through the Canongate, was taken, and, for the most part, burnt; the environs were likewise laid waste. During the whole of this singular courtship, Hugh Willoughby distinguished himself so much that he was knighted at Leith on the 11th of May, by the Earl of Hertford, Commander-in-chief; and on this occasion a dragon was added to his ancient coat of arms.

I need scarcely here observe that the Earl of Hertford was the same Edward Seymour whose marriage with Edward Willoughby's sister-in-law we have already mentioned. He was brother to Jane Seymour, Edward's mother; obtained the honor of knighthood in 1553; and in 1536, when Henry the Eighth married his sister, was

great-grand-daughter of the before-mentioned Mary Brandon. Now (in June, 1846) Lord Francis Egerton has been created Viscount Brackley, of Brackley, and Earl of Ellesmere. His Lordship, as is well known, assisted Agassiz in the publication of his work on the fossil fishes of the old red sandstone.

created Viscount de Beauchamp. At Edward's birth (in 1537) he became Earl of Hertford, afterwards Knight of the Garter, and then Lord Chamberlain. In 1544 he was appointed to the chief command in the north; for as at that time England had a frontier, a land-force was required, besides the " wooden walls" along the coast, for its defence. On the 6th of February, 1547, he knighted Edward the Sixth, his nephew, who had then just succeeded to the crown. This was his first act after taking into his hands the reins of government as Regent appointed in the will of Henry the Eighth. On the 10th of February he became Lord Treasurer, on the 16th Duke of Somerset, and on the 17th Lord Marshal of England, and received the title of Governor of His Majesty, Protector of the English Realm, and Lieutenant-General of the whole army. He had a palace built for himself, in the Strand, by an Italian architect, which edifice (Somerset House), renovated and much enlarged in 1775, is at present the focus of science in England. Here, since 1780, the Royal Society has held its meetings; and here, since 1781, the Antiquarian, and at later periods the Astronomical, the Geological, and other learned societies, as well as the Senate of the London University, have assembled. Here are King's College, where Daniell taught Chemistry and Wheatston gave lectures on Natural Philosophy; the free School of Design in the halls, where formerly were the public exhibitions of paintings; and moreover a number of offices, partly occupied by the Naval Department, partly by that of Taxes, the Poor Law Commission, &c., &c. Somerset's brother, Sir Thomas Seymour, who, together with Sir Hugh Willoughby, went in 1539-1540 to receive Ann of Cleves, became, on the 16th of February, 1547, Baron of Sudley and Lord High Admiral. He married the widowed Queen, Catherine Parr On his family escutcheon Sir Hugh Willoughby bore very old military blazonry, not often met with, three double (united by a thong at top) "water bougets," buckets formerly used to carry water on the back in camp, and which can still be seen in Lord Middleton's coat of arms. These water bougets, the ancestor of the family, then called Bugg, but who took the name of Willoughby from the places belonging to him, adopted in his escutcheon as far back as the thirteenth century.

Sir Hugh Willoughby remained constant to his military calling, and fought bravely in several campaigns. During the latter part of the hostilities with Scotland, under Somerset's administration, he defended Fort Lowder, so called by the Scots. This is the present Castle of Thirlestane, in Berwickshire, near the town of Lauder on the river Leader, from the vale of which Lord Lauderdale, to whom Thirlestane likewise belongs, derived his title in 1624. This fortress, as well as the others then in the possession of the English, were assaulted and besieged by the Scotch and French, in 1549-1550, in the most fierce and obstinate manner. Broughty Castle, on the Firth of Tay, was taken on the 20th of February, 1550, and the whole of the English garrison put to the sword without mercy: but the valiant Sir Hugh was determined not to yield Fort Lowder, and the resources at his command for its defence were already so much exhausted, that all the pewter vessels in the place had been cast into balls, when peace was concluded.

Sir Hugh Willoughby married Jane Strelly, a daughter of Sir Nicholas Strelly, of Strelly, near Wollaton. We find him again in 1551 on the frontiers of England and Scotland, and likewise in the East marches, doing active military service. Sir Hugh had one son, Henry, whose name is met with in the accounts of Sir Francis Willoughby (the builder of Wollaton House) from 1578, with a yearly allowance assigned to him of twenty pounds out of the Wollaton property.

The ruin of Somerset, which commenced in 1549, and ended, at the beginning of 1552, with his execution (he had already removed from his path the High Admiral Baron de Sudley, who had intrigued against him), probably interfered with Sir Hugh Willoughby's further advancement in his military career. He nevertheless retained the intimacy of some who held office under the Regency; and it is deserving of remark, that they were especially persons, more or less connected with the naval department.

The Duke of Northumberland succeeded Somerset in his high position in the Regency; and, as we have seen, commanded in 1544, as Lord Admiral (he was then Viscount de Lisle), the fleet which conveyed to Scotland the troops, amongst whom was Sir Hugh Willoughby. Edward Clinton (Baron of Clinton and Say), who returned from Boulogne in 1550, succeeded the Baron de Sudley as Lord High Admiral of England, Ireland, and Wales, as well as of their dependencies and Islands; of the city of Calais, and the territory belonging to it; and of Normandy, Gascony, and Aquitaine. With this new naval commander, Sir Hugh was likewise acquainted, for they had both been knighted by the Earl of Hertford, on the same day. It was Lord Clinton, who in 1547, as Admiral of the North sea, took Broughty Castle, on the Firth of Tay, when Hertford won the battle of Pinkey.

In King Edward the Sixth's autograph journal there is the following entry on the 4th of July, 1551: "I was banketted by the L. Clinton at Deptford, where I saw the ships Primrose and Marie Willowby launched." The last must have been named after Mary Salines, who was the mother of Catherine Brandon, and she again the stepmother of Frances Grey. Mary Salines was by birth a Spaniard, and formed one of the court of Henry the Eighth's first consort, Catherine of Arragon, through whose friendly interposition she became the wife of the rich William Willoughby, the last Baron d'Eresby of the original line. She presented him with a daughter; and this was the Catherine Willoughby, named after that Queen, whose personal charms, as well as considerable inheritance, induced Charles Brandon, Duke of Suffolk, to marry her (she being his fourth wife), after the death of the King's daughter, Mary Tudor; whence she became the step-grandmother of Lady Jane Grey. The nephew of this Mary Willoughby, who received the name of William, after her husband, was the same on whom, on the 20th of February, 1547, the title of Baron of Parham was bestowed; and his son married Margaret Clinton, the daughter of the Lord High Admiral. Catherine

Willoughby, after the death of the Duke of Suffolk in 1505, became the wife of Richard Bertu, to whose son Peregrine, the extinct title of Eresby was granted. Her two sons by the first marriage, Henry Duke of Suffolk, and Charles Brandon, both died within a few hours of each other, ten days after the naming of the ship after their grandmother, viz. on the 14th of July, 1551.

We have seen that, in the year 1512, Lord Willoughby de Broke, in compliance with the wish expressed by King Ferdinand, invited Cabot to enter into the service of Arragon. This Lord Willoughby's name was Robert, and he was the second, and at the same time the last, Baron de Broke of that line. His second wife was Dorothy Grey, the sister of Thomas Grey, second Marquis of Dorset, who at that time (in 1512) was the Commander-in-Chief of the British Army in Arragon. We know further, that this Thomas Grey's daughter Ann, sister to Henry Grey, Duke of Suffolk, and also aunt of Lady Jane Grey, was the wife of Henry Willoughby, Sir Hugh's nephew. It may perhaps be as well here to observe, that Elizabeth Willoughby, mother of the then Earl of Arundel, Henry Fitz-Alan, was a daughter of the beforementioned Lord Willoughby de Broke, and that the Earl of Arundel married Catherine Grey, the elder sister of Ann Willoughby. Thus Cabot's introduction to Ferdinand, King of Arragon, was brought about by a relative of Sir Hugh Willoughby; and, consequently, we may infer that this circumstance contributed to Cabot's appointing him to the command of the great

North-Eastern Expedition to Cathay. To be connected with the Grey family was, indeed, at that time, a powerful recommendation.

Cabot's proposal for a voyage of discovery fell under the cognizance of the Lord High Admiral, Lord Clinton; and I find, from manuscript documents, that he expressed himself ready to issue the necessary orders for levying the seamen required. I also possess a copy of an unpublished letter, written, in the King's name, by which Sir Hugh was authorised to man and equip the three vessels, as well as to maintain the necessary discipline on board.

Richard Chancellor was proposed as second in command of the expedition by Sir Henry Sidney, father of the still better known Sir Philip Sidney. Henry Sidney was brought up with the young Prince Edward; for his father, Sir William Sidney, was Chamberlain and Steward of this Prince's Household. This led to his being appointed, when Edward became King, one of his four Privy Chamberlains; and he was most favored by his confidence. In the year 1550 he was knighted, and in 1552 married Northumberland's daughter, Mary Dudley, whose brother, Guildford Dudley, became in 1553 Lady Jane Grey's husband. Sir Henry Sidney recommended Chancellor to the company as a man in the highest degree fitted for carrying out their purpose, and as one whom he knew most intimately from daily intercourse ("quotidiano convictu hominis ingenium penitus habeo perspectum et exploratum").

It appears that Richard Chancellor had already, at some earlier period, made a sea-voyage, although not as commander; for in the year 1551 he accompanied Captain Roger Bodenham in the barque Aucher, belonging to Sir Anthony Aucher, which went to Chios and Candia with merchandise, leaving the Thames in November, 1550, though she was unable to sail from Plymouth until the 13th January, 1551. She was nearly taken by the Turks. Her homeward cargo consisted of wines, and the pilot's name was William Sherwood.

Chancellor must also have been in France, for in his description of the Czar Ivan Vassilovitch's warlike preparations, he says: "I have seen the pavilions of the Kings of England and France, which are beautiful but do not equal this."

He appears to have possessed talents for mechanism, for he had a quadrant of five feet radius, constructed according to his own directions, with which he made observations after his return from Russia, in company with John Dee, in whose Ephemerides (1554 and 1555) they are mentioned. This instrument John Dee, who calls it an excellent one ("one excellent, strong, and fayre quadrant, first made by that famous Richard Chancellor, wherewith he and I made sundry observations"), was used at a later period by Bromfield, at that time Lieutenant of Artillery, who had improved it; but it was destroyed ("most barborously spoyled, and with hammers smytt in peces"), together with the rest of his instruments, during his astrologic-alchymical travels on the Continent (in 1583-1589), which, fortunately for himself, did not extend to Russia. Dee also says, that he possessed an astronomical quadrant of ten feet radius, the staff and cross of which were very curiously divided, "in the same manner as Richard Chancellor's quadrant."

Richard Chancellor was a widower, and had two sons ("reliquit abiens (1553) duos filios parvulos orphanos futuros si asperior aliquis casus eum sustulisset"): one he took with him on his second voyage to Russia (in 1555), in order to show him the city of the Czar. The other, Nicholas, was sent in 1550, when an apprentice, from London to Moscow, and especially recommended to the agents there by the directors of the company, who had already given this orphan boy a good school education in London—"He hath been kept at writing schoole long; he hath his algorism and hath understanding of keeping of books of reckonings."

Nicholas Chancellor was, in 1580, sent to manage the trading department of the maritime expedition dispatched under Arthur Pet, of Ratcliff, and Charles Jackman, of Poplar, in search of Willoughby's Land, as well as to make an attempt to advance to the Eastward of Waigats and Nova Zembla, and so reach China. Chancellor was fortunately on board Pet's vessel, the George, for Jackman's, the William, was lost with all her crew, it never having been heard of. Hakluyt prepared for this expedition a list of the articles to be taken, as well as instructions for the merchant ("a note and caveat for the merchant"), consequently for our Nicholas Chancellor. I discovered in England the journal of this voyage, in the hand-writing of the latter. In Hakluyt's collection of 1599 is to be found the diary of the same voyage, kept by Hugh Smith. I congratulated myself on finding Chancellor's Journal, but afterwards discovered that it had been published in Hakluyt's first and rarer edition of 1589. I have likewise a very slight sketch, drawn by Arthur Pet, and copied in England, of the position of both vessels at Nova Zembla in August, 1580. Nicholas Chancellor must, moreover, have accompanied Martin Frobisher on the second of the three voyages undertaken by the latter in 1576, 1577, and 1588. This appears from the following note, written by John Dee in 1577 :—" The North Cape (was) first so named by the worthy of æternall good fame and grateful memory, my derely beloved Richard Chancelor, father to this Nycholas Chancelor, whose diligent, painful, and faythful service is known both in the Moscovy Region, and now in the Atlanticall northwest attempt." On this second voyage the Charles Jackman, who afterwards perished in the expedition to Nova Zembla, was chief officer; and after him an inlet was named Jackman's Sound. We afterwards find Nicholas Chancellor as purser on board a new Edward Bonaventure, which in 1582 sailed with the Leicester Galleon, under Edward Fenton's command, to double the Cape of Good Hope, with the intention of reaching India and China. In the lists of stores served out to both vessels I found a saltwater-distiller included.

On the part of the mercantile community, Sir George Barnes, then Lord Mayor of London, and one of the Sheriffs, William Garret (a name afterwards changed into Gerrard, and now into Garrard), exerted themselves considerably in furthering the execution of Cabot's project. Sir George Barnes' son, likewise Sir George, became Lord Mayor in 1586; he married Sir William Gerrard's daughter Ann. Their descendants write their name Barne, and are the proprietors of Sotterley and Dunwich Park, in the county of Suffolk, as well as of a house in London, No. 37, Grosvenor-street. Sir William Garret was Lord Mayor in 1555, died in 1571, and was buried in St. Magnus the Martyr's Church, in Lower Thames-street. His son, likewise Sir William, married an heiress of Sir John Gresham. The property was transferred in 1567, by will, to Charles Drake, a relative. The family of Drake Garrard own Lamer Park, in Hertfordshire.

Here we are reminded of another family of merchants, that of the Greshams. Sir Thomas Gresham was, in his time, the most accomplished merchant in London. He had studied at Cambridge; he then acquired a knowledge of commerce with his uncle, Sir John Gresham, and from 1551 was employed as Financial Agent of the Regency in the Netherlands, for which reason he was sometimes called the Royal Merchant. Almost immediately before Sir Hugh Willoughby's and Chancellor's expedition, he addressed a letter (on the 16th of April, 1553) to the Duke of Northumberland, in which, perhaps for the first time in England, he called commerce a science which required study. The following is a passage in his letter: " Please your Grace, how ys yt possibell, that ayther a mynstrellplayer or a shoye maker, or anny craftye men, or any other that haythe not bynne browght vppe in the syence, to have the pressent understanding of the feat of the merchaunt adventurer? To the wyche syence

I myselfe was bound prentisse 8 years, to come by the experyence and knowledge that I have." To Thomas Gresham the first London Exchange, of which he laid the foundation-stone in 1566, owed its existence. His father, Sir Richard, had already, in 1537, proposed to build an Exchange in London. When Queen Elizabeth went to see the Exchange in 1579, she honoured Sir Thomas with a visit. He established, where the Excise Office now stands, a public academy, named after him Gresham College, where astronomy, geometry, medicine, and other sciences, were taught, and which was the cradle of the Royal Society, but has since been shamefully neglected.

From the establishment of that Society in London until the great fire in 1666, and again from 1673 until 1701, it held its meetings at this place. There also was its Museum of Nature and Art, described by Dr. Grew in 1681. At the time of Willoughby's expedition, Sir Thomas Gresham was at Antwerp, but his uncle and commercial guide, Sir John Gresham, the elder, took up Cabot's project with warmth, and placed himself at the head of the Company which had resolved on carrying it out. He had engaged in foreign trade since 1517, at times as far as the Levant. As Sheriff of London in 1547, during his brother Sir Richard's mayoralty, he was knighted; at Edward the Sixth's accession he was an alderman; and the following year (1547—1548) Lord Mayor. J. W. Burgon, the biographer of the Greshams, in "The Life and Times of Sir Thomas Gresham, 1839," is in error in supposing that a younger Sir John Gresham—viz., the nephew of the one mentioned, and the elder brother of Sir Thomas—was the person who interested himself in Willoughby's expedition. This younger Sir John Gresham was with Hugh Willoughby at the reception of Ann of Cleves, for, in a manuscript list of the persons appointed for this purpose, " yonge Gresham's" name is to be found. In 1547 he accompanied the Protector Somerset to Scotland, and received the honour of knighthood from him after the battle of Pinkey; he was likewise, in documents as late as 1550, termed "Sir John Gresham the yonger—knight." What Burgon, vol. i., page 370 to 372, says of him must be slightly alluded to, viz., that he died in 1560, leaving but one daughter behind him. Sir Thomas' only son died in 1564, unmarried; and he himself died in 1579. The last direct descendant of Sir John Gresham, the elder, was the baronet of his name who died in 1801, whose daughter and heiress married a step-brother of the first Marquis of Stafford, and step-great-uncle of the present Duke of Sutherland, and, consequently, likewise of his brother, Lord Francis Egerton,* and his sisters the Duchess of Norfolk and the Marchioness of Westminster.

There is a portrait of Edward the Sixth, by Hans Holbein, in the Imperial Hermitage (Hall 47, No. 19), from the Royal Collection in England, dispersed during the troubles in the reign of Charles the First; it came from Lisbon with the pictures of the Houghton Gallery, which were purchased by the Empress Catherine the Second.

A portrait of Sebastian Cabot, probably also painted

* Now, 1846, Earl of Ellesmere.

by Holbein, found its way at the same time to Scotland from Whitehall, and is at present in the possession of the Harford family, at Bristol.

Sir George Barnes and William Garret or Gerrard are painted by Holbein in the picture in the Hall at Bridewell, in London, which represents Edward the Sixth as he, in 1553, consequently in the year of Willoughby's and Chancellor's expedition, is delivering the charter to the Lord Mayor Barnes, who is clothed in scarlet. This picture was engraved by Vertue.

At the Imperial Hermitage there is a highly valuable portrait of Sir Thomas Gresham by Sir Anthony Moro, which I was aware had arrived in Russia with the collection from Houghton, but could not at first discover it: with no small pleasure, however, I met with it in Hall 47, No. 13. In the catalogue of the Picture Gallery at the Hermitage, this portrait is described at page 480 in the following manner: "Portrait à nù corps d'un homme vêtu de noir, assis dans un fauteuil, tenant les gants dans la main droite; ses traits portent l'empreinte d'un charactère serieux et méditatif." It was thus unknown that the portrait of the famous Sir Thomas Gresham was there.

Sir Hugh Willoughby's portrait is at Wollaton House; and Sir Nisbet Willoughby, a few years since, had a copy of it taken by Barker, the painter, at Nottingham, for the great picture hall at Greenwich (No. 1).

On the 11th of May, 1553, the three vessels appointed for the service weighed anchor at Deptford for China, and passed Greenwich, where the court resided, the sailors dressed in light blue, and the ships firing guns. Unfortunately, Edward was already too ill to show himself, as it was expected he would do. The undertaking excited general interest, for it was a new and important one. Up to that time, no English vessel had doubled the North Cape, or, at all events, sailed to the eastward of Wardhuys. The North Cape had not yet received this name, which was first bestowed during this voyage of Richard Chancellor and Stephen Burrough: the Russian vessels had long named it "Murmansky Noss," which means Nose or Cape of the Normans.

Two of the vessels, the "Bona Esperanza," and the "Bona Confidentia," on board of the first of which were Sir Hugh Willoughby, as commodore, and William Gefferson, as sailing master, while on board of the other, Cornelius Durforth commanded, sailed far to the North, where Willoughby, on the 14th of August, came in sight of land, probably that part of the coast of Nova Zembla, lying between the Northern and Southern Goose Cape, Gussinü Noss. The main-land of Russia appears to have been seen by them for the first time, on the 23rd of August.

Sir Hugh Willoughby set his foot on Russian soil either on the same day or perhaps one day earlier than Chancellor, who landed on the 24th of August. On the 14th of September a fresh landing was effected on the Lapland coast, in a bay westward of the Island of Nokujeff, where pretty good anchorage was found. Willoughby now sailed with both vessels along the Lapland coast, in a south-easterly direction towards the White Sea; and, had he continued this course, would probably either have reached the monastery of Ssolovetz, or joined Chancellor at Nenocksa. He appears, however, only to have advanced as far as a spot long in bad repute with Russian coasting vessels; the tongue of land called the Svatoi Noss (perhaps the mysterious Wattunäs, the Waternose of tradition), which, with Kanin Noss, forms, as it were, the gate of the White Sea.

CHAPTER II.

EARLY RUSSIAN VOYAGES—INTERCOURSE BETWEEN RUSSIA AND WESTERN EUROPE.

OF Cape Svatoi Noss, the point gained by Sir Hugh Willoughby, and other places on the Lapland coast, Herberstein received an account from Gregory Istoma as well as from Vassily Vlassy and Demetrius Gerassimoff, but his version of their communication, which he entitles "The Voyage to the Sea, called the Icy or Frozen Sea," differs so much from the original, that it is very difficult to recognise the places meant; on which account the narrative of our countrymen is much less highly appreciated than it deserves to be.

Although the above-named Russians were but interpreters employed in the Embassy, they are, nevertheless, worthy of special notice; for through them Western Europe, in the first half of the sixteenth century, became more closely acquainted with Russia, by means of the accounts which were given to the world. In proof of this we may mention that, through their knowledge of the Latin language, they were placed in a position to give the desired information, which they then made known by means of the press. At an earlier period we had employed

Greeks in our diplomatic missions abroad, who returned to Russia from Rome and Constantinople, and spoke Italian. Gregory Istoma appears to have been the first of the Russian interpreters who learnt the Latin language, and from him Herberstein obtained a great amount of information. He was not only one of the Emperor Maximilian's interpreters at Moscow, in 1517, but travelled also with him afterwards (in 1517 and 1518) as far as Innspruck and Halle, and from thence back to Vienna.

According to Herberstein, Gregory Istoma made his first voyage round the North Cape in the reign of Ivan Vassilovitch, in the year 1496; and it appears, by documents in the Danish archives, that in 1507, he was sent by Vassily Ivanovitch, to Denmark, where he probably learnt Latin. Herberstein, who calls him "homo industrius," and a "discreet and modest man," came to Russia for the first time in 1517, in company with Gregory Demetriovitch Sagräshly, who was on his way back from Germany, in consequence of the state of Poland. Istoma was the interpreter who, when Herberstein set out from the waiting station, at Nicola to Chlinsk, came to meet him at a spot not far from the mansion, for the purpose of announcing that he was to alight from his horse, in order to listen to the greeting sent in the name of the Czar by Timothy Constantinovitch Chludeneff (not Chaldeneff), who had been appointed his host at Moscow. Herberstein was very glad to be enabled to speak Latin with Istoma; and his desire to receive information with regard to Russia, which had been increased by Matthew Lang, the Salzburg Cardinal, was so great, and he asked so many different questions as they rode into Moscow, that his host knew not what to think of such unusual curiosity. Herberstein says, " When I heard the interpreter speak Latin, I conversed with him in that language as we rode in. I was delighted to have the means of doing this, for as the country was unknown to us, I much wished to obtain a complete knowledge of it, and to be enabled to delineate it correctly in our maps. My host soon asked what I had said, and as I had a Lithuanian with me, I drew upon myself some suspicion." It appears as if Istoma, in the first instance, was not permitted to have much to do with Herberstein, but subsequently it was he who prepared his official dispatches; for example, that in which he proposed to separate Smolensko from Poland; but then, if Herberstein had been prevented from sounding Istoma freely at Moscow, soon afterwards he had an opportunity of doing what he wished, for the latter was sent with the secretary Vladimir Ssemenoff Plemännikoff, towards the end of 1517, when Herberstein returned, on an embassy, to the Emperor Maximilian. To their care was Herberstein committed until their arrival at their destination, and they journeyed in a great measure together by Wilna, Cracow, Vienna, and Salzburg. On their arrival near Innspruck (at the end of March, 1518), where the Emperor Maximilian at that time resided, two persons of high rank came out to pay their respects to them.

Herberstein himself had hastened on a little, in

order to give preliminary notice to the Emperor of their approach, and instructions were given to him to be present at their reception. After formal speeches on both sides, delivered by Istoma on the part of the Russians, they entered the town on horseback, Plemännikoff between the two officials, and Istoma behind him with Herberstein on his left. In the town itself, he likewise rode by his side to the audience, and after this was over, the same order was observed in their progress to their quarters. At the audience Plemännikoff, who was only a secretary, was requested by the Emperor to deliver his speech sitting and with his cap on his head. His Majesty also ordered the interpreter Istoma to sit down, but he did not, for he interpreted standing. Herberstein was commanded to take care that whilst Plemännikoff and Istoma remained at Innspruck, they should want for nothing. As Herberstein had been present at Moscow, at the Feast of the Assumption of the Virgin Mary, held in the cathedral church, in the Kremlin, which was so named after this feast, and set apart for the solemn service of God by the Patriarch, in the presence of the Czar, the Emperor was desirous that our countrymen should likewise visit the church at Innspruck, on Palm Sunday, and for this purpose sent Herberstein to the Bishop of Brixen; but this man was a bigot, for he decided, after due deliberation, that it should not be allowed as they were not members of the Romish Church.

After a week' residence at Innspruck, Herberstein escorted them to Halle, in the valley of the Inn, whither the Emperor had gone, and the latter had high mass sung for them there, by his choir *à demi-voix*. Herberstein, in speaking of this, remarks, " This pleased the Russians, who said that it was much better to perform God's service in a lower or softer voice." When they had taken leave, Herberstein accompanied them down the Inn and Danube, as far as Vienna, where they were to await the arrival of the Emperor. From Vienna, Plemännikoff and Istoma travelled homewards with Maximilian's newly-appointed Ambassadors, Francesco da Collo and Antonio de Conti, who were to endeavour to negotiate a peace between Russia and Poland, and who had likewise accompanied them and Herberstein from Innspruck to Vienna; and they all reached Moscow together, in July, 1518. To Istoma the merit is due of having obtained for his country, during his stay at Innspruck, the services of a number of skilful gunners, with whom he entered into contract. This must have required great tact; and Herberstein informs us how it was managed. His words are: "as the Envoy was desirous of enlisting gunners, and was unable to do so publicly, he gave his servants money, in order that they might go to the common women about the court, in the evening; and through the solicitations of the latter, five persons expressed themselves willing to proceed to Moscow."

To these five master-gunners Istoma gave money wherewith to buy themselves horses and travel to Lubeck, where they embarked for Livonia, and thence proceeded to Moscow. Two of them died soon; the third, by name Walch, became blind, and returned to his native country with Herberstein, in 1526, with the Czar's leave. The other two, Niclasen, from the neighbourhood of Spires, and Jordan, from Halle, in the valley of the Inn, Vassily Ivanovitch refused at that time to discharge. They had acquired considerable claims to his gratitude on the occasion of the advance of Mahomet-Girai, Khan of the Crimea, to Moscow. Niclasen was to have defended the Kremlin at that time with the celebrated heavy artillery; and it was even desired that he should place it in haste at one of the gates, ready for service. Jordan was present at the retreat of the Tartars at Old Käsan, the capture of which the Khan had contemplated, Unauthorised by his commander, he seized a favourable opportunity to open a heavy and unexpected fire with his artillery, on the multitudes of Tartars who were within his reach, and spread so great a panic among them, that they all fled in haste, leaving behind them a document drawn up by the Khan, which had been intended for the Czar, wherein the unconditional surrender of Moscow was demanded. Hans Jordan's trade abroad was that of a cannon-ball founder. He married a Russian woman; and he it was who, in 1526, imposed on Herberstein the absurd story that wives in Russia considered the blows they received from their husbands, as so many proofs of their love. His words are: "Jordan has told me himself that his wife loved him much more than she did before, because he had beaten her." Istoma, as well as other interpreters of that time, are mentioned in our public documents with the title "Maloi," before their names, which in this case does not mean either great or elder, but a subordinate position. Herberstein writes his (Istoma's) name Isthumen, Ystumen—(Istonium).

Vassily Vlassy was, in 1517, interpreter to Herberstein. He understood German as well as Latin, and is considered to be the source whence Dr. John Faber (Heigerlin) derived his description of the religion of the Russians, published at Tübingen, in 1525. Soon after the appearance of this work, it was sent to Herberstein, by the Archduke Ferdinand, whose secretary as well as father confessor and counsellor, Faber was, with the request that he would complete it, as far as possible, during his residence in Russia. Herberstein was at that time on his second journey to Moscow; and in his company, returning with the Prince Ivan Iarosslavsky Sassekin, from the Emperor Charles the Fifth, then in Spain, was Vlassy, from whose hints the pamphlet had been composed at Tübingen but a few months previously.

Herberstein, in comparing Vassily Vlassy with Istoma, calls him "a tolerably good man," for he learnt to know the one as well as the other, during his first residence at Moscow, in 1517. It was he who, two days after Herberstein's arrival there, on the 20th of April, was sent to him by order of the Czar, accompanied by Jelisar (Jelka) Sergejeff, the Chamberlain Chludeneff's deputy, at the house of the latter, in order to repeat to him the announcement made by the Chamberlain on the previous day, that the audience was fixed for the day following. The Czar further arranged that Vlassy should go to Herberstein on the morning of that day, to announce to him that, besides his Chamberlain, the Boyar's son, Gregory Fomin ssün Ivanoff, with the Secretary Missur Munechin, should escort him. At the audience, Vassily Vlassy was the interpreter. At an earlier period he was much engaged in the translation of religious works into Russian. Maxim, the monk, by us generally called Maksim the Greek, came to Moscow from Mount Athos, as is well-known, in 1506; and after he had looked over the Greek writings found at that time in the Kremlin, in great numbers, he was requested to translate several of them; but as he did not understand Russian, Vassily Vlassy and Demetrius Gerassimoff were united with him for the purpose of rendering his Latin translations into Russian, by which means Vlassy became better acquainted with church affairs. He and Maxim alone are the writers of the abstracts 31 to 51 of the commentaries on the History of the Apostles by Chrysostom, &c., which were translated by order of the Patriarch, in 1520. In 1525, he was sent as interpreter with the Envoy Prince Ivan Jarosslavsky Sassekin, and the Secretary Ssemen Borissoff Trofimoff, to Madrid, to Charles the Fifth, who had been elected Emperor of Germany, in 1519; and when they returned to Russia in January, 1526, Herberstein, who, with Leonard, Count of Nugarolis, was dispatched to this country, travelled with them. Our Envoy was obliged to make rather a long stay at Tübingen, and Dr. Faber, a zealous Catholic, availed himself of this opportunity to obtain from Vassily Vlassy the information with respect to the Russian religion, which he immediately published, in 1525, under the title of "*Epistola de Moscovitarum juxta Mare Glaciale Religione*," which the Archduke Ferdinand sent to the two envoys from Augsburg, on the 1st of February, 1526, in order that during their residence at Moscow they might complete the work, by giving a good account of the distinction between the two churches, and of the doctrines and rites of the Russians ("erit nobis hæc inquisicio et labor omnis vester perjucundus"). It is highly probable that the Archduke's counsellor, Dr. Faber, induced him to order this investigation to be made. Herberstein was thus enabled to acquire much of the desired information on the road. Vlassy was called by us "The Latin and German Interpreter." Faber says of him, "Germanice et Latine mediocriter callebat."

Demetrius Gerasimoff, a Russian, who has been confounded with two Greeks who bore the name of Demetrius, communicated about that time, in 1525 and 1526, all the information in question, to the author Paulo Giovio, and thus furnished the latter with materials for the account of Russia, which met with such a good reception by the public, and was published with Herberstein's commentaries. Gerassimoff, the summer before Herberstein's second arrival at Moscow, visited Rome and did not return until 1526, when the latter had already been a considerable time with us.

Gennady, Archbishop of Novogorod and Pskov, had, probably at the commencement of the year 1493, requested a Greek of the name of Demetrius to give his opinion, 1st, on the Triple Hallelujah; 2nd, on the Sclavonic translation of the first verse of the 32nd Psalm; and, 3rd, on the calculation of the seven thousand years from the creation of the world. According to the Greek chronology, indeed, those seven thousand years had already elapsed without the world coming to an end, as was so much dreaded at this period. Demetrius' reply, entitled "The Triple Hallelujah and the Seven Thousand Years," is dated in 7001 (1492-93). In my opinion, the author is no other than Demetrius Manuilovitch Trachaniot, who arrived at Moscow from Rome, in 1472, with Sophia, the bride of the Czar, Ivan Vassilovitch, as Envoy Extraordinary from her two brothers, Andrew and Emanuel.

Although he returned to Rome at the commencement of 1473, and in 1474, when again sent by Sophia's brothers, remained at Moscow but a short time; still, at a later period, he took up his residence with us altogether. Gennady applied to him in order that he might learn the opinions of a Greek; the position of the latter at Court, too, may have induced the Archbishop to write to him. In 1500 he was present at the marriage of Ivan and Sophia's daughter Theodosia with the Prince Vassily Dassilovitsch Cholmsky, and likewise had the honour of going in procession to the church, together with his elder brother Jury and his own son, whose name was also Jury, close to the sledge of the Czarina Sophia and her daughter, the bride Theodosia. His son, the above-named Jury, accompanied him to Moscow, in 1472. This younger Trachaniot deserves to be somewhat better known, for Herberstein often met him. He was keeper of the seals and treasurer to the Czar, Ivan Vassilovitch, until the death of the latter, and is mentioned as such in the Czar's will, in which golden crosses were likewise left to his father, Demetrius, and his uncle, Jury, as mementoes of Ivan. He was much beloved at that time by the young Prince Vassily, Ivan and Sophia's son, and had conceived an idea that the latter might, perhaps, marry his daughter, for the counsellors, of whom he was one, adduced several reasons why it would be right that the young Czar should marry a native. "Of this counsel (says Herberstein) George the younger, the treasurer, was the originator, for it was most agreeable to him, as he hoped that his own daughter would be selected." Jury was generally called Juschko Maloi, because he was the younger, but not, as Adelung imagined, because he was small and weakly. This appellation was given to him at first in order to distinguish him from his uncle, Jury Staroi, the elder; and afterwards he continued to be so designated, for Herberstein still called him George, the younger.

In the index to Pantaleon's translation of Herberstein, he appears as "Georgius the younger, a trusty counsellor," but certainly this would lead at once to his being recognised as Jury Demetriovitch Trachaniot. Vassily Ivanovitch, when sovereign, valued him to the last very highly, for he was "his dearest counsellor, treasurer, and chancellor."

Nevertheless he fell into disgrace for a short time, in consequence of the counsel he gave in church matters; and in 1516 this was also participated in by his wife, because she and another lady had spread the report that Solomonia Vassily's repudiated wife had given birth to a son, soon after her taking the veil under the name of Sophia. The Czar, however, could not keep his favourite long out of office, and "restored him to honour in another capacity, for he was learned and experienced in many things. When the Czar had need of him, and he had been brought to the stairs of the palace, several of the most distinguished counsellors were ordered to bring him up, together with the sledge in which he sat; but after his disgrace, when he was ascending the stairs softly by himself, the Czar heard of it, and his anger was kindled: he ordered him to be carried up as before, and when they had deliberated together on various matters, he was conveyed down stairs again."

Jury Demetrovitch Trachaniot was almost always one of the persons of rank, whose duty it was to converse with Herberstein at the private audiences given to him by the Czar at his residence in the Kremlin, in the hall situated near the river Mosqua. He it was who endeavoured to prove to him the right of the Czar to Lithuania and Poland, in consequence of the descent of the Hungarians, Moravians, and Poles from the Ugri. For no one at the Court (in 1516) had Herberstein such high esteem as for Trachaniot. I think it right here to remark, that the "Dobrago Dadiana," twice mentioned by Adelung, as a work written by Herberstein, never existed. This name has originated in an erroneous reading of the following passage in our public reports:—" The Czar, on Herberstein's arrival, ordered that a good Boyar's son and a scribe should be appointed to do him the honours." The selection fell on Gregory Fomin, son of Ivanoff, and on Missur Munechin. When Herberstein took up his residence a second time at Moscow, he sought Trachaniot in vain, for he says: " I could not find my old friend, George the younger."

Let us now turn to another Demetrius. According to the wish of Gennady, the Archbishop of Novogorod, who filled this office from 1485 until 1504, one Demetrius had procured some historical data at Rome with reference to the white bishop's mitre, which he had obtained, not without much entreaty, from Jacob, the church librarian. He sent them to the Archbishop by Foma Salareff (also written Sareff and Lareff), a Russian merchant. This Demetrius was, I believe, the Demetrius Ivanovitch Raleff or Lareff, who came to Moscow from Constantinople with his parents and his brother Emanuel, in 1485. He was employed on a mission with the latter to Rome, Venice, and Milan, in 1488, and returned to Moscow at the beginning of 1490 in the suite of Andreas, the brother of the Czarina Sophia, and was also accompanied by the unfortunate physician Leo, who was beheaded on the 22nd April, at Moscow, because the young Ivan had died on the 6th March, under his treatment. They likewise brought with them several engineers and skilful craftsmen, amongst whom was the architect, who completed the Granovitaja Palace, and erected "shot towers" over three of the gates of the Kremlin.

Emanuel Ivanovitch accompanied the two miners, who, in 1491, discovered copper ore in the Zilma, a river falling into the Petschora. Demetrius Ivanovitch was despatched in 1493 with the secretary, Demetrius Saizen, to John, King of Denmark, at the same time that John Jacobson (Ravensberg), ambassador from the latter, was on his way back, and returned in 1494 with David, the Danish herald. In March, 1499, he was again sent with Mitrofan Karatscharoff, by way of Cracow and Hungary to Italy, for the purpose of engaging architects, cannon-founders, and a few other workmen for Russia. His other fellow-travellers were Alexis Jakovleff Golochvastoff, besides several Russian merchants. He was to go down the Don, and across the Black Sea to Constantinople, with a view of obtaining some privileges for Russian commerce. It is probable that Salareff, the before-named Russian merchant, accompanied him to Italy, and that the work, as well as the memoir of Demetrius Manuilovitch, were brought away by Salareff from Rome for Archbishop Gennady.

Raleff did not return from his mission until November, 1504, and Gennady had already been removed from his office in July of the same year. In 1506, we find Demetrius Raleff engaged in the campaign against Kasan. The historical description of the introduction of the white bishop's mitre sent to Gennady, of which there are several copies, afterwards gave rise, as is well known, to continual discussions, and at last was rejected as apocryphal by the great assembly of the church held at Moscow in 1607, at which three patriarchs were present. The third Demetrius was our countryman, Gerassimoff, who, when at Rome in 1525, signed himself Demetrius Erasmus, and who must have been born in 1465, and received the first rudiments of his education in Livonia, where he also learnt Latin. He was employed in several missions abroad as interpreter, and availed himself of the opportunity which offered for improving himself at the court of the Emperor Maximilian ("dum in aulâ Cæsaris omnis generis hominum refertissimus versaretur, si quid barbarum quieto docilique ingenio inerat, elegantium morum observatione detersit"). At the same time he was employed, as already mentioned, with Vassily Vlassy, in the translation of the church writings undertaken by Maxim, the Greek; and the most important, and, indeed, the first work on which they were engaged was the Commentaries on the Psalms. Both Russians merely translated into their own language the text rendered into Latin by Maxim from the Greek. Had Gerassimoff himself been a Greek, it is not likely that he would first have required a Latin translation of that work. The Commentaries on the Psalms, moreover, although approved of by the metropolitan and by the assembly of the church, shared the same fate as the majority of Maxim's other translations and writings, for they were never published. A beautiful manuscript of the commentaries, copied in 1692, is to be met with in the Synodal Library at Moscow.

Maxim's activity in the Kremlin came to an end about the year 1525, and this was the most memorable period in Gerassimoff's life. Paolo, the Genoese, recommended by Pope Leo the X., came to the Grand Prince Vassily Ivanovitch in 1520 to lay before him a project for converting the Caspian Sea, the Oxus, and the Indus, into a route for carrying on a trade between Moscow and India. The idea was, to receive the productions of the latter country, and afterwards distribute them to the various European States, by which means Spain and Portugal would not alone derive all the advantage of a trade with India. This plan, however, was not encouraged by the Russians, for it happened that half a century earlier Afanassy Nikitin, a merchant of Tver, succeeded in finding a road to India and back.

In 1525 Paolo came to Moscow a second time with the aforesaid project, bringing with him a letter from Clement VII., which also related to an union between the Greek and Roman churches; but after remaining with us for two months, he was obliged to bend his steps homewards, without attaining either of his objects; and our Demetrius Gerassimoff was appointed to accompany him to Rome, provided with a letter from the Czar to the Pope. The latter assigned him a handsome residence, had him clothed magnificently in silk, gave him a bishop for his cicerone, granted him a friendly audience, and requested Paolo Giovio, the savant, a native of Como, but not bishop of that place, to become better acquainted with him. This person found him to be well informed ("humanarum rerum et sacrarum literarum valde peritum"), and managed to obtain from him a great deal of information about Russia, which was published at first in 1537, and then in 1545 and 1551, with the title "De Legatione Basilii Magni Principis Moscoviæ liber." The Legation, or Embassy, here mentioned, was composed neither more nor less than of the interpreter Demetrius Gerassimoff, who must be considered as the source of this description of Russia, which is justly preferred to that of Herberstein for its comprehensiveness. In order to cite an example of the abundance of useful productions to be found in his country, he narrated the comical story of the peasant, who, as he was gathering honey in a hollow tree, slipped to the bottom and remained there until he was drawn out by clinging to a *med-wed* (a judge of honey, *i.e.* a bear), which descended backwards into the cavity. Gerassimoff returned to Moscow in July, 1526, and with him came Johannes Franciscus de Potentia, whom the Pope appointed to the bishopric of Scara, in Sweden, but whom Gustavus I. refused to recognise. He was sent, as legate from the Pope, to discuss Polish affairs with the Czar, and received instructions, *en route*, from King Sigismund. Gerassimoff occupied himself afterwards at Novogorod, at the request of Makary, Archbishop of Novogorod and Pskov, in the translation of Bruno's Commentaries on the Psalms, which Cochleus published at Leipzig in 1533, under the title of " Psalterium Beati Brunonis, episcopi quondam Herbipolensis a Johanne Cochleo Presbytero restitutum et Hebraica veritate adauctum."

In our academical library there has been, since 1763, a manuscript copy in good condition of this translation of Bruno's works by Gerassimoff, with a few additions by the latter; and another copy with the same additions is preserved in the library of the church of St. Sophia, at Novogorod. Gerassimoff concluded his work on the 15th October, 1535.

The translator remarks, that he undertook the work in obedience to the command of the Archbishop. Upon the whole, a comparison of Gerassimoff's work, in 1535, with that completed by him and Vassily Vlassy, more than a quarter of a century earlier, would not be altogether uninteresting, for it would show the improvement made in the Russian language. Demetrius Trachaniot, the Greek, called himself, in 1493, in his letter to Gennady, Demetrius Staroi, the elder. The Demetrius Raleff, the Greek, who, about the year 1500, sent a treatise to Gennady from Rome, signed himself Mita Maloi, the younger, to distinguish himself from Trachaniot. Demetrius Gerassimoff, the Russian, called himself, in 1535, Demetrius the Scholastic, by which he meant the scholar. Another of his appellations was Demetrius Tolmasch (the Interpreter), but Demetrius Raleff, the Greek, was likewise so called. Demetrius Gerassimoff was also designated as Mitä Maloi and Tolmatsch Latünskoi. From these indefinite appellations arose the mistake, into which, as we have said, our historian fell. In the dictionary of the Russian church writers, the translator of Bruno's Psalterium is considered to be the author, or, at all events, the editor of the historical description of the white bishop's mitre; and to the same person is ascribed, in the catalogue of Rumanzoff's Manuscript, the Essay, written in 7001, on the Hallelujah and the Seven Thousand Years considered to be the period of the world's existence. Lehoberg, of Krug, in the "Enquiries, in order to elucidate the Ancient History of Russia," erroneously states that Gerassimoff was at Rome in 1522, for in the date given by Jovius, "Anno septimo millesimo tricesimo tertio Aprilis," "tertio" refers to the year (7033, *i.e.* 1525), and not to the day of the month.

The substance of what we have been enabled to gather from Istoma's and Gerassimoff's communications to Herberstein, with reference to the early voyages of the Russians to the Icy Sea, is briefly as follows:—

Even before Vasco de Gama made his first voyage round the southern extremity of Africa, some Russians, commissioned by their sovereign, had sought their way by sea round the northernmost Cape of Scandinavia, induced to do so by the relations then existing between Sweden and Russia.

They sailed from the Dwina in very small vessels, which could be hauled over tongues of land when not very broad, and proceeded along the coast of the White Sea to the right, then crossed over to the left or Ter shore, and so followed this course northwards, leaving the Petzeroy Sea on the right, to the beforementioned Cape Svatoi Noss. The western side of this narrow tongue of land, which stretches out from the main to a distance of nearly ten nautical miles, in a north-north-west direction, forms, with the broad shore to the south, the inlet of Svatoi Noss; and into this rushes the flood tide, almost parallel with the slope of that part of the Lapland coast, from the north-west. The vast bulk of water there accumulated at the extremity of the *cul de sac*, is now turned against the current, so that part of it is compelled to force its way back along the spit, at the end of which this eddy, flowing out of the inlet, encounters the general tide-waves at an obtuse angle : a violent commotion ensues in the sea, which, by the Russians is called Suloi or Suvoi, and is observable at a distance of ten versts * from the shore. Herberstein gives a sketch from Gregory Istoma's verbal communication of his voyage round Svatoi Noss, and of the dangers he encountered; but as he did not clearly understand the cause of the unusual commotion of the water, called the Suvoi, his description of it is obscure. Herberstein, moreover, was unable to conjecture what rock it was of which Istoma relates that the master of his vessel offered it secretly a mess of oatmeal mixed with butter, in order to be permitted to pass it. He was ignorant that this rock (the chimney), called Woronucha, is scarcely a cable's length distant from the pointed and low projecting Cape Svatoi Noss, and that only at half-tide it begins to be visible above the surface of the sea ; on the contrary, he imagined that it was a huge and lofty mass of rock—in fact, a mountain. That Istoma, however, meant no other rock than the Kamen Woronucha, which is invisible at high water, has been confirmed by

* A verst is about three-quarters of an English mile.—Tr.

Anthony Jenkinson. When the latter came to Russia for the first time, in 1557, he wrote in his log-book: "On the 7th July we arrived at a Cape called Svetinose, which forms the entrance into the Bay of St. Nicholas. Off this Cape lies a great stone, to which vessels, when passing it, took care to make an offering of butter, meal, and other victuals; for they imagined, that if this were omitted, their barks or other craft would necessarily be lost, as, indeed, it has often happened." We ought not, therefore, after such direct testimony, to allow ourselves to be deceived by the erroneous name of Semes, given to this rock by Herberstein. He found it just as easy to change Istoma's Latin word Kamen, written in Latin Camen (a rock), into Lemes, as to transmute Borsü, which means greyhounds, into the hitherto undeciphered word Kurtzi.

In the account of the coursing match, in which Herberstein took a part in the presence of the Czar, Vassily Ivanovitch, he says: "When they had uncoupled the hounds, they followed in a body, making a great outcry which could not be restrained; and then certain swift hounds were let loose, which they call Kurtzen (Kurtzos dictos)." Adelung endeavoured to explain the word Kurtzen by the canis cursalis of the middle ages. In reference to the word Lemes, it might also be possible that Istoma mentioned that he passed not only Svatoi Noss, but the Seven Islands, Sem Ostronoff; and that Herberstein, in his notes, confounded this Sem with the rock Kamen Woronucha above mentioned. Almost all the Russian names were, moreover, much mutilated at that time. Even in the year 1555, Stephen Burrough turned Ivanovskige Kresti into Swan Crist, and Cape Teriber into Cape Sowerbeer.

When Istoma and his companion undertook a long voyage to Wardehuus, they did not endeavour to sail round the Peninsula of Rubatschy, which projects to a great distance and would have required a considerable circuit, but kept near the coast of the mainland and entered the Gulf of Motover, which is formed by that coast and the south-eastern part of the Peninsula. Thence, that is, from the harbour situated at the extremity of the Gulf, and named Nova Zembla, in 1823, by Captain Lieutenant, now Admiral, Lütke, after his ship,—the four vessels, as well as baggage, had been dragged over the neck of land, here very narrow, which connects the Peninsula of Rubatschy with the main, into the largest, the northernmost, of the two Volokoff inlets,—they sailed round Murmansky Noss to the west coast of Norway and into the Drontheim Fiord. From Drontheim they journeyed by land with reindeer as far as Bergen, and from thence on with horses to the coast opposite Copenhagen.

Herberstein is scarcely to be excused for saying that Dront (Drontheim) is situated two hundred miles to the north of the Dwina, and that Bergen lies between mountains enveloped in darkness (midnight). Istoma travelled to the Dwina by way of Novogorod, but Vlassy from Moscow by way of Pereslavl, Rostov, Jaroslav, and Vologda; the greater part of the distance from Rostov was traversed by water.

In the direction here described, this voyage was made by Istoma, in 1496, and, as Herberstein says, at a later period also by Vlassy, but the latter proceeded first to Bergen by land. Both returned from Copenhagen by the Baltic Sea, and through Livonia to Moscow; but in 1501 Jury Manuilovitch Trachaniot made the tedious voyage round Murmansky Noss in the opposite direction on his way home to Russia from Denmark.

Jury Manuilovitch Trachaniot, one of the Greeks who came to Russia from Rome, pre-eminently belongs to that interesting epoch when Russia entered into relations with Western Europe, which he himself was active in promoting. On the 11th of February, 1469, he arrived at Moscow, deputed by the Papal See to offer the hand of Sophia (Fominischna), the last Greek emperor's niece, then resident at Rome, to the Czar Ivan Vassilovitch, who had been a widower since 1467. When the Princess Sophia was on her way to Moscow in 1472, as *fiancée*, Demetrius Manuilovitch, brother to Jury, was, as already mentioned, in her suite with his son Jury; Jury Manuilovitch came somewhat later to Russia, and remained there. Through Ivan's marriage with a descendant of the line of Greek emperors, the double eagle came into the Russian escutcheon, and in consequence of the repeated journeys which then took place from Russia to Italy, many useful artizans came to Moscow, whose works are still to be seen in the Kremlin. The attention of Germany was likewise at this time directed to Russia, for, in 1486, the Emperor Ferdinand the Third gave

Nicolaus Poppel, a polished and travelled German, a letter of introduction to Ivan Vassilovitch. It appears that besides acquiring a general knowledge of Russia, he was in the first place to endeavour to ascertain whether an union could not be brought about between a son of the Emperor Maximilian, at that time King of Rome and a widower, and one of Ivan's two daughters, Helena and Feodosia, or whether either of them was inclined to marry any other member of a royal German house, of Saxony, Baden, or Brandenburg. On his return, in 1488, Poppel found the Emperor at Nuremberg. He gave him and the Diet a long account of the greatness and power of Russia, as well as of the distinguished qualities of its ruler, whereupon he was sent, officially, to Moscow, without any colleagues, both by the Emperor Ferdinand and his son Maximilian, King of Rome and there he made the before-mentioned proposals. In March, 1489, Jury Manuilovitch Trachaniot and Poppel were dispatched as envoys from the Czar to the Emperor and the King, accompanied by Ivan Chalepa and Constantine Aksentjeff, who were native Russians. Besides attending to the more important affairs of the mission, Trachaniot and the latter were commissioned to engage a miner, a metallurgist, a military engineer, an architect, and a skilful silversmith. A few years previously, before Poppel had brought about relations with Germany, the Czar had requested Matthias, King of Hungary, to send him a like number of practical men following these callings.

In 1489, the King of Rome presided in the name of his father, the Emperor, at the Diet held at Frankfort on the Maine. Our embassy was received by the King in the Council-house, in the presence of many of the sovereigns who had come to the Diet. Trachaniot, who understood neither Latin nor German, made a speech to the King in Italian, which was replied to, likewise in Italian, by Dr. George Von Thorn. He delivered as a present from the Czar three suits of furs, one of sable, one of ermine, and the other of squirrel. Chalepa and Aksentjeff, who were called the ambassador's knights, each brought a suit of squirrel-skins. On the following morning, Trachaniot had a private audience, and afterwards visited the Emperor, who at that time was seventy-four years old, and received him very graciously, but gave him no letter to the Czar, so that on his return to Moscow, in 1490, he only took one from Maximilian, King of Rome. The next ambassador sent by Maximilian was the before-mentioned Dr. George Von Thorn, who was not admitted to an audience by the Czar in the presence of his sons Vassily and Jury, but specially in that of the Czarina Sophia, to whom he presented a piece of grey cloth and a parrot.

Karamsin, misled by our chronicles, says that Jury Trachaniot was sent in 1499, as ambassador from Russia to Rome. This is an error which has evidently arisen from his mission to the King of Rome being mistaken for one to Rome. After staying at Moscow somewhat less than six weeks, Jury Trachaniot and Dr. Thorn travelled back to Germany, in August, 1490, the former accompanied by the secretary Vassily Kuleschin. Besides the diplomatic matters with which they were entrusted, they were to announce to the King of Rome that the Czar was ready to give him his daughter in marriage; and they were, moreover, to engage a good physician, for Leo had already met his tragical end. They found the King at Nuremberg, remained with him from March until June, 1491, and returned in the autumn to Moscow, where soon afterwards Dr. Thorn appeared as ambassador for the second time, to announce that as the King had received no answer from Moscow for a length of time, he had come to the determination of marrying Anne of Bretagne. He was followed, however, by the intelligence that the King of France had dissuaded her from the match. When Thorn returned to Germany in the spring of 1492, he was commissioned to give King Maximilian to understand, amongst other things, that he might still obtain the hand of one of the Czar's daughters, either for himself or for his son Philip. Jury Trachaniot was dispatched soon afterwards, charged with the same communication, and accompanied by two secretaries, Michael Jaropkin and Ivan Kuritzin, the latter of whom was burnt as a heretic in 1505. They were received by the King of Rome at Colmar, but returned to Moscow in June, 1493, without anything being settled, and the Grand Duchess Helena was married to Alexander, Grand Duke of Lithuania, and afterwards King of Poland. The before-mentioned Vassily Kuleschin, who was now treasurer, was present at the wedding at Wilna. After Jury Manuilovitch Trachaniot with his brother and nephews had been honourably employed with reference to the nuptials of Ivan's daughter

Feodosia with Cholmsky, in February, 1500, and had participated in the festivities consequent thereon, he, together with the accomplished statesman, Secretary Vassily Dalmatoff, was sent to Denmark, in April, in company with the Danish ambassadors, John Anderson, Andrew Cristenson, and Andrew Glob, who had arrived in February; and from thence Trachaniot, together with Dalmatoff and the Danish herald, returned to the Dwina, in August, 1501, doubling the North Cape, as already observed. That this Jury Staroi, together with his brother and nephews, were mentioned in Ivan's will, has been previously stated. Vassily Dalmatoff had been engaged in 1477 at the subjugation of Novogorod, and, in 1493, he was employed in the missions with regard to the projected marriage of a daughter of Ivan with Conrad, Prince of Masovia, but at a later period, in 1509 and 1510, he was the principal agent in the final overthrow of Pskov. Herberstein relates of him that Vassily Ivanowitch held him in high esteem ("charus principi et inter intimos secretarios habitus"), but sent him into confinement at Belosero, where he died, and then confiscated the whole of his property, because he had pleaded poverty in order to avoid proceeding on a mission to the Emperor Maximilian, entrusted to him by the Czar. His brothers, Nemetz (Theodore), and Sachar were sent to meet Herberstein in 1517, and again were his conductors on his homeward journey from Moshaish as far as the frontier beyond Smolensko.

A Scotchman by birth, who in the series of communications made by our interpreters, as well as by Herberstein, and preserved in our archives, is merely designated by his christian name of David, made the northern voyages as herald from the King of Denmark, not only with Istoma in 1496 and 1507, but with Jury Trachaniot in 1501. I have an idea that his family name was Cocker, or one somewhat similar to it; but it was by no means Gerold, or Gerlad, as he is incorrectly named in our series of translations, as well as in the Danish writings.

This herald has received the altogether erroneous family name of Gerold, through an incorrect reading and translation of the Latin letters from King John of Denmark; for the title of herald, "David Heraldus" (noster) has been taken for a surname—in Russian the sound of g being given to the h. This has given rise to the name of Gerald, and the latter again has been changed into Gerlad; but his real name we must expect to find in the Danish archives. I discovered, in a copy of the Latin translation of a letter from the Czar, Vassily Ivanovitch, to King John, the words, "Vestrum oratorem heraldum magistrum, David Kocken." Hence, I may be allowed for the present to assume that his family name was Cocker; and this well deserves to be taken into consideration, for on the copy preserved (and of which I have availed myself) by the former Chancellor, Couzt Rumanzoff, taken from an original document to be found in the private State archives of Copenhagen, there is this note: "Ex chartâ coævâ Archivi Regii secretioris accurate exscripsi, Grimus Johannes Thorkelin archivi Regii secretioris Præfectus." I wished much to see the original of the letter I have quoted, on account of the word Kocken. Istoma's name, too, is not once correctly written in any of Herr Thorkelin's authentic copies. As a further proof out of the Danish writings that the word Herald denotes the office and not the surname, a quotation may serve from Huitfield's work: "Danmarkis Regis Kronicke II. p. 1075;" and which is again to be found in his "Kong Hansis, Kronicke, p. 270." Here it is "Kong Hansis, Sir Herold, Master David, &c." It is unfortunate that the family name was not here added.

Herberstein tells us that Master David was a Scot, and that one of that nation should be found in King John's service need not appear remarkable, for James the Fourth, at that time King of Scotland, was John's nephew, James the Third having married his sister Margaret in 1470, in consequence of a proposal made by Charles the Seventh, King of France, and received the Orkney and Shetland Islands as her dower. At the conclusion of a treaty between Denmark and Scotland (with England one had existed since 1490), an embassy was sent, in May 1493, from the latter country to Copenhagen; and probably David accompanied it. King John earnestly wished the Czar Ivan Vassilovitch to make up his mind to seize Sweden, which had become faithless to the Danish Crown, or at all events its neighbouring dependency, Finland; in return for which he promised his assistance against Lithuania. The name of the Danish ambassador who came to Moscow in July 1493, to settle the terms of an offensive and defensive alliance, and who was the first envoy to Russia from that country, is nowhere mentioned; and the mission with which he was charged, so far as it regarded the plot against Sweden, was kept as secret as possible in Denmark. Nevertheless the author of the "Swedish Rhyming Chronicles" received intelligence of it, and he says briefly in his verses that "the Dompropst of Roschild was sent by King Hans to Russia." Messenius copied this in 1620, as Dolin did likewise in 1750, without examination; and Schlegel in 1769 erroneously believed that Master David and this Dompropst were one and the same person.

In my opinion the Danish envoy who arrived at Moscow in July, taking Gothland, Livonia, and Novogorod *en route*, was no other than John Jacobson, "Jeas Ibson, or Jebson, or Jpson," who seven years afterwards became Bishop of Roschild, and was of the Ravensberg family. His father sent him when a youth to Cologne with a tutor in order to study at the University, which was at that time famous. An unsuitable matrimonial engagement, which he there contracted ("*turpi amore captus est libidine cæcus, uxorem duxit meretricem quandam, nomine Christinam*") was annulled on his return, through his father's interposition, and Jacobson became a canon and priest in the Cathedral at Roschild. King John took him with him as his secretary in 1482, on the occasion of the journey which he undertook to Schleswig and Holstein, as well as to Hamburg for the purpose of receiving oaths of allegiance from those places to himself and to his younger brother, Prince Frederick. Somewhat later we find Jacobson appointed provost or superintendent of the Monastery of Dalby in the province of Schonen, and previously to this he was Dean of Roschild. He was entrusted by King John with a mission to Scotland and England; and in 1500 at the decease of the Bishop of Roschild, Jacobson was installed in this high office. Shortly after he became a Bishop he was sent to Opslo, in Norway, accompanied by Heinrich Krumeridge with a fleet, for the purpose of reducing to obedience the Norwegians, who had fallen off from their allegiance to their Sovereign.

Knut Alfson, their leader, was slain on board the Bishop's own vessel; and we learn from history that Jacob was suspected of secret concurrence, not only in this act, but in the murder of the Lord High Steward (Reichshofmeister), Paul Laxmand, in 1502. For the rest, he is represented as a learned man and great politician; but, moreover, as very sensual and ostentatious ("*regem ipsum vivendo sumptuose et splendide superavit*"), although, it must be said, in his behalf, that he conferred many favours on the poor and needy. He maintained several hundred horsemen at his own cost for the King's service. He died in 1512, in embarrassed circumstances, at the Castle or Palace of Hintholm, after the canon Langurn, his successor at a later period, had already officiated for him for some time. He was buried at Roschild, the ancient residence of the Kings of Denmark, where many of them repose in the main aisle of the old Cathedral Church, which was visited by Peter the Great in 1716, and he was accidentally discovered in 1753, in his episcopal robes, with the paten and chalice placed on his folded hands. By the way, I here remember that the sarcophagus of Duke John the younger, of Denmark, who died at Moscow in 1602, was placed in this Cathedral in 1642, after having been interred in the first instance, with the permission of the Czar Boris Fedorovitch Godunoff, in an arched vault in the Lutheran Church, a plain building in the German quarter. It is well known that he married the beautiful and accomplished Grand Duchess Xenia Borissovna Godunoff, only daughter of the Czar, who, three years afterwards, met such a cruel fate. Near a pillar, where the length of body of Christian the First was observed, Duke John's grave was likewise pointed out to Peter the Great, in 1716. Joachim Beck, son-in-law of John Jacobson's brother Joachim, who lies buried near him, had an epitaph written for John the Bishop, in which are the following lines : *—

" When employed on an embassy to England and Scotland, he so conducted himself, that his name is held in most pleasant, grateful, and glorious remembrance, both by the English and Scotch, whom he persuaded to enter into a truce, though engaged in sanguinary warfare, with their armies stationed in face of each other, maddened with rage, and with banners flying, ready to commence the fray—a fact worthy of being handed down to posterity. Such was the effect produced, even on foreigners, by that man's august majesty of voice and countenance; and such was the authority of his name in matters of great import!"

* See Appendix A.

Unfortunately we are not informed in what year Jacobson visited England and Scotland, but at the end of February, 1493, we find that a Danish Embassy, consisting of a chancellor or secretary of the King, his brother, a doctor and a herald, was to start for London. From the epitaph we are led to believe that Jacobson was in Scotland in 1497, and that he was there employed by King James the Fourth in negotiating the truce concluded in that year. The King of England on his side likewise made use of a stranger for that purpose, Don Pedro Ayala, who had come to England on the occasion of the projected marriage of Arthur Prince of Wales with Catherine of Arragon, who, on his death, became the bride of his brother Henry.

At the same time that political matters were discussed, the marriage of the English Princess Margaret, Henry the Seventh's eldest daughter, with James the Fourth King of Scotland, which had been talked of in 1495, but was not celebrated until 1503, appears to have been brought on the tapis. This marriage must be considered as the foundation of the union between England and Scotland, which took place in 1603, a hundred years later. If John Jacobson was in England and Scotland, after his visit to Russia, he would naturally have been enabled to give an account of this country and Moscow, in both those kingdoms. It appears as if at that time the English court had begun to take notice of Russia. In the first year of the reign of Henry the Eighth, in 1510, a *bal costumé* was given in the Parliament Hall, at Westminster, at which the King himself appeared in Turkish costume; but Henry Stafford, at that time just created Earl of Wiltshire, and the Baron Fitzwalter, afterwards Viscount and Earl of Sussex, presented themselves in Russian dresses, with caps of grey cloth "in two long gounes of yelowe satin traversed with white satin, and in every bend of whyte was a bend of cremson satin, after the fashion of Russia or Ruslande, with furred hattes of greye on their hedes, either of them havyng an hatchet in their handes and bootes with pykes turned up." Probably there were similar "goodly bankets" at the nuptial festivities of the King of Scotland and the Prince of Wales.

It may still be mentioned that, in 1496, a treaty of commerce was concluded between King John of Denmark and King James the Fourth of Scotland. Jacobson's missions to Russia did not take place, as Huitfield wrote, for the purpose of settling the boundary question, but as already said, in order to request assistance against Sweden, which had attached Lubeck and other Hanse towns to its interest, and excited them against Denmark and Russia. A letter from Kemi, at the mouth of the river Kemi, somewhat to the eastward of Tornea, was made public in the spring of 1490, which was intended to irritate foreigners against Russia, and justify the execution of a great number of Russians. Therein are described the repeated inroads of the Russians during a series of years, into North and East Bothnia, where, availing themselves of the peace then existing, and under pretence of carrying on their traffic, they effected an entrance, and then fell on the defenceless inhabitants, who lost not only their property but their lives, in the most cruel manner. The villages of Kemi, situated on the north-eastern shore of the Gulf of Bothnia, Ijo and Limingo, were stated to have been burnt; the Russians, it was alleged, asserted that the whole salmon fishery in the northern part of the Gulf of Bothnia belonged to them, and indeed that this was the case, not only on the eastern side, as far as Pyhäjoki and down to the Hanakiffvi Rock, but likewise on the Swedish side as far down as Biureklubbe in the parish of Skelleftea; and then in the north, the eastern half of the river Kemi, up to Rovaniem. The inhabitants moreover were obliged, it was said, to pay three white furs (squirrel-skins) per head.

Hanakiffvi or Hanlickivi is a rock about fifteen fathoms in circumference, and rises more than three fathoms out of the water, on the shore of the Gulf,— there must have been inscriptions upon it. Biureklubbe is a rock on the opposite or western shore of the Gulf.

Orta, a place two miles from Ulea, had been appointed as a limit, which the Russians were not to pass; but as at that time this again happened, Hans Anderson, the governor, slew one-and-twenty persons, whilst the remainder fled towards the White Sea. The Orta in question was situated on a small island in the river Ulea.

Near the Chapel of Muhos, likewise on the river Ulea, four miles from the place of that name, there must have been a stone three ells high, and of the same breadth, named Ruskonkivi, on which three boundary marks were cut, the lion for Sweden, a cross for Russia, and a hammer for Lapland. In 1492, the Czar Vassily Ivanovitch built the Castle of Ivanogorod opposite to Narva, as a defence against Livonia; in 1493 he entered willingly into the alliance, which was proposed to him by King John of Denmark; and it was with a view to conclude this definitively that Demetrius Ivanovitch Raleff and the secretary Demetrius Saitzeff were without loss of time sent to accompany John Jacobson on his return to Denmark. Demetrius Raleff was, as we have seen, employed in 1488 on a mission to Italy, and was afterwards absent from 1499 until 1504, during which time he sent from Rome his treaties on the *White Bishops' Mitre*. He must have thoroughly understood Italian, as well as Latin, and was thus enabled to make himself understood by Jacobson on their route; with King John, there was at that time a learned Italian doctor of laws, of whom it is known that in the sea-voyage he made with the King to the Imperial Diet at Colmar in Sweden, he nearly lost his life, for the ship on board of which he was with the documents, caught fire. Jury Manuilovitch Trachaniot returned from his last mission to Rome just after Raleff's departure, otherwise he would probably have gone with Jacobson to Denmark; for, on his journey homewards, he was sorely handled in the Danish possessions, and made a complaint on the subject. For the rest, he appears to have been more employed on missions connected with matrimonial matters. The "Rhyming Chronicle" refers to Raleff and Saitzeff where two Boyars from Russia are mentioned; it also informs us that in all, no less than twenty Russians went to Denmark at that time, and that they embarked at Revel. Perhaps Gregory Istoma was in this company, for the Chronicle acquaints us that some Russians remained behind in Denmark in 1493. The treaty, drawn up in Latin, was celebrated at Copenhagen on the 8th of November, and we possess a copy of it. John promised assistance against the Duke of Lithuania, but he also required aid* "against his adversaries, and especially his enemy, Swanton, who had usurped the government of the kingdom of Sweden. It was stipulated that when either of them attacked Swanton, who acted as Governor of the kingdom of Sweden, or Captain Eric Sture, at Wyburg, or any such other rulers in the kingdom of Sweden as were faithless and rebellious subjects, notice should be given to the other party to the treaty."

The Ambassadors of the one were to have free passage through the territory of the other, "viam mundam in terris et aquis absque impedimento habebunt." Trade and commerce were likewise taken into consideration; but that King John promised the Czar Vassily Ivanovitch part of Finland, according to Messenius, Aeyräpää, Lasche (Jaskis), and Sawolax, does not appear in this document.

With Raleff and Saitzeff now came to Moscow the herald David, who probably had already accompanied Jacobson to that city the year before. They were the bearers of the treaty; but, as they could not return by way of the Baltic Sea, on account of the season, and moreover the danger they would run from Sweden and

* See Appendix B.

her allies, the King had them conveyed to Marstrand in Norway, a place at that time situated at its southern extremity; and there, by his order, they received guides and reindeer, with which to travel round Sweden through the Norwegian territory. The Swedish "Rhyming Chronicle" expresses great disapprobation that the King should have made the Russians acquainted with the road through Norway. According to Hintfield, some of them returned by way of Narva (Ivangorod). Master David, the companion of Raleff and Saitzeff was, so far as we can ascertain, the first Scotchman who ever visited Moscow. If Istoma went to Copenhagen in Raleff's suit, in 1493, he must also have returned before the decease of Dorothea, the Queen Mother, in 1495, after which hostilities openly broke out on the side of Sweden; for we find from Herberstein, that in 1496 his expedition set out from the Dwina, and proceeded across the White Sea and the Northern Ocean, and so round Murmansky Noss, to Drontheim in Norway. In the last mentioned year it was impossible to travel by the usual road, because Russia was waging a bloody war in Finland; whilst on the other hand, a Swedish fleet had arrived from Stockholm at Ivangorod (near Narva), then but four years built, which was plundered and destroyed. Previously to this, towards the end of the year 1495, our army, composed for the most part of inhabitants of Pskov, had been encamped for some time before Viborg, without effecting anything.

In February, 1496, Russian troops from Novogorod, where the Czar Ivan Vassilovitch had taken up his quarters in 1495, were again in Finland, into the south-western part of which they had probably penetrated on the ice of the Gulf. The winter was particularly severe; nevertheless they committed great ravages, and before the thaw came on, in the month of March, had already returned to Novogorod. About this time a fresh and powerful body of Russian troops, led by the two Princes Uschatoi, and recruited in the country around Ustjug, Onega, and the Dwina in the present government of Uleaborg, as far as Kemi and Tornea, at the north end of the Gulf of Bothnia, reached Kalikself, belonging then, as it does now, to Sweden; and likewise harassed the inhabitants of the north-eastern part of the eastern shore of the Gulf, where several places and rivers, not easily to be recognised by their Russian names, are mentioned, viz., Ijo (Ia); Hankifindas (Hechtbrecht); Ulea, where Uleaborg now stands; Limingo; Lumijoki; Sükajoki, named after the fish, Sigi (Salmo lavaretus), and Salo. A part of the troops must, nevertheless, have arrived further south, in July, in the present Knopio, as well as in the Viborg, government; for the "Rhyming Chronicle" says that the towns of Jokkas and Oloffsborg, *i. e.* Nyslott, were burnt.

Arzubuscheff writes in 1838, that this considerable Russian host embarked on the river Dwina, and proceeded by the White Sea and the Northern Ocean, round Murmansky Noss, to the places where it encamped, consequently to the Gulf of Bothnia. Into this remarkable error he appears to have been led by Letopissetz, a native of Archangel. Herberstein mentions that Istoma learnt Latin in Denmark, and it is likely that he did so under the tuition of John Jacobson, the King's "Archigrammaticus."

As Istoma was now our first interpreter and understood Latin, and as Herberstein, by his means, made himself acquainted with the history of our country, it is as well here to observe, that in 1493 Istoma arrived at Copenhagen, and either remained there then for some time, or resided there at a somewhat later period; so that opportunities were not wanting for him to attain a knowledge of that language. The University was founded in 1474, under the patronage of the then Bishop of Roschild, who, together with the Dean and the Provost of the Cathedral of that place, formed the Senate of the University. The first students were from Cologne, where Jacobson had studied, who, as we have seen, was himself Bishop of Roschild in 1500, as well as Chancellor of the University of Copenhagen. The Latin language was thus brought to Russia from Cologne by way of Copenhagen; and John Jacobson Ravensberg contributed towards its introduction. The Latin treaty of 1493 is interesting to us, because in all likelihood it was drawn up by him; and our copy must have been compared, in the first instance, with the Copenhagen original, and then published.

My conjecture that Jacobson came to Moscow in 1493 as ambassador from Denmark, is confirmed by a statement just discovered by me, in the manuscript registers used by Karamsin and called the Archival, because they are preserved in the Archives at Moscow. I found the Christian name of the ambassador to be John. In 1499, Ivan Vassilovitch demanded the hand of King

John's daughter Elizabeth, for his son, the Grand Duke Vassily; in consequence of which a Danish Embassy, consisting of Master John Anderson, Dr. Andreas Christenson, and Master Andreas Glob, was sent to Moscow, where they arrived in February, 1500. In order still further to urge on this marriage-business, Jury Manuilovitch Trachaniot was dispatched in April with the same individuals, to King John, as already stated; but they soon sent back intelligence, before they had reached their destination, that Elizabeth had married Joaquim, Margrave of Brandenberg; and nothing more explicit is mentioned in history with regard to this Embassy. Karamsin merely gives a quotation (B. 6, note 434) from the Annual Record, mentioning Master John Anderson; and he is no other than the Jens Anderson, so well known in Danish and Swedish history by the nickname of Baldeneck, being so named from his bald head.

He was the son of a shoemaker, had studied at Merseburg, and resided for some time in Italy. After his return to Denmark he became King John's private secretary; and in 1502 was installed in the Bishopric of Odensee, on the Island of Funen. He was a clever man, and frequently employed in State affairs. After Laxmand's murder he was presented with the palace of the deceased; and history throws on him likewise some suspicion of having participated in this deed. He, however, appears to have ventured to give the King a warning hint of what was intended, by means of a favorite. In 1503, he was sent to Cardinal Raymund, the Papal Legate, at that time resident at Lubeck, for the purpose of effecting Queen Christina's deliverance from Stockholm, by the promise of a large sum of money. Between 1504 and 1508 he built the Episcopal Palace at Odensee. In 1520 he attended at the coronation of Christian the Second, King of Sweden, and had a share in the massacre at Stockholm, which succeeded the festivities. He it was who made the speech to the different classes of the people, in order to persuade them to recognise the King, and afterwards proposed that all those executed should be burnt in three heaps. King Christian the Second nominated him in the same year to the Bishopric of Strenguas, in Sweden; but during the siege of Stockholm, in 1521, he escaped to Denmark, where the King, it is not known why, had him removed from one prison to another, and at last to Hammershuus, on Bornholm Island. The Lubeckers released him in 1522, when they captured the island, and after the flight of Christian the Second he returned to Odensee. In the year 1529 he disposed of this Bishopric for money to Knut Gyldensterna, and returned to Lubeck, where he died in 1539.

As I have been obliged to mention the massacre at Stockholm, I will here add a few words with reference to a man who was likewise, though indirectly, connected with it, and who was for some time in Moscow, the already-mentioned Johannes Franciscus de Potentia, a Neapolitan monk. He was sent to Denmark in 1520, by Pope Leo the Tenth, as commissioner to examine into Church affairs in the north, and particularly distinguished himself in instituting enquiries into the Stockholm massacre. The principal blame was thrown on Dietrich Slaghök, who was a countryman and relative of the infamous Sigbrit, mother of Dyveke, Christian the Second's mistress (on whose account Herberstein was sent to this King in 1516); he was of a barber's family, and after being a priest in Denmark, became Bishop of Skara in Sweden, in 1520. In consequence of the investigation made by Johannes Franciscus, at the beginning of 1522, Slaghök was first placed under the gallows, and then, after the executioner had bound him to a ladder, he was thrown on a burning pile of wood. In 1526 Pope Clement the Sixth appointed Johannes Franciscus to the Bishopric of Skara, in Slaghök's stead, and he was about to commence his journey to Sweden, to take possession of his see, when he met Demetrius Gerassimoff, and accompanied him from Rome to Moscow. Hence Herberstein says of him, without however mentioning his name, " that he was a schismatic and titular bishop of Scara." King Sigismund, on Johannes Franciscus' passage through Poland, gave him written instructions so to frame his proposals to the Czar, with regard to peace with that country, that the latter might be induced to believe that that peace was not sought by the king; he wished, moreover, to have Smolensko back again, to which end Herberstein afterwards exerted himself fruitlessly.

Andreas Christenson was a Carmelite and Doctor of Theology. I find him mentioned in 1519, on the occasion of the removal of the convent of Carmelites from Landscrona to Copenhagen, to a new building erected for the purpose, for he was then appointed

Magister provincialis. The third Dane who visited us in 1499 was Master Andreas Glob, who next appears in 1512, as secretary to Bishop Jens Anderson Baldenach, of Odensee, the same with whom he came to Moscow; and at a later period he was provost of the Cathedral of the same place. In 1520 he was sent by King Christian the Second to Segeberg in Holstein, to convey some records from thence to Sonderburg; many of the most important of which are conjectured, probably with reason, to have been destroyed at that time. He seems to have established himself afterwards at Gamborg, on the west coast of Funen, and to have inhabited at times a delightful country-house on the neighbouring Island of Svinoe, in the Little Belt. A chest presented by him to the Church at Gamborg bears this inscription, "Andreas Glob, Anno Domini, MDXXII," and it is believed that he was buried in this church; but the characters on the stone said to cover his grave have long been illegible.

Jury Manuilovitch Trachaniot and Fretjak Dalmatoff, who accompanied the three envoys whom I have here described on their return to Denmark, must have been with King John in Sweden, at the commencement of the year 1501, for the chronicle of that time relates that at an Imperial Diet then held at Stockholm, a Russian envoy was present, and that a portion of Finland was promised by the King to the Czar Ivan Vassilovitch. To this the fresh revolt of the Swedes must have not a little contributed. Sten Sture took Stockholm, and at once seized the Queen, who had remained behind in the Castle. Knut Alfson then went to Norway, and roused the whole country to rebellion; on which John Jacobson Ravensberg, Bishop of Roschild, was sent thither likewise, in order to counteract his operations. It was on account of the insurrection which then became general in Sweden and Norway that Trachaniot and Dalmatoff were unable to travel back to Russia by the usual route; and thus is explained why they sailed round Murmansky Noss, to the Dwina, in August, 1501. It may be that, in order to avoid Svatoi Noss, they made their way through Russian Lapland, to the coast of the Kandalax Gulf, and then re-embarked; for it appears that they passed the Convent of Solovetz. In their company was David the Herald, who had made the voyage round Murmansky Noss with Istoma, in 1496, in the opposite direction. When Ivan Vassilovitch, in 1503, wished to send David and his companions, escorted by a single messenger, back to King John, who was in Denmark, he dispatched the secretary Mikita Semenoff Moklokoff to his son-in-law Alexander, King of Poland, and Duke of Lithuania, to procure a safe-conduct for the going and returning through those countries. Two passes were consequently issued for them at Cracow on the 13th January, 1504, one in Russian for Lithuania, and one in Latin for Poland, and Moklokoff brought them to Moscow.

After the demise of the Czar Ivan Vassilovitch, which took place in October, 1505, David arrived at Moscow with a letter addressed to the deceased, and delayed his return until 1507, when a new messenger,

Johannes Plagh, dispatched by King John, reached the Czar Vassily Ivanovitch, and both the herald David and the messenger Plagh were sent together with Gregory Istoma back to Denmark. Here, at that time, at Nykiobing on the "Falster," a species of congress had assembled to discuss the affairs of Lubeck, where Lubeck, French and Scotch envoys met. As the letter dispatched from Moscow to King John, by Vassily Ivanovitch, was probably composed by Istoma, our first Latin diplomatist, I cannot altogether refrain from quoting it. It is as follows:*—" Most serene and dear brother, we send you many and friendly greetings. We write to your Highness, inasmuch as your Highness sent your spokesman and Herald, Master David Kocker, to our Father John, Emperor, Grand Duke, and Lord of all Russia. By the will of God, our Father has departed in the Lord. Subsequently your messenger, John Plagh, came to us with your credentials and letters, for whereas your Master David brought a message from you after the death of our Father, your messenger, John Plagh, has acquainted us again with your wish that, as Divine Providence has willed that our Father should depart in the Lord, we should be united with you, as our Father was, in fraternity and friendship, against all enemies; and that we should also send a messenger to you our brother John, the King, together with your messengers. Truly we desire to have the same friendship and fraternity with you our brother John, King of Dacia (Denmark?), Sweden, and Norway, as you had with

* See Appendix C.

our Father; and we now send you our ambassador Yschonia, together with your ambassadors. God willing, your ambassadors will reach you together with our ambassador Yschonia (Istoma), who bears these our letters. We desire, moreover, that your letters to Us be conceived in the same strong terms of friendship as those you wrote to our Father; and that you order your seal to be affixed to these letters in the same manner. And we request that in the presence of our ambassador Yschonia (Ystoma) you kiss the cross on those your letters to us, and that you send them to us, so confirmed, by your ambassador, together with our ambassador Yschonia (Istoma), sealing up your said letters in the same manner. And, God willing, when Our aforesaid ambassador returns to us with your ambassadors, bearing your letters so ratified, and when the same have been seen by us, we shall write to you letters in return—the same word for word as yours—and shall also order Our seal to be affixed thereto. On the same letters, We shall kiss the cross in the presence of your ambassador, and then we shall send you Our letters so ratified together with your ambassador. And so, with God's assistance, we request that you will sign, and send us back our ambassador Ysconia (Ystoma) without delay. Dated at Moscow on the seventieth (*sic*) day of July, in the year seven Thousand and Fifteen."

It would be very easy to set down almost to a letter the Russian words of the sketch from which Istoma composed this masterpiece. We also possess a copy of the sketch of King John's reply to Vassily

Ivanovitch. It thus commences :*—" John, &c., King. —To the Emperor of all Russia, health and sincere and fraternal love in the Lord. Dearly beloved Brother and Confederate,—Your Majesty's ambassador Yscania (Ystoma) applied and came to Us, with David our Herald on such a day, exhibiting and presenting your letters. From which letters we have clearly understood that you wish in all things to follow the footsteps of the Lord John Vassily of pious memory, and especially to enter into brotherly friendship and confederacy with Us—and so to frame our letters with reference to such friendship and confederacy, and send them to you by our aforesaid Ambassador N. and Yscania (Ystoma). We therefore, by these presents, address and transmit them to you, greatly desiring and requesting that you will send Us letters from you containing the assurance of the same friendship and confederacy—O Prince, our brother, father-in-law, and parent!"

Here follows a description of what had happened when King John went to Sweden, at the commencement of 1501, and where at that time, as already mentioned, our envoys Jury Manuilovitch, Trachaniot, and Dalmatoff must also have been; and then,† "after we had entered our kingdom of Sweden with a few followers, in accordance with their wish, in order that the natives might not be too much exasperated, they obstinately opposed us, just as the Jews did Christ; and then it pleased God that we escaped in person out of the hands of these our rebellious Swedes. Thus

* See Appendix D.   † See Appendix E.

the aforesaid Swedish rebels still occupy the whole of our kingdom of Sweden, and detain it, contrary to the law of God, contrary to justice, and contrary to the fidelity they have sworn to us. For which reason we are moved to beg Our Brother and Confederate to bear in mind the iniquity of our rebellious subjects."

In 1514, David the herald came to Moscow for the first time, as envoy from King Christian the Second, and was then already named in our annals David Staroi (the elder). In the spring of 1515 he returned to Denmark, with Ivan Mikulin Jarro Ssabolotsky, the ambassador, and the secretary Vassily Beloi, in order to negotiate a treaty of friendship and alliance with that King; and all three came back to Moscow in the autumn of the same year, to report the progress they had made, and to form arrangements with reference to this compact.

In 1516 David returned to Copenhagen with the secretary Nekrass Dalmatoff. Herberstein writes that he "made acquaintance with Master David, the envoy of the King of Denmark," but although it is neither very clear from his German nor from his Latin description, whether he and David met at Moscow, in 1517, or at Nykiobing in 1516, it is nevertheless probable that he saw him at Moscow; for in a letter written in July, 1517, by the Czar Vassily Ivanovitch, to King Christian the Second, it is explicitly stated that "Master David Gerhold" had presented himself as messenger from the King, and had requested that Danish merchants might be permitted to reside at Novogorod and Ivangorod, and there have churches of their own; to which the Czar had consented. Now, as Herberstein arrived at Moscow on the 18th April, 1517, he doubtless there met the Danish herald David, who had been for more than twenty years an acquaintance of Istoma's; and it was probably David himself who was the bearer of the Czar's letter of July.

It is remarkable that, in the translation of the Russian letter into Danish, the incorrect name of the herald should have been preserved. From this Danish translation from the Russian, Büsching took his German one, and made the name Gerolt (Magazine III, p. 178); thus the corrupted name of Gerold was transmitted by us to Denmark in writing, and afterwards returned to us in print. The treaty of alliance concluded between Vassily Ivanovitch and Christian the Second, was similar to that established, by John Jacobson's medium in 1493, with King John, and dated at Moscow the 2nd of August, 1517. Thus it is probable that David the Herald was at that time in Moscow. Herberstein remained there until the end of November. In the Imperial Archives in the Kremlin, there were formerly six original letters from the Danish Kings, John and Christian the Second, to the Czars Ivan and Vassily; and just the same number of rough sketches of epistles from the two latter to those monarchs.

I have already pointed out the probability of Cape Svätoi Noss being called by voyagers Watternäs, or Wassernase (Waternose), on account of the whirlpool which foams at a short distance from it. It was necessary that I should call attention to this Suvoi, for I consider that it contributed very considerably towards preventing Sir Hugh Willoughby from continuing his voyage farther in a south-easterly direction towards the White Sea. According to the journal kept by him, we find that, on the 14th of September, he ran into a bay on the Lapland shore, where he met with convenient anchorage; and there is no doubt that this was the large bay in which the island of Nokujeff is situated. How long he remained here is not stated, but it is probable that he weighed anchor again on the following day, or, at all events, on the 16th of September, in order to continue his course along the south-eastern coast. Now, however, the winds were quite contrary, and in tacking his vessels, he must have fallen in with the line of breakers stretching out from Cape Svatoi Noss in a north-north-west direction. That his two ships were the smallest in the expedition we are aware; for the largest was only of one hundred and twenty tons' burthen. As the wind now blew directly against the current, the Suvoi must have been in a very disturbed state, and Sir Hugh, who could not understand why his ship spun round so violently, gave orders, on the 17th of September, that both vessels should put back, probably during the flood, which set in early on this day, for he intended to return for shelter to the bay which he had left shortly before, behind the island of Nokujeff. He could not effect this, however, on the same day, and it was not advisable to attempt it during the night, for he knew, from his previous survey, that there was a small isolated rock in the middle of the bay. Sir Hugh's two vessels, therefore, the Esperanza and the Confidentia, entered Nokujeff Bay only on the 18th of September.

If the difficulties encountered by Istoma, and David the Herald, as well as by several earlier voyagers in navigating along the Lapland coast near Svatoi Noss, by reason of the Suvoi, which probably induced Sir Hugh Willoughby to return to the harbour, are no longer so much dreaded, this is very naturally explained by the difference in the size of the craft now employed, as well as by the perfection now attained in all branches of navigation, through our being at present in possession of excellent charts, and from the knowledge we have acquired of the cause and nature of the Suvoi itself. For the rest, Diaz, who perished in 1500, had, in my opinion, less grounds for naming the southernmost point of Africa, reached by him on the 1st of May, 1487, Cabo Tormentoso (Stormy Cape) than our voyagers round Murmansky Noss had for bestowing a similar appellation on Svatoi Noss; for although the dangerous whirlpool there met with is not permanent, still it continually starts into existence at regular intervals of six hours, whilst Diaz merely had to struggle against the violent and adverse winds which he casually encountered. In an unpublished memoir, dedicated to the illustrious Emperor Alexander, which gives a description of the Lapland coast, from the fishing colony in Lumboa Bay to the fishing town of Plotna, situated near the Svatoi Noss Bay, behind Joakan Island, the whirlpool is very fully described, and we find that it is even now, at the commencement of the present century, considered very dangerous for small fishing craft; for when these are accidentally drawn into it during foggy weather, they are exposed to great perils, and, indeed, are often altogether lost. This memoir forms the first volume of a work which the author, Anthony von Poschmann, who was attaché to the Polish embassy, intended to write on the fishery established on this part of the Lapland coast; the nautical part appears to be derived from the observations and inquiries made in 1800, by the naval Lieutenant Kordjukoff.

There is a manuscript description by Poschmann of that part of the Lapland coast situated in the neighbourhood of Svatoi Noss. The second volume was to contain further information with reference to the cod, herring, and other fisheries, and especially some plans for the encouragement of this branch of industry. Until very lately an opinion prevailed among the seamen along the coast, that there were worms at Svatoi Noss which perforated their vessels, but were driven away by a spell.

For the positive certainty that the bay, in which Sir Hugh Willoughby took shelter on his return, was situated to the westward of the island of Nokujeff, we are again indebted to Anthony Jenkinson, who, when near Cape Svatoi Noss, in 1557, made the following entry in his logbook, on the before-mentioned 7th of July, viz.: "Note, that we yesterday (on the 6th July) passed the spot where Sir Hugh Willoughby perished with the whole of his crew, and which is called Arzina reca, which means the river Arzina." Jenkinson was enabled to point out the place, because he had some one with him who, two years previously, had been at the mouth of the Dwina when both Sir Hugh Willoughby's vessels were brought there. This was Robert Best, who now served as interpreter. The short description given to us by Sir Hugh Willoughby himself, in his journal, of the harbour, or rather bay, which to him was nameless, is altogether applicable to the bight on the west side of Nokujeff Island, formed by the coast lying opposite to it. He says: "This harbour stretches into the land for a distance of about two leagues, and is half a league in breadth; the land is high and rocky." According to the description given by Captain Lieut. Reineke in 1842, and which is based on Affanassjeff's measurements in 1840, the western Nokujeff Bay is six versts and a half in length, three in breadth at the entrance, and one and a half in the middle; and to the south runs almost to a point. The rocky island (a peninsula at low water) of Nokujeff towards the north, viz. seaward, is the highest land on this part of the coast, and here Willoughby was completely protected against the south-east wind which at that time blew very strong. He may have sailed up to the southernmost point of the bay, where the Drosdovka falls into it; but it is probable that he cast anchor, if not at once, at all events afterwards, in the small bay formed at the mouth of the Varsina which is on the west side of the large one; for in both places there are soundings of six fathoms, which was the depth at the spot where he anchored.

CHAPTER III.

MELANCHOLY END OF SIR HUGH WILLOUGHBY—CHANCELLOR'S VISIT TO MOSCOW.

SIR HUGH WILLOUGHBY merely intended to await a change of wind in the bay in which he had anchored; but he was doomed to disappointment, for shortly afterwards a severe winter set in, with frost and snow. The moon since the night of the 21st to the 22nd of September had been on the wane, and at the end of a week Sir Hugh doubted the possibility of proceeding further, and resolved to winter there. Three parties, which were sent three and four days' journey, in different directions, to search for inhabitants, returned unsuccessful, for all the fishermen had already departed far into the interior for the winter: the days became shorter and shorter, and after the 25th of November our voyagers saw no more of the sun even at mid-day. No one was aware of any means of guarding against the cold, and, indeed, nothing had been brought for the purpose; for at that time they had no idea in England what a winter in Russia, or in the northern regions in general, was; moreover, the country surrounding Nokujeff Bay was quite bare of wood, so that at that spot were frozen to death, with Sir Hugh Willoughby, the strong crews of both vessels, consisting of sixty-five men. Most of them may have commenced their eternal sleep during the night of more than a month's duration, from the 25th of November to the 29th of December; but from a signature of Willoughby, it is ascertained that he was still alive at the end of January, 1554. Probably before his decease he was even several times rejoiced by a sight of the sun at midday; but what a scene of horror it shone upon! Two frozen-up vessels full of stiffened corpses, and only partly discernible through the snow which had drifted over them, towards which the looks of the remaining unhappy voyagers, now but half alive, were involuntarily turned, as, hopeless, and deprived even of the comforts of religion, they were despairingly awaiting the same fate. The chaplain was with Chancellor. Willoughby's vessel had two surgeons on board, Alexander Gardiner and Richard Molten, who first embarked at Harwich. In the Esperanza there were three, not, as Hakluyt writes, six, and on board the Confidentia the same number of merchants.

In summer many fishermen frequent the Lapland coast, which, as before stated, is uninhabited during the winter months; and by them were discovered in Nokujeff Bay the English vessels, with their dead crews, their merchandise, and all their gear. So soon as the Czar Ivan Vassilovitch received information of this calamity, through Chancellor, he ordered the Dwina Namestnick (Governor), Prince Semen Ivanovitch Mikulinsky Punkoff, to have all that was found on board the vessels, and in the boats, conveyed to Cholmogoru, there to be kept for a time under seal. Fofan Makaroff, together with some other persons (Kossitzin,

Rosselsky, and Jepichoff), were charged with the execution of this order. This happened in the spring of 1555.

Forty-two years later (1596-97), eleven Dutchmen, with Jacob Heemskerk and Wilhelm Barentz, lived through a winter, certainly in the endurance of many hardships, on the northern side of Nova Zembla, which had not been revisited, but they found sufficient drift wood for fuel, and for building a hut. It is worth mentioning that, as their vessel was locked up in the ice and useless, they patched up their two boats in such a manner that with them they succeeded in reaching the Lapland coast from Nova Zembla; and that these boats, after their arrival at Kola on the 1st (11th of September, 1597), were brought to the chief inn by permission of the Vaivode of that place, there to be preserved " in remembrance of their unheard-of voyage."

We are indebted to this incident for a view of Kola as it was at that time, with the large inn at a distance from it, in the middle of which a large pair of scales was suspended. It happened that the Dutchmen, with both their small craft, reached the Lapland coast (although singly, for they were separated at some distance to the north of Kanin Noss) in the neighbourhood of Nokujeff Bay, in which the English were frozen up in 1553-54. Heemskirk appears to have arrived at the bay behind the island of Kitai, where Kongloe Stanovischt is situated; and here he entered a dwelling, in which there were thirteen Russians, by whom he and his companions were received very hospitably. The other boat had already reached the coast not far from the same place, and the crews consequently united. After they had remained here a few days to recruit their strength, and had decided on naming the spot Comfort Bay, they again started together, with the idea of proceeding to Wardhuus, but were compelled by bad weather to run into an inlet to the westward of the Bay of Kola, where they found a house inhabited by three Laplanders, who confirmed what they had already ascertained from the fishermen at Lem Ostronov and Kildin—that there was a Dutch vessel at Kola. The master turned out to be Johann Cornelis Ryp, who had been their companion the year before; and they now returned to Holland in his vessel, and, consequently, were enabled to leave their boats behind them at Kola.

Although this place has already been mentioned in our work, it is not on that account by any means to be considered as important, or, indeed, as permanently settled or colonised. The Laplanders from the Murman Sea, who were baptized in 1533, were from the Kola River, Tutoloma (so it is called in the Annual Record), and Svatoi Noss. Missionary priests had been sent to them from Novogorod for the purpose of founding two churches in Lapland, one dedicated to the Annunciation, and the other to St. Nicholas. Although Stephen Burrough, during his fortnight's stay in the Bay of Kola, saw as many as thirty huts, with at least four-and-twenty men in each, these, for the most part, were not inhabitants of the place, but people who had congregated from the southern districts to engage in the walrus and other fisheries. A considerable time must have elapsed before an important settlement was formed where Kola now stands; for when, in 1565, a Dutch ship, despatched from Wardhuus in search of Philip Vinterkonig, arrived there to pass the winter, the whole place contained but three houses, the inhabitants of which fled into the forest at the sight of the vessel. In the following years the population increased, and more vessels visited the place. Until the year 1582, when some Danish vessels committed divers acts of pillage, there was no Vaivode at Kola or Malmuss, for the taxgatherers for the north of Lapland had generally dwelt at Kandalaksch. The first Vaivode, Averki Ivanovitch, constructed the store and the road for the Norwegians in 1582; and the second, Maxaka Fedorovitch Ssudimontoff in 1583 built the small fort, with the towers at the corners, the remains of which are still to be seen. To this the monastery of Petsch, destroyed by the Finns in 1590, was transferred. Between the fort and the store, and the market, at that time, flowed the Kola, which has since scooped out another channel, and by this means formed a kind of island, called Monastürsky Ostrov.

In the autumn of 1595, Ivan Samoilovitsch Salmanoff was Vaivode, and it was probably he who welcomed the Dutch vessels. With the assistance of the present excellent charts of the Lapland coast, for which we are indebted to Admiral Lutke and Captain Lieutenant Reineke, the small views and charts of

Gerhard de Veer, who passed the winter at Nova Zembla, are now rendered intelligible, which previously was not the case, for the names seldom stood in their proper places. In Veer's illustrated descriptions, published in 1598 in Dutch, Latin, and French ("Vaerachtige Beschryvinge, Diarium Nauticum, und Vraye Description," &c.), is a chart, in which the Svatoi Noss coast is placed on the other side of the Bay of Kola. Nokujeff Bay, owing to the rock which is so prominent an object in the middle of the entrance, is not to be mistaken, but the name of Mokogef is there given to it. Northwest of these are to be seen the two boats; consequently, the view was taken after they had united a second time. In later editions of Veer's illustrated account, in that, for example, by Hulsius, dated 1612, the Russian hut, and Heemskirk's boat, in which Veer himself was, are represented in a circular bay with a narrow entrance; and Veer tells us that they found their way into it through a number of rocks. It admits of no manner of doubt that this was the Bay of Kruglaja (which means circular), formed by the island of Kitai. On an eminence, the height of which is estimated by Reineke at two hundred and sixty feet, two Dutchmen from the other boat are sketched in the act of discovering from thence the hut and Heemskirk's craft; the other boat is to be seen coming out of a bay situated in a north-west direction, which must have been that of Dvorovaja. According to Hulsius (1612) the name of Mokogef is incorrectly placed here, but that of Comfort is to be read near the houses in the Bay of Kruglaja, where now also there is an encampment. Varsina is erroneously placed opposite to the Seven Islands. Afterwards we have both boats lying in a bay west of that of Kola, where also the house mentioned in the account is set down, together with the three Laplanders and the great dog—probably this was the Bay of Ura. Another Laplander, who was hired on the neighbouring hills, is now to be seen as companion to the Dutchman, despatched from thence to Kola, or rather to the ship. The latter commanded by Ryp, lies in Kola Bay, not far from the fort and the opposite store. The two boats are observed once more sailing into the bay towards the vessel. The salt works, which stand on the right shore of the bay, at the distance of three miles and a half from Kola, are likewise pointed out, and on one of the already-mentioned pages a boat is to be seen borne over land by six men. Veer's Illustrations make us tolerably well acquainted with the Russian mode of building huts at that time. It is scarcely necessary that I should remind my readers that the ever-memorable Barentz died soon after the return from Nova Zembla, and that it was the same Heemskirk who went to India from Holland with the Expeditions in 1598 and 1601. Detachments from these fleets contributed considerably to the extirpation of the Dodo at the Mauritius. Heemskirk met with his death in 1607, as admiral in the sea-fight near Gibraltar. He was interred in the old church at Amsterdam, where a monument was erected to his memory.

That at the period when it occurred, so little was written about Sir Hugh Willoughby's melancholy end is explained, on the one hand, by the fact that, in 1553, when the expedition set out, the Wollaton family, as already observed, was represented by Thomas Willoughby, a youth only thirteen years of age; and that, at the death of the latter in 1558, his successor Francis was only eleven. At the time of the voyage, moreover, and at its conclusion, the attention of England was directed to Church and State matters, far too weighty to allow of the sympathy of the public being much excited for Sir Hugh Willoughby's fate. Immediately after his departure from England, the tranquillity which until then had existed was disturbed, and very stormy times succeeded. On the 6th of July King Edward the Sixth died, and on the 10th Lady Jane Grey was proclaimed Queen. Arms were taken up on all sides; Mary ascended the throne, and Northumberland was executed. The revival of the Roman Catholic religion, as well as the Queen's intention to marry Philip of Spain, son of the Emperor Charles the Fifth, by which it was believed that England's very existence as an independent nation was endangered, gave rise to many insurrectionary movements. Wyatt advanced upon London, but was seized and beheaded. The prisons were filled with persons of rank; and at the same time that Sir Hugh's blood froze in his veins on the Lapland coast, that of his young grand-niece, Lady Jane Grey, was shed on the scaffold in the Tower, almost simultaneously with that of her husband, Lord Guilford Dudley, to whom she had been married very soon after the departure of our vessels. Shortly afterwards that of her father, Henry Grey, the brother of

Ann Willoughby, and of his and her brother Thomas Grey, was to flow. In July Mary's marriage with Philip was celebrated. Religious persecutions without number, the burning of many Protestants, pregnant women even not excepted, and the proceedings of the Inquisition, so occupied men's minds at that time, that neither Chancellor's so-called discovery of Russia, which became known in London in 1554, nor the intelligence afterwards received of the tragical end of Willoughby and his fellow voyagers, possessed sufficient interest to attract the attention of the public in any great degree.

At Wollaton House, near Nottingham, which belongs to Lord Middleton, some clothes are preserved which are supposed to be those found on the body of the frozen Sir Hugh Willoughby. Pennant relates that a servant at Wollaton House, when he showed Sir Hugh Willoughby's portrait to a stranger ("a whole length in large breeches, according to the fashions of the times") was wont to say, that it represented him in the attitude in which he was frozen; ("from his meagre appearance the servant tells you that it represents the attitude in which he was found starved"). It is difficult to imagine that any one of his unfortunate companions who may have survived him should have thought of taking the portrait of his corpse; and certainly it was not done by any of the fishermen who discovered the vessels in the spring. Be it as it may, the scene at Nokujeff in 1553-54 well deserves to have been portrayed by a more skilful artist, as John Pinkerton confesses in his book of travels,—" A general Collection of the best and most interesting Voyages and Travels," in the frontispiece to the first volume, 1808.

It were desirable, that, as a proof of our gratitude for merits so long since proclaimed, and not unworthy of a period so fruitful in events, an everlasting monument should be erected; not only in commemoration of the achievement of which Cabot was the instigator, and which led to the immediate intercourse of England with our country, but in honour of Sir Hugh Willoughby, the leader of this maritime expedition, so memorable in history and productive of results, who, with no less than sixty-five Englishmen, became the victim of his bold undertaking. The year 1853, indeed, the three-hundredth anniversary of the establishment of friendly relations between England and Russia, would have been the most appropriate for the erection of such a monument.

The black and rocky edge of the Island of Nokujeff, which, rising to a height of four hundred feet, stretches far into the sea, and is one of the most lofty and conspicuous objects on this coast, would be particularly suitable for the site of a testimonial which might be constructed of Russian and British granite. The British factory at St. Petersburg, in common with the Russian Company in London, would certainly be glad to contribute their aid to such an undertaking. Lord Middleton, too, might perhaps wish to lend some assistance towards it, for Sir Hugh Willoughby was one of the members of the family of his ancestors.

The consideration whether such a monument might

not be combined with a lighthouse, to be erected on the spot I have named, so as to be rendered useful to shipping, and instrumental in the preservation of human life, does not fall within my province. The Genoese are now about to erect a monument to their Columbus; Cabot has none, either in his native city of Bristol, or in the metropolis of Great Britain. The place of burial of the discoverer of North America, where England, as well as Russia, has now such important possessions, is not even known, although he died either in or near London. The Willoughby expedition to which Richard Chancellor, who visited the Czar Ivan Vassilovitch at Moscow, belonged, was the last great undertaking promoted by Cabot; therefore the monument at Nokujeff might be likewise a memorial of him.

It may as well here be remembered, that, just at the time when Cabot made his voyage of discovery, in 1497, to North America, Don Pedro de Ayala was in England as agent from Spain, with reference to the marriage of Catherine of Arragon, and probably made arrangements for Cabot's visit to his Court. In the following year, 1498, Columbus reached the continent of America.

The Edward Bonaventure, which was the third vessel of Cabot's expedition, was separated from the other two on the 30th of July, 1553, by a heavy storm in the North Sea, and waited for them in vain for a whole week at Wardhuus; which place had been named as the rendezvous in the event of such an accident occurring. She then entered the White Sea, and reached the coast near the mouth of the Dwina, with forty-seven persons on board, besides Richard Chancellor, Stephen Burrough, and John Buckland. The name of the before-mentioned chaplain was John Stafford, that of the physician Thomas Walter (in a MS., Water). There were two merchants, George Burton, who traded as far as the Cape, and Arthur Edwards. We might likewise mention not only John Hasse, because he at that time wrote something about Russia, but Arthur Pet, William Burrough, Richard Johnson, John Sedgwick, and Edward Passy, because, as well as Chancellor, Stephen Burrough, Buckland, and Edwards, they paid Russia a second visit. I have also found the name of Passy written Pacie, according to Hakluyt; but I cannot but imagine that the latter, on a subsequent occasion, has made the name Price. If this be the case, the Edward Price who came to Russia on the second voyage was no other than this Passy.

Nenocksa was the place, where, for the first time Russian bread and salt were placed before these guests who had so unexpectedly arrived from England. At Nenocksa itself salt is extracted from the water by boiling. The Convent of St. Nicholas carried on the salt distillery at Nenocksa. By an edict of the Czar Ivan Vassilovitch, issued in the year 1545, permission was granted to that convent to extract salt from the surrounding brine, and to lay down pipes for the purpose. Salt is yet distilled at this place, as well as at Rura, and other neighbouring spots.

The convent of the miracle-working St. Nicholas situated to the East of Nenocksa, close to the Korelian mouth of the Dwina, must have been the first place visited by the English. From a description given of the church and the possessions of the convent, scarcely two years previous to their arrival, we are made acquainted with what they saw there, and with the names of the persons then inhabiting it.

Chancellor must now have assumed the character of an envoy (Pussol) from England. With several of his shipmates he ascended the Malokurje and Dwina as far as Cholmogorü, the chief magistrate (Fofan Makaroff) of which town, with his colleagues, sent a report of the arrival of the English to Ivan Vassilovitch. This happened in October. It must have been a very hard winter, for Chancellor related to Adams in London that the people remaining on board the vessel suffered very much from the cold: " Nautæ certe nostri, qui in nave remanserant, ex inferiori stega in foros scandentes, tam subita, lipothymia nonnunquam sunt correpti, ut intermortui subinde ruerunt; tanta erat illic rigentis cœli inclementia." In the hermitage of Pertomin, erected in Una Bay in 1599, the Czar Peter, at the time of his visit to the Dwina in 1694, spent three days, and there himself put together a wooden cross with an inscription, which he also assisted in carrying to the sea-shore, and erecting in grateful remembrance of his preservation; for in the passage from Archangel to the Convent of Solovetz he had been in great danger of losing his life in a storm. For his deliverance he was indebted to the resolution and dexterity of the steersman Antip Timofeeff, who piloted the craft happily into the Bay of Una. Did the Czar at that time call to mind that this Bay in 1553-54 was the first on the North coast of Russia in which a foreign vessel anchored? Chancellor's vessel was brought, by direction of the magistrates, to winter in the Bay of Una to the West of Nenocksa, and Chancellor started in a sledge on the 23rd of November, to travel to the residence of the Czar, without waiting to receive his invitation or permission. This, however, met him on its way from Moscow.

The arrival of the English in Russia took place almost at the same time as some of the most important events in our history. The Czar Ivan Vassilovitch had not long before returned, covered with glory, to Moscow, after the conquest of Kazan. Astrachan was soon afterwards compelled to open to Russia a passage to the Caspian Sea. Siberia, ignorant of the golden treasures contained in her soil, sent offerings of sables and grey squirrel-skins as tokens of subjection to the ruler of Russia; her Prince and people did homage to the Czar; and thus was the first step made towards taking possession of that immense country, so rich in metals, and from whence North America was soon afterwards reached.

Twelve days after Chancellor's arrival at Moscow, the Czar's Secretary, Ivan Michaelovitch Viskovatü, who at that time presided over the Department of Foreign Affairs, announced to him that Ivan Vassilovitch would admit him to an audience, whereat he was not a little rejoiced. This person was, just at the time of Chancellor's visit to Moscow, under examination on account of his accession to the Baschkin heresy. The ignominious fate which he suffered in 1570 in consequence of his alleged treason against Russia, in favour of Poland, is known. Alexis Fredorovitch Adascheff, Ivan's favourite, was present at the reception of Chancellor, who was accompanied by the two merchants, Burton and Edwards, and handed to the Czar an open letter from King Edward the Sixth, of which several copies had been supplied to each vessel of the Expedition in different languages, for all rulers whose countries they might visit ("Ad Principes septentrionalem ac orientalem mundi plagam inhabitantes juxta Mare Glaciale, necnon Indiam Orientalem.") In this document England's especial desire to enter into treaties of commerce was evinced. Amongst other things there is the following paragraph :*—" We have permitted the honourable and brave Hugh Willoughby, and others of our faithful and dear servants who accompany him, to proceed to regions previously unknown, in order to seek such things as We stand in need of, as well as to take to them from our country such things as they require. This will be productive of advantage both to them and to us; and establish a perpetual friendship and an indissoluble league between them and us, whilst they permit us to receive such things as abound in their territories, and we furnish them with those of which they are destitute." After the audience, Chancellor and both the merchants had the honour of being admitted to the Czar's table.

Chancellor took a great deal of trouble in acquiring as much information as he could as to the commercial

* See Appendix F.

capabilities of Russia, this being the point most interesting to England. We are in possession of the result of his observations in an English letter, written by him to his uncle Christopher Frothingham; and Clement Adams has imparted to us, in Latin, the communications made to him by Chancellor, with reference to his travels. Eden, in 1557, wrote that he had been told by Chancellor that at Moscow he had met with an ambassador from "the Kinge of Persia, called the Great Sophie," who was dressed in scarlet, and had said much to the Czar in favour of the English, for England and her commerce were not unknown to him. (" The ambassador was appareled all in scarlet, and spoke much to the Duke in behalf of our men, of whose kingdom and trade he was not ignorant.") Our annals contain no information with reference to this visit of a Persian ambassador to Moscow in 1553-54. Chancellor himself, and after him Adams, describe the pomp with which two ambassadors were dispatched to Lithuania. Hasse states that, whilst he was at Moscow with Chancellor, a great ambassador arrived from Livonia "for the assurance of their privileges." This must have been the Embassy, an account of which has been handed down to us, and consisting of the military chief of Livonia and the Bishop of Dorpt. John Hasse, who accompanied Chancellor, described, for the information of the body of English merchants, the Russian coins, weights, and measures, as well as the customs' duties; he, moreover, gave a list of the commodities produced by Russia, and recommended Vologda as the most suitable place, after Moscow, for the establishment of a second depôt for English wares. He profited also by the detention at Wardhuus, by making himself acquainted with the weights used there. Of stockfish and salmon, he says that they come to Cholmogoru, from a place not far from Wardhuus, named Mallums. This must be Malmuss, identical with Kola.

In compliance with Chancellor's request that the establishment of commercial relations might be permitted between England and Russia, a letter was dispatched by the Czar Ivan Vassilovitch to King Edward the Sixth, but the latter had died on the 6th July previous. It was thus possible for so long a period to elapse before the intelligence of such an important event could reach Russia from England. What a contrast this affords with the present time! According to this letter ("Gramota"), English merchants were to be well received in Russia, and empowered to carry on their trade without hindrance. The document is not only interesting, because it was the first received in England from Russia, but deserves to be still better known, because Hakluyt, in publishing an English translation of it in 1599, was led into an error in expressing the title of the Czar Ivan Vassilovitch, as it appears that Astracan, Siberia, and Livonia are placed earlier in the Czar's title than really was and could be the case. In the Czar's letter of February, 1554, neither Astracan, Siberia, nor Livonia is named.

I have sought in vain in England for the original of this letter from the Czar, but believe I have discovered the first English translation made from it, and have, moreover, copied for myself that translation of which Hakluyt must have availed himself. This MS. is much injured by fire, but I have been enabled to supply what was wanting, from an earlier copy. All three copies prove that Hakluyt, in the publication of his " Principal Navigations" in 1599, has taken an unpardonable liberty, for the names of the countries governed by the Czar were not only illegible, but he has taken the Czar's titles from later documents, so that Ivan Vassilovitch, at the commencement of 1554, is represented as " King of Astracan, Lord and Great Duke of Livonia, and Commander of the whole of Siberia." Hence Karamsin is led to believe that the Czar was then, in February, 1554, so designated, although our annals, even in 1555, make mention of an embassy sent to him at Moscow by Lediger, the ruler of Siberia, with offers of submission.

As Karamsin says nothing of Astracan and Livonia, he appears to consider it possible that Ivan Vassilovitch, even in 1554, had assumed the names of these countries in his title. Hakluyt's error of 1599 is the more remarkable, since in his earlier, and, for the rest, very rare work, published in 1589, he has given the Czar's title correctly. He seems also to have seen the original Russian letter, for he describes the Russian writing, as well as the seal affixed to the document, with the knight in armour fighting with the dragon. It was written on paper, and there was also a German translation of it. The older English copy, discovered by me, appears to have been taken from this German one, and again, indeed, by a German in London. I met with it in a volume which must once have belonged to the

Herald's College, but which since has been in the possession, amongst other persons, of Sir Robert Cotton, and at last of the celebrated antiquary, Richard Gough, who died in 1809. At the sale of his effects by auction, in 1810, this volume was purchased for the British Museum. On the back of page 175, and at page 176, we find the following:—"The copye of the lettre which was sente to Kinge Edward, A.D. 1554. The almyghtie power of God, with the feare of the hooly Trynytie: a right Christian belever, we greatiste Lord John Vasselevitch, by the grace of God Emperour of all Russes: and greate Duke Volloidemersque: Moskosque: nogrottsque: kassanque: placestosque: Smallentsque: Tweresque: Iverdsque: permysque: vettsque: bolgorsque: and of other lands Emperour and greate Duke to Newgorod in the lowe countrey: chernegofsque: Rasusque: Wollotsque: yerzeffsque: belsque: Rostosque: yeraslawsky: belowesbersque: udorsque: obdorsque: flondynski: with dyverse other lands: lorde on all the northe side and petisioner. In primis greattist and famous Edward Kinge of England: our gracious word, with good and friendlie remembrance in all reason from our Christian faythfull greate taking auctoritie by commanndment of the hyghest of our Awncestrye: this our lordlie writinge to a kinglie desyre, accordinge to the peticon of one Richard, trewlie sent with the reste of his fellowshippe whern he shall trewlie com to you. By yt celf the 20 yere of our lordshippe to our seacoste ys com folk in one shyppe theade Rychard, withys felowshippe and have said that they arre frinds they have desyred to com within our lordlie dominion, and accordinge to theyre requests they have fullye grauntid, and have byn in our lordlye howsse in presence of our sight, and hathe desyred us accordinge to Your kinglie requests that we wold permytt Your marchants to travaile to our subiects and dominions, to occupie withall manner of wares, without hynderaunce, staye, or Interrupcon, and hathe geven us your lettre, in which lettre ys written the like request, to manner of men in theire dominions, wheresoever they shal happen to com sent by Your trewe servaunte, Hughe Willowghbie the which Hughe Willoughbie in our dominions hathe not arryved, and whereas Your sservante Rychard ys com to us, we wythe christian trewe assurance in no manner of wyse will refuse his petision, and by our faythful grante, we will not forsake thye request, by the which Your ymbassett that You sent to us, the same thy Imbasset with good ffree will to passe to us and from us withowt anye hynderance or losse, with suche message as shall com to us, the same message to retourne to thie kingdom well awnswerid withall suche marchaunts as shall com forthe of Your lande withall manner of ware, if they will traveile to occupie within our bordours, the same marchants with free marchandise in all our lordshippe, withall manner of ware and uppon all manner of ware frelie to travele owt and in, without hynderaunce and losse accordinge to this our lettre, and as ffurther assurance of our worde we have caused our signet to be sett to this our lettre, written in our lordlie howsse and castle the Musco. In the yere 7042" (it should be 7062) "the monethe of februarye."

As Hakluyt, according to his usual custom, has thought proper to alter the translation of which he availed himself, so as to suit his own fancy, I here give it exactly as it is to be found in the British Museum (Otho E. pages 49 and 50). The pieces burnt out I supply in Italics from a copy taken before the accident, and which I met with in the Lansdowne collection, 141, page 342. It is as follows:—" The Almightie power of God and the *incomprehensible* hollie Trinitie of our rightfull *christian beliefe*. We greatest Lord Ivan Vassileuiche *by the* grace of God Emperour of all Russia *and great* Duke Vslademerskij, Moskous*kij*, *Cazanskij*, Psouskij, Smollenskij, Tuerdskij, Yogors*kij*, *Permijsk*, Veatskij, Bolgarskij, and other lands, *Emperor* and great Duke of Novagorodas and in the *lowe* countreys cheringosskij, Rezanskij, Volots*kij*, *Rzesskii*, Belskij, Rostouskij, Yoroslanskij, Belocherskij, Ovdorskij, Obdorskij, Condinskij and many other *countries*, Lord over all the north Cost greetinge. Before all right great and of honor worthye Edward Kinge of England, our most hartie and of good zeale with good intent and frendlie desire and of our holie Christian faith and of great governaunce and in the light of great understanding our answere by this our honorable writinge unto Your Kinglie governaunce at the request of your faithful servaunt Richard with his company as he shall wisely lett You know, is this. In the strength of XX tie year of our governance be knowne at our sea coast arived a shipp with one Richard and his companie, and sai*d that he was* desirous to come into our dominions a*nd according* to his request hath seene our lordshipp *and our heires*" (at Otho, E 3, this certainly stood, " eies." Hakluyt also so has it) "and hath declared your Ma-ties *desire* that wee schould graunt unto Your subj*ects to goe* and come and amonge our dominions *and subiects* to frequent free merkett with all sort of *merchandizes*, and uppon the same to have ware for the*ir retorne*, and they delivered unto us Your letters *which declared* the same request. And uppon that we *have geven* order wheresoever Your faithfull servaunt *Hugh* Willobe lande or touche in our dominion*s to be* well enterteyned which as yet is not arri*ved the* which your servaunt Richard can declare. A*nd we* with Christian beliefe and faithfullness and *according* to Your honble request and my hõble commande*ment* will not leave it undonne. The which both wilbe You to send unto us with your shipps *and* vessells when and as often they may with good assurançe to see them harmeles. And yf You *send* me one of Your Ma-ties Councell to treat with us whereby Your countrey merchants maie with all kind of wares and wheare they will make their mar*ket* in our dominions and ther to have the*ir free market* with all free liberties through my who*le domi*nions with all kinde of wares and of all kinde of *wares* to come and goe at ther pleasure with*out any* of ther lett damage or impediment accor*ding and* by this our Lettre or word with my seale and this my will or Lettre wee have co*manded* to be undersealed. Written in our dominion *in our* Towne and our Pallace in the Castell of *Moscovie* in the yere seven thousand and sixtie the *second* month ffebruarye."

CHAPTER IV.

ESTABLISHMENT OF THE RUSSIA COMPANY—CHANCELLOR'S SECOND EXPEDITION.

CHANCELLOR and his companions quitted Moscow in March, 1554; awaited the favourable season for leaving the Dwina, and returned to England in the Edward Bonadventure. This vessel had the misfortune to fall in with, and be robbed by, the "Flemings," on the passage, but the ship's company reached London with the letter addressed to Edward the Sixth by the Czar, which was delivered to Queen Mary. Chancellor everywhere related how graciously he had been received at Moscow by Ivan Vassilovitch.

A new company was now formed in London by some merchants and a few persons of rank, which had for its object the discovery of unknown countries in a north-east as well as north-west direction, and was established by special charter, granted by Philip and Mary, on the 26th February, 1555. Cabot was appointed President of the same during his life; and as Chancellor had already obtained from Ivan Vassilovitch the assurance of special favour for England, an exclusive privilege was conferred on this company to trade with Russia. This company has often changed its name in the course of time. It is now known under that of the Russia Company, although it does not retain its earlier privileges. I have before me the names of all its founders, which are nowhere published. Amongst six persons of high rank, one was William Howard, Earl of Effingham, at that time Lord High Admiral of England. In the account given of him in the latest edition of Burke's Genealogical and Heraldic Dictionary of the Peerage and Baronetage of the British Empire (under the head of Effingham) it is stated that in 1553 he was employed as Ambassador to the Czar of Muscovy, and that this was the first embassy from England to Russia; but this altogether groundless assertion must be expunged from the next edition of the Peerage.

Besides those six noble persons, there were one hundred and eighty-four other members, of whom we may here mention—Sebastian Cabot, Sir Henry Sidney, Sir William Cecil, Sir William Peter, Sir George Barnes, William Gerard, Thomas Offley the elder, and John Dymock, because they made themselves useful to the Company in various ways; but Richard Chancellor, Stephen Abroughe (Burrough), John Buckland, Arthur Edwards, George Burton, Thomas Banister, and John Sparke, because they had been in Russia. The list of the original members preserved in the Cottonian collection of MSS., in the British Museum (Otho E 3, pages 49 and 50) is unfortunately half burnt, as well as many other documents of this section, so that the last half wants all the leaves. In the Lansdowne collection, No. 141, pages 343 and 352, I found a copy from which I was enabled to supply what was wanting. Hakluyt has considered it necessary to acquaint us with merely the names of the noblemen connected with the company.

Great pains have been taken in England to represent Chancellor's arrival at Nenocksa in the light of a discovery of Russia by England. Hakluyt, even in 1598, wrote as follows:—" Wil it not in all posteritie be as great a renoune unto our English nation to have bene the first discoverers of a sea beyond the North cape (never certainly knowen before) and of a convenient passage into the huge Empire of Russia by the bay of St. Nicholas and the river of Dwina; as for the Portugales to have found a sea beyond the Cape of Buona Esperanza, and so consequently a passage by sea into the East Indies; or for the Italians and Spaniards to have discovered unknowen landes so many hundred leagues Westward and Southwestward of the streits of Gibraltar, and of the pillers of Hercules." It is, therefore, worth while to ascertain whether Willoughby and Chancellor, before their departure, had been able to acquire any knowledge of the White Sea, the Dwina, and the north-eastern part of Russia.

We know that the earliest information of a voyage round Norway, viz., round Murmansky Noss (since 1553 called the North Cape) was drawn up by Alfred, King of England, who was equally well qualified to wield the sword and the pen, and who is considered to be the creator of the first English fleet. He wrote down his information from the accounts of Other, the Norman, who in Burik's time, or somewhat earlier, probably in the last quarter of the ninth century, had undertaken a sea-voyage from the west coast of

Norway to the White Sea. It is remarkable that the oldest description of a voyage to our northern coast should have been written by a King's hand, at the same time that we are indebted to an Emperor, Constantine the Fourth, Porphyrogenitus, for the first intelligence with respect to the earliest voyages made by the Russians in the Black Sea.

It appears to me to be by no means certain that the river visited by Other was, as is generally supposed, the Dwina, into which Erik Blodyxa, with Harald Gräfäll, Thorer Hund with Karli and Guastein, as well as certainly many other coasting voyagers ("biarm afahrer"), had sailed up to the commencement of the Mongolian period (1252); for it may have been the river Mesen that Other entered. In the White Sea, or to speak more accurately, in the Bay, into which the river Mesen falls (Mesen Bay), there is an island to the left, that of Morshovet, so called after the walrus, "Morshü." Herberstein, in 1549, wrote it "Mors," and Pantaleon, the translator of his Latin work, in 1563, capriciously added, "or death." Miechov, the Pole, rendered it in 1517 the fish "morss." Chancellor, in 1554, says: "a fish, called a Morsse," and Adams also, in 1554, makes it "bellua Mors nominata." To the left lie the "Morshowuja Koschki," *i. e.* the Walrus sandbanks or shoals. Other tells us that, to acquire information respecting the walrus fishery, was the principal object of his voyage, for the walrus teeth, the ivory of that period, were valued very highly; and the ropes used for shipping were made from the hides of the same animal. This account, by the way, is a proof of the great antiquity of navigation in those waters. Alexis Fedorov Okladnikoff, an inhabitant of Mesen, possessed of much experience, assures me that twenty years ago a great many walrusses were killed on the east side of the entrance into the White Sea, between Kija and Kanin Noss. The stations were at the little rivers Salmitzu and Bolschija Bugranitzu. Herberstein mentions that walrusses were abundant at the mouth of the Petschora; and Chancellor says: " Those who kill them live at Pustosersk." The first writes: " At the mouth of the Petzorn they talk of remarkable animals, called mors, which are about the size of an ox, live in the sea, and have two long teeth in the upper jaw. Only those are killed which have the beautiful white teeth, of which handsome knife-handles are made." The most productive walrus-fishery is even now on the Gulaiev shoals, opposite to Petschora Bay, on Waigat, and on the West Coast of Nova Zembla, but in Other's time these animals may have been abundant on the island called after them, and on the coast south of Kanin Noss.

As Other presented King Alfred with some walrus teeth, from the White Sea, these were the first articles brought to England from the waters, which wash the present Russian coast. Probably Other took not only teeth, but hides with him, so that these would be the earliest known articles of exportation from the White Sea to Norway. I cannot here refrain from observing that I found Alfred's description of Other's voyage, preserved in the British Museum, near William Cecil's journal, from 1552 to 1557. Cecil first married Mary, a sister of Sir John Cheke's, and then Mildred, the daughter of Sir Anthony Cooke. As Cheke and Cooke were tutors to the young Edward, Cecil became well known through them, not only to the Protector Somerset, but to the young monarch himself, and attained considerable honours. As he was likewise active in commercial matters; for example, in 1551, when the monopoly of the Steelyard was abolished, we may easily infer that Alfred's account of Other's voyage was laid before King Edward, and that many conversations took place on the subject between Cabot, who had access to the Court, and Edward, who was eager after knowledge, and before whom plans were often laid relating to naval affairs.

We cannot inform our readers whether Cabot, for whom King Alfred's description of Other's voyage must have possessed great interest, had any knowledge of it; but he had it in his power to procure the published Italian translation of Herberstein's work on Russia ("Commentari della Moscovia"), in which are to be found the voyages of our Istoma, and David the Danish herald, round Murmansky Noss, together with notes on the Icy Sea, the Dwina, the Petschora, and the Oby. It had been published in 1550, at Venice, where Cabot spent his youth; and annexed to it is the map of Russia, drawn up by Giacomo Gastaldo, the Piedmontese Cosmographer, in which, not only the Icy Sea (it is merely a portion of the White Sea), but the rivers Dwina, Mesen, Petschora, together with the Zilma (where ores had been found), and likewise the Oby, are set down. The latter issues from a large sea, on the right, the eastern, side of the map, viz. the Kithai Sea (Kythay lago), and the account of it given in the book is, that it was "il lago di Kithai, dal quale il gran chane di Cathaia, il quale gli Moscoviti Czar Kythaiski appelano, ha il nome." How much such a geographical notice must have interested the projector of the north-eastern expedition to Cathay! It is scarcely to be doubted that Cabot received this book, together with the map, from Venice. Of Finland and Wardhuus, Sir Hugh Willoughby and Chancellor had accounts in their possession; for they had agreed, that in case their vessels were separated in the North Sea, they should wait for each other at Wardhuus. As the navigation between Wardhuus and the Dwina was then described by Herberstein, from Istoma's narrative of his voyage on the Icy Sea, the way there was pointed out, and Cabot may have thus been made acquainted with it. Now Demetrius Gerassimoff explained, in his description of Russia, annexed to Herberstein's work, that if a vessel sails from the Dwina along the shore to the right, she will probably reach Cathay; and Gerassimoff's account was published in Latin, first in 1537, and then in 1545 and 1551.

Germany had received a considerable amount of information with regard to Russia in 1488, through Poppel, as well as from 1489 until 1492, through Jury Trachaniot, Chalessa, Aksentjeff, Kuleschin, Dr. Thorn, Jarophin, and Kuritzin. When the Diet met at Frankfort, in 1489, sable, ermine, and squirrel skins were presented to Maximilian, King of Rome; and, soon afterwards, furs of a similar description were offered in payment to the metallurgist and other artizans engaged for Russia. Soon after his return to Germany, Poppel dispatched a person to the north-eastern districts of Russia, in order to procure one of the Woguls, "who eat raw flesh," as well as a live moose-deer, for the German Emperor, Frederick the Third. Michael Snups travelled to Moscow, in 1492, for the purpose of undertaking a journey to the Oby, and giving a geographical, and, especially, a scientific account of that region, but Ivan Vassilovitch would not permit him to proceed.

In Ramusio, we find that a Russian displayed a map to a scientific person at Augsburg, in order to demonstrate that it might be possible to reach the Spice Islands and countries, *i. e.* India, by way of the Icy Sea. This may have been Vassily Vlassy, on his way back from Spain, in 1525, with the Prince Ivan Jaroslavsky Sassekin; if not, it was Demetrius Gerassimoff, either on his way to Rome with Paulo (centurione), or on his homeward journey with Johannes Franciscus de Potentia, the Bishop nominated by the Pope to the See of Skara, in Sweden, who was never recognised by Gustavus Vasa, as we have already mentioned.

The Russian peltries, about the time of Willoughby's expedition, were in considerable request in England, as well as elsewhere; as many of the portraits painted by Hans Holbein in that country, from 1526 to 1534, testify. I will only cite, as examples, that of Warham, Bishop of Canterbury, who died in 1532; that of the Chancellor, Sir Thomas More, who was executed in 1535; and that of Queen Anna Boleyn, who was beheaded in 1536.

The Queen of Poland, Helena Ivanovna, towards the end of the year 1503, requested her father, the Czar Ivan Vassilovitch, to send her a fur of the black sable, with the fore and hind feet and claws on; and his reply, in March, 1504, was, that where the sables were caught both their legs were cut off; but that he had given orders that some should be preserved for her as she desired, and that when he had received them they should be immediately forwarded to her.

In 1527, Herberstein brought with him from Moscow to Germany, some living ermines and squirrels (from which the grey fur is taken), but lost three of the latter on the way, at Dubrovna.

In April, 1555, Chancellor was again dispatched to Russia with the Edward Bonaventure, and furnished with a letter from Philip and Mary to the Czar, dated the 1st of April, and drawn up in Greek, Polish, and Italian, wherein His Majesty was thanked for the gracious reception he had accorded to Chancellor on the occasion of his first visit to Moscow, and a renewal of his favour for that commander and the persons with him, together with further encouragement of commerce, were solicited. In the English sketch of this letter I find a confirmation of my former conjecture with reference to the age of the translation communicated by me, of the Czar's Russian dispatch of 1554, for in some passages the identical words there used appear: for instance, in the following: "Your Maiestie have granted that all marchants with al manner of wares, if they wil travel or occupie within your dominions, the same marchants with their marchandises in al your lordship very freely, and at their libertie travaile out and in without hinderance or any manner of losse: further, that our ambassadours shall with free good will passe to and from you without any hinderance or losse, with such message as shall come unto you, and to return the same to our kingdomes well answered." Thus that translation was the official one, and in accordance with which the reply was composed.

It is likewise evident from this sketch, that at Chancellor's first visit to Moscow, some of his companions were admitted with him to an audience, and to the Czar's table, for mention is made of it in the same document: "Your Majestie did call Chancelour and certaine of his company to your emperiall presence and speech, entertayned and banqueted them with all humanitie and gentleness." From the royal privilege of 26th of February, 1555, it appears that these were the merchants, George Burton and Arthur Edwards. "Lord John Basilivitch, Emperour of all Russia, did not onely admitte the captaine and marchants our subjects into his protection and princely presence, but also received and entertained them very graciously and honourably."

Stephen Burrough remained this time in England, and John Buckland, who on the first voyage was his lieutenant, was now the sailing-master. Chancellor took one of his two young sons with him. At the same time came two merchants, appointed to be commercial agents in Russia. The name of one of them was George Killingworth, that of the other Richard Gray.

Killingworth had been a draper in London. The company particularly reckoned at that time on a ood sale of cloth in Russia; and the result proved that they were not mistaken. It was the period when sheep-skins began to make way for kaftan. In London, the broadcloth exported to Russia cost the company, one piece with another, £5 : 9 : 0, if dyed of the usual colours; but scarlet came to £17 : 13 : 6; and fine violet to £18 : 6 : 6. The rouble then passed for sixteen shillings and eightpence, but was considered to be worth only thirteen shillings. I have often found in the imperial edicts conferring grants, the words "lukno lundüsch," which simply mean London cloth. At Cambridge I found a MS. from which I learnt that a description of broadcloth afterwards exported to Russia, was called by the English merchants lundish cloth. The first important shipment of cloths from England (two hundred and nine pieces) arrived in the Dwina in the year 1557: it was accompanied by five hundred and eighteen pieces of kerseys, from Hampshire, which in London cost £4 : 6 : 0 the piece. No less than four hundred of them were sky-blue, consequently this colour must have been particularly in request; of the remaining pieces forty-three were blue, fifty-three red, fifteen green, five ginger-coloured, and two yellow.

The shipment likewise included some cotton stuffs, (twenty-one bales, at £9 : 10 : 0,) pewter vessels (nine casks,) sugar, &c. The prices of Russian produce, at that time, were: wax four pounds, tallow sixteen shillings, and flax from twenty to twenty-eight shillings per cwt.; and train oil nine pounds per ton.

During the first few years of its existence, the company wished to confine its imports principally to the articles here named, but contemplated the subsequent introduction of hemp and tar, in the shape of cables, and ropes coated with the latter substance. With regard to furs, they imported an assortment, for the directors wrote, "as for sables and other rich furres, they bee not every man's money." Killingworth, soon after his arrival at Moscow, in 1555, purchased five hundred weight of flaxen yarn, at eightpence farthing the pound, for exportation to England. The company had probably heard from Napea, or from Robert Best, that in Russia and Tartary much steel was manufactured ("we heare that there is great plentie of steele in Russia and Tartarie, and that the Tartar's steele is better than that in Russia"). The directors consequently desired, in 1557, to see some samples of it, and that of Ustjug and Tula Uklad must here have been meant. The latter might be correctly called Tartar steel, for it was prepared for the most part behind the line on which Russia's wooden walls (an abattis of forest trees) were erected against the Tartars; at all events it is worthy of being historically recorded, that England was desirous of procuring steel from Russia. German steel was then much dearer in London than it was in 1551, at the time of the abolition of the Steelyard monopoly. Intelligence had also reached London, that Russia was rich in copper ("that there is great plentie of copper"), in consequence of which there was a great desire to see samples of it, and obtain more detailed information. Three roubles in coin were then procured from Moscow, in order that they might be assayed, and their true value ascertained. Killingworth was only, for about two years, at the head of the trading department at Moscow, and made journeys to Novogorod, Pskow, and Cholmogorü. When he first arrived at Vologda, in 1555, a merchant offered him twelve roubles for a piece of broadcloth, and four altins for a pound of sugar, but he would not sell at these prices. For the rent of a house at Vologda, in which he stored the greater part of the goods which he brought with him, he paid, from the middle of September until Easter 1556, ten roubles.

Richard Gray, the second chief of the trading establishment, energetically undertook to set up a rope manufactory at Cholmogorü, for which the principal workmen were sent out from England, in 1557. On the 14th of April, 1558, he and Robert Best were shown Ivan Vassilovitch's crown, together with the great ruby on a wire; his jewels, which were costly, but most miserably set; and the Czar's rich robe, covered with large pearls and heavy stones. He was then requested that, on his return to England, which was soon to take place, he would ascertain whether he could not purchase some similar, and if possible, more costly jewels, pearls, and gold stuffs, to add to the Czar's stock. In February, 1559, Gray was at Cholmogorü, and had an idea of proceeding thence to the annual fair at Lamposhna. This place, situated on an island eighteen versts beyond the present chief town of Mesen, was at that time one of considerable commercial importance. Lamposhna was the Makarjev of that time, for it was the place where the commodities from that part of Russia, situated on this side of the Dwina, were bartered for the produce of the fisheries on Nova Zembla, Waigat, and other islands; and for the articles brought by the Promuschlenniks from the country of the Samoiedes, as well as from Ugria and the whole of the north-eastern regions then known.

Many varieties of peltries and reindeer hides, as also those of the walrus and their teeth, were conveyed by means of reindeer, from Pustosersk and other places, to Lamposhna, where, twice a year, a fair was held, frequented by Russian merchants, mostly from Cholmogorü. The bartered wares were brought to Cholmogorü by way of Pinega, and from thence, those destined for exportation, before the English had found their way to the Dwina, were sent to Novogorod; but Russia was provided with them by way of Vologda and Moscow. John Hasse, 1554, mentioned Lamposhna as situated between Pinega and Pustosersk ("Penninge, Lampus, and Powsetzer"). He says that, amongst other things, cloth, tin and copper utensils ("cloth, tinne, batrie") were taken there for barter, from Cholmogorü. Chancellor enumerates the different peltries, and says that they were conveyed, together with the "fishteeth," on reindeer ("on harts"), to Lampas, for sale; but that from the latter place the articles obtained by barter were taken to Cholmogorü, where the yearly fair was held, on St. Nicholas' day. In imitation of him, Adams relates, when speaking of that fair, that the goods were conveyed to Lamposhna on the backs of reindeer ("Mercimonia cervorum dorsis ad oppidum Lampas feruntur"). Chancellor did not express his meaning quite so clearly by "on harts," but if he supposed that the reindeer were loaded with the goods, he was mistaken, for they were placed on sledges; and these were drawn by reindeer. From Richard Johnson we learn, that twice a year a fair was held at Lamposhna; and Gray wrote that, in 1559, more people congregated at Lamposhna than had been the case for ten years previously. ("This lent, 1559, cometh to Lampas such a number of men of divers nations, with wares, as hath not been seen these ten yeeres.") He especially mentions the Ugrians ("thither came many out of Ugori"), and likewise names the Cholmogorü merchants, who had already arrived there. He had himself taken a quantity of cloth (kerseys) for the purpose of bartering.

Lamposhna is incorrectly set down on our maps, for the true situation of this place is on Lamposhensky Ostrov, the southernmost and largest of the dozen islands formed in the channel of the river Mesen, to which names are given, and which are covered with fertile grassy meadows. The narrower part of the right branch of that river, eastward of those islands, is here called Kurja Creek. On the south end of the said island, which is about twelve versts in length, the town of Lamposhna, which contains two churches, is built; and before it the small river Schukska flows from the west into the Mesen. A winter road, which has four stations, leads from thence to the town of Pinega. Lamposhna is at present the seat of the administration of a district of crown serfs ("Wolostnoje Prowlenie"). Inquiries should be instituted as to the age of the place, as a mart: perhaps it was frequented by the coasting voyagers (Biarma-fahrer). In the spring, parts of the old buildings must at times be be washed away by the freshes. The Russian word Poshna (a meadow) appears to be the root of the present name.

Several other young merchants accompanied Chancellor, in his second voyage, for the purpose of being employed, as well at Moscow as at several other places in the interior of the country, in the management of commercial matters. Some of them are to us invested with special interest, because they have given accounts, in writing, of matters relating to trade as then carried on, and of other subjects. The following individuals came to Russia, for the first time, with this expedition: Henry Lane, Christopher Hutton, Robert Best, and others. Henry Lane, in 1557, was appointed third agent, and to him we are indebted for several notes on the establishment of the trade. One portion of them was drawn up by himself, the other is to be found in the correspondence communicated by him for publication. Although he was originally appointed agent to the company at Cholmogorü, he afterwards filled the same post at Moscow, and quitted Russia in 1560.

Henry Lane was an accomplished person; he wrote sundry papers with reference to the early period of the residence of the English in Russia, and particularly on the audience granted by the Emperor in 1555, at which he was present. He mentions that Stephen and William Burrough were the first who laid down the island of Waigat on a chart (" an island called Waigatz, first by them put into the carde or mappe"). On another occasion he describes how, shortly before his departure from Moscow, in 1560, a commercial difference with Schirai Kostronitzky, and some other Russian merchants, was legally settled by lot in favour of the English Company. He returned to England with Jenkinson, and in 1556 was the company's agent at Antwerp and Amsterdam.

In the previous year, Raphael Barberini, an Italian, sought, as further on I shall show, to establish a trade between Antwerp and Russia, and in 1554 obtained for himself a privilege for that purpose from the Czar Ivan Vassilovitch. In 1567, when the Muscovite merchants, Tverdikoff and Pogreloi, came to England, he acted as interpreter to them, as well as he could, at the audiences granted to them by Queen Elizabeth. In an account given afterwards, in 1582, of the presents brought by these Muscovites from the Czar, which consisted of furs, Lane speaks with much warmth in praise of them, whilst he censures the introduction of all kinds of silk stuffs. " At that time (1567), that princely ancient ornament of furres was yet in use; and great pitie but that it might be renewed, especiall in court and among magistrates; not onely for the restoring of an olde worshippfull art and company (he means the skinners' handicraft and guild), but also because they be for our climate wholesome, delicate, grave, and comely; expressing dignitie, comforting age, and of longer continuance, and better with small cost to be preserved, then these new silks, shagges, and ragges, wherein a great part of the wealth of the land is hastily consumed." The greater part of the early commercial correspondence of the English in Russia, to us so interesting, which Hakluyt has published, was communicated to the latter by Lane.

Christopher Hudson was for some time at Nishny-Novogorod; and afterwards, for two years, principal agent at Moscow, where, as I have ascertained from his autograph letter to Cecil, some articles were sold for twenty times their value. This Hudson signed himself Hoddesden. He had been a clerk to Sir George Barnes, and remained seven years in Russia. The above-mentioned letter I found amongst Pepys' papers, at Magdalen College, Cambridge. At Nishny-Novogorod (Novogorod in the confines of Russia) he sold the same cloth (sorting cloth), a piece of which, with all expenses thereon, until its arrival at the spot, came to but six pounds sterling, for seventeen roubles, which, as he himself says, according to the value of money at that period, amounted to nearly three hundred per cent.; consequently the rouble was almost equivalent to the pound sterling. Hudson was for two years at the head of the English factory at Moscow, and relates, amongst other things, that he sold goods which had cost him £6608 for £13,644, and on which, consequently, there was more than two hundred per cent. profit. In 1562 he returned to England, where he carried on business on his own account; but four years afterwards he was again employed by the company in extending the trade with Narva. I have in my possession copies of the letters written by Queen Elizabeth on the 16th of March, 1566, to the Kings of Denmark and Sweden, for the purpose of recommending him to their protection during that disturbed period. In these letters he is called "Christophorus Hoddesden, mercator Londinensis, spectatæ quidem et probitatis et fidei vir." Elizabeth had likewise written previously to both kings on the 4th of December, 1565, assuring one, as well as the other, that the company's vessels were employed in conveying no articles used in military operations.

In 1567, Hudson was again sent to Narva with £11,000 worth of cloth, kerseys, and salt. The directors wrote to their agent, William Rowley, at Moscow, on the 18th of April: "We have sent M. Christopher Hoodson this year to the Narva (whome we think to be arrived ther by this tyme) about 200 clothes, 200 kersaies, seven ships laden with salt and other wares, to the value of £11,000, and shippes to the burden of about 1300 tonnes, ther to be laden, and the wares solde, and the (w)hole returne to be made this summer, if it be possible." Hudson informs us that, notwithstanding the unfavourable state of affairs at that time, he obtained for the company a profit of forty per cent. In 1569 Hudson again quitted London for Narva with three shiploads of goods, and remained there himself as chief of the factory established by him in the first instance. He wrote to the company by the same vessels on their return, that in the following spring, 1570, they might send him thirteen ships, as he then hoped to be enabled to load them all. He recommended that they should be well provided with artillery, because it was likely that they would meet with numerous freebooters; indeed, he himself had encountered several on his last voyage to Narva.

The command of the fleet of merchantmen which, according to Hudson's desire, sailed from the Thames, was entrusted to William Burrough, who really did meet six Polish piratical vessels on the 10th of July, near the large island of Tüter (Tuttee). One of them fled, another was burnt by him, and the other four he brought, together with eighty-three of the crew, to Narva, where the prisoners, with the exception of one, who had formerly saved the lives of several Englishmen, were delivered over to the Vaivode. The report sent to the Czar of this occurrence was signed by Hudson, as chief of the factory, and Burrough. Hudson afterwards had to contend with a great deal of unpleasantness, because the company accused him of doing business on his own account, and claimed a hundred pounds from him as fine and compensation money. The letter without date to "Syssel," who, in 1571, became Lord (Baron) Burleigh, which was discovered by me at Cambridge, was written by him with reference to this circumstance. Hudson mentions in it that he came to Russia in 1553, and that two years later, in 1555, he was sent from Moscow to Nishny-Novogorod with cloth; but in this he was mistaken, for he visited Russia for the first time in 1555.

In 1562 he returned to London, and in 1566 was sent by the London Company to Narva, there to open a factory on their account.

Robert Best was, in 1556-57, enabled to act as interpreter to our envoy Nepeja, and likewise to Jenkinson. He was at first of essential service in the shipwrecks which took place on the Scottish coast, and we are indebted to him for some information on Russia. Robert Best was, in my opinion, the author of an exceedingly interesting article, published by Hakluyt. This paper contains a description of the journey of Nepeja and his English companions from the convent of St. Nicholas to Moscow, and several ceremonial audiences and banquets given by the Czar, as well as a visit made by Best to the richly-endowed convent of Troitzki; and, moreover, some observations on the Czar himself, on holy water, and the ceremonies on Palm Sunday at Moscow; on baptisms, weddings, and funerals in Russia in general, and, lastly, an account of the artillery practice, which, at that time, took place every winter at Moscow. As the author was unknown, this communication was not thought much of. I will here quote some passages from it. The word Zar Best writes for his countrymen, otesare. He says, "This word otesare his Majesties interpreters have, of late dayes, interpreted to be emperor, so that now he is called Emperor and Great Duke of all Russia. He is no more afraid of his enemies, which are not few, than the bobbie of the larks ('bobby' is the lark-hawk—*Falco subbuteo*). I think no prince in Christendome is more feared of his owne nobles and commons then he is, nor yet better beloved. He delighteth not greatly in hawking, hunting, or any other pastime, nor in hearing instruments or musicke, but setteth all his noble delight upon two things—first, to serve God, as undoubtedly he is very devoute in his religion; and the second, howe to subdue and conquere his enemies." Thus did an Englishman describe the Czar Ivan Vassilovitch in the year 1558.

On the walls of the convent of Troitzki, Best found some metal cannons ("it is walled about with bricke very strongly, like a castle, and much ordinance of brasse upon the walls of the same"), and in the ten cellars some very large casks ("of an unmeasurable bigness and sise: they conteine six or seven tunnes a piece"). Every winter, in December, there was artillery-practice at Moscow, as already mentioned. The clumsy ordnance was dragged to a place set apart for the purpose, and then wooden houses, built expressly, and filled with earth, were fired at. For the muskets, blocks of ice, six feet in height, and two in thickness, were used as targets, which were set up close to one another in a row, about a quarter of a mile in length. On the 12th of December, 1557, Best, accompanied, probably, by Dr. Standish, and other Englishmen who had arrived at Moscow not long before, was present at the artillery-practice. He saw the Czar Ivan Vassilovitch arrive on horseback, with a scarlet cap on his head, ornamented with pearls and precious stones, and dressed in richly-embroidered stuff. The boyars, and other nobles, habited in gold brocade, preceded him, three abreast, and the procession was opened by five thousand arquebusiers marching, in parties of five, each with his firelock on his left shoulder, and the match in his right hand. ("The Emperor's Majestie, and all his nobility, came into the field on horsebacke, in most goodly order, having very fine jennets and Turkie horses, garnished with gold and silver abundantly. The Emperor's Majestie having on him a gowne of rich tissue, and a cap of skarlet on his head, set not only with pearles, but also with a great number of rich and costly stones. His noble men were all in gownes of cloth and gold, which did ride before him in good order by three and three, and before them there went 5000 harquebusiers, which went by five and five in a rank, in very good order, every (one) of them carrying his gun upon his left shoulder, and his match in his right hand, and in this order they marched into the field, where the ordinance was planted.") For the harquebusiers (in Russian, pischtschalniki,) a stand of boards was made parallel with the blocks of ice, somewhat raised, and at a distance of about twenty-five fathoms from them, and on it they placed themselves.

After the Czar had taken possession of the spot intended for him, the pitchtschalniki commenced firing at the ice, and continued until it was altogether shattered to pieces. The mortars followed, and then the fire of the clumsy artillery was directed, all at the same time, at the houses. They commenced with the smaller, and ended with the larger guns, and this was thrice repeated. ("They have faire ordinance of brasse of all sortes, brises, faulcons, minions, sakers, culverings, cannons double and royal, basiliskes long and large; they have six great pieces, whose shot is a yard of height, which shot a man may easily discerne as they flee; they have, also, a great many of mortar pieces, or potguns, out of which pieces they shoot wild fire.")

I may here observe, that between Chancellor's first and second visit to Moscow, two large cannons had been cast there—one in September, 1554, weighing one thousand two hundred pounds, with a mouth fifteen inches in diameter: the name bestowed upon it by the Czar was Kasan, between Novogorod and Pskow. The other gun was completed just before Chancellor's second visit to Moscow, in September, 1555; it weighed one thousand and twenty pounds, and had a mouth fourteen inches in diameter: in the name given to it by the Czar, Astracan was placed between Kasan and Pskow. It is remarkable that, on Chancellor's return to London, in 1554, from his first visit to Moscow, he mentions the capture of Astracan. Eden says, in his translation of Peter Martyr's Decades, published in 1555, "At Richard Chancellor his being in Moscovia (1553-54), fyrst Duke John Vasilivich, that now reyneth, subdued all the Tartars, with their regions and provinces, even unto the great citie and mart towne of Astrachan and the Caspian Sea." Chancellor must certainly have meant the previous subjection of Astracan, in 1552, for Ivan Vassilovitch first received intelligence of the decisive conquest of that place on the 29th of August,

1554; but Chancellor had already taken his departure from Moscow in March, and, consequently, it is very probable that he sailed from the mouth of the Dwina at the end of August.

Here, likewise, might be adduced that statement often made, even in an Imperial Gramota of 1570, that Chancellor had been three times in Russia; but even if he did go to England for a short time, during the winter of 1555-56, Eden's book was then already published.

Best thus describes the Czar's crown, together with other insignia of royalty, and some articles of clothing, shown to him on the 14th of April, 1558, before his departure from Moscow: "His Majesties crowne being close under the top very faire wrought (of gold), was adorned and decked with rich and precious stones abundantly, among the which one was a rubie, which stood a handfull higher than the top of the crown upon a small wier; it was as big as a good beane; the same crown was lined with a faire blacke sable, worth, by report, forty robles." The Czar's wand ("possoch") is thus described by Best: "A staff of goldsmith's worke, well garnished with rich and costly stones." Henry Lane relates of Best, that being "a strong, willing Englishman," he offered himself, in 1560, as a proper guard to accompany the before-mentioned Russian merchants (Schirai and Kostronitsky), in the interest of the English Company at Moscow. The former had already sent Russian produce to England, by means of the latter, and now desired to export more than, according to Lane, the agent's account, they could collect.

Best's offer was not accepted by the Russian merchants, and the matter was then decided by lot. I possess the copy of a letter, dated the 21st of April, 1565, from Queen Elizabeth to Dr. Albert Knopper, the Councillor of Frederick the Second, King of Denmark, wherein she requests him to render assistance, in case of need, to Robert Best and William Rowley, who were at that time on their way to Narva, with a cargo of cloth, on account of the Russia Company. I found a copy of the letter of which Robert Best was the bearer, in the public Library at Cambridge. It is dated the 24th of January, 1571, and Best is not named in it. The Queen says, " De his singulis cæterisque rebus Serenitatem Vestram sigillatim magis certiorem facere poterit is qui has perfert." In a letter taken by Best, addressed to John, King of Sweden, his name is likewise omitted, merely the words "præsens hic nuncius" being used.

At a later period, at the commencement of 1571, Best was dispatched with a letter from Queen Elizabeth to the Czar Ivan Vassilovitch, who, as we shall see, was not at that time well disposed towards her, because he had not received a satisfactory reply to the private overtures made to her in 1567 through Jenkinson. In a fit of bad humour, consequent thereon, he withdrew the privileges conceded to the English Company. Intelligence of this was forthwith transmitted to London, and the directors made a representation to the Queen, which led to the prompt dispatch of Robert Best by way of Sweden. The Czar Ivan Vassilovitch did not reply to the Queen until some months after the burning of Moscow, in August, 1571, from the Alexandrian suburb. From this letter it appears, amongst other things, that he himself had conversed with Robert Best. In the English translation this is mentioned as follows: " Having asked your ambassador Best, he hath spoken unto us by the same words that were wrytten in your letter, and we have caused answere to be gyven unto hym upon his talke accordinge as we have wrytten unto you in our letter." The particulars we shall give in their place.

Thomas Hawtree was, for some time, the company's agent at Vologda, and I have discovered some traces of him in England. In the Library of Trinity College, Cambridge, I found a small MS. work, which belonged to this Thomas Hawtree when he was at Vologda. In his hand is written, "Thomas Hawtree, of London, marchaunt of the Moscovia;" and further on, in another hand, "So sayeth the worthie merchant of Winchcombe, with the winching paynted spoons and brass cups." This is one of the three works which, in the Catalogus librorum manus creptorum Angliæ et Hiberniæ (of 1697), are numbered 626, and are defined as " 3 books in the Russian language."

Amongst the MSS. in the Bodleian Library at Oxford, I found a small Russian book, in which Hawtree wrote: " This boke cost one roble, one altyne, and 2 d (engi), and was wrytten in Colmogov, and bounde at Vologda, the 7th of November, anno 1557." In 1601, the latter work was presented to the Library at Oxford by Dr. Lancelot Browne, chief physician to Queen Elizabeth. In the before-named catalogue it is numbered

2903, and inserted as "Liber lingua Russica seu Moscovitica." As Hawtree paid a visit to England soon after 1557, it is probable that he left the work behind him as a souvenir for his relations or friends there. In 1560 he returned to Russia. In 1567 he, with Jenkinson and some others, authenticated with his signature the translation made by Ralph Rutter of the privileges which at that time had been obtained. In the following year he, with several others, was pointed out by Queen Elizabeth, in a letter to the Czar, dated the 16th of September, as one who carried on business for himself in an illegal manner. Nicholas Chancellor, the only son of Richard Chancellor, was likewise there similarly named. I also found, in the Ashmolean Museum at Oxford, in a small book, several papers, which were written at Cholmogorü in 1557. According to an account given by "Trytiak Afnute, of Coboylove," the Pereslawl (Salessky) Lake appears to have risen three times on the 16th of May of that year, and a procession to the church was resolved upon in consequence.

On the 13th of June a fearful thunderstorm raged at Cholmogorü, accompanied by great heat, when the lightning struck several spots, and set fire to and killed several persons in the suburb, as well as in a country house of the Czar's ("in a nosad of the emperor's"). I mention this chiefly because we happen to possess accounts of the weather just at that time, at a distance of $2° 34'$ north from the eastern side of the Lapland coast, at Tri Ostrova. Stephen Burrough, who was then, with his brother William, on a voyage in search of the ships Confidentia, Esperanza, and Philip and Mary, which had not reached England, writes in his journal, that when near Cape Orlov (named by him Cape Race), it became so cold on the evening of the 10th of June, through a storm from the north, after a thick fog, that sails and ropes were quite covered with ice, and he thanked God that he was enabled to take refuge behind the Three Islands (Trii Ostrova), two leagues further south, where he cast anchor. The gale and cold lasted not only until the 13th, on which day the great sultriness was felt at Archangel, but till the 16th, and Burrough found it impossible to put to sea until the next day, on account of the very great quantity of ice.

Lastly, we have Richard Judde, who was probably a relative of Sir Andrew Judde, an active member of the company in London.

The persons I am about to name were with Chancellor on his first voyage: Arthur Edwards, merchant, who travelled with Richard Johnson to Persia in 1565, and afterwards, repeatedly, up to 1579, in which year he ended his life at Astracan.

Richard Johnson, who in 1556 accompanied the Burroughs in their voyage to Waigat, was, at the beginning of the year 1557, in the country of the Samoides, but, at the commencement of 1558, at Novogorod. In the same year he went with Jenkinson to Little Bokhara, but at a later period, in 1565 as chief of the third expedition to Persia.

John Sedgwick, who, in 1557-1558, bought up hemp and flax at Novogorod and other places.

Lastly, Edward Price, that is, if this name be identical with Passy and Pacie. He paid a rouble and a half at Novogorod for Berkovety hemp; white flax cost three roubles; and at Vologda the price of hemp was two roubles and a half.

Besides the Edward Bonaventure another vessel was dispatched from London, the Philip and Mary, under the command of Captain John Howlet, and on board of her was John Brooke, who was to ascertain, at Wardhuus, whether a trade with England could not be established there. It is nowhere stated whether this vessel sailed as far as the mouth of the Dwina. The Edward reached it on the 23rd June, and her cargo was conveyed in barges hired at Cholmogorü, to Vologda, where it arrived on the 11th September. Part of her crew must have remained there, but the remainder accompanied Chancellor to Moscow, which they reached on the 4th October. Killingworth wrote that he, Chancellor, Lane, Price, and Best, reached Moscow together; but Lane names Edwards instead of the two last. In England I discovered a letter from Hudson, written from Jaroslavl on the 7th November, 1555, wherein he says that on that day full three thousand sturgeons were exposed for sale in the market at Moscow, and that he purchased one for seven altins; at Dantzic he must have paid nine marks for one not so good; the latter was the *Acipenser sturio* of Linnæus, but ours (the Russian ones) were mostly the *Acipenser Güldenstädtii Brandt* (in Russian, *ossetr*).

The Secretary, Ivan Michaelovitch Viscovatü, invited the chiefs to his house—received them with great civility—requested to be allowed a perusal of the royal letter—took care to procure them suitable quarters and provisions; and obtained an audience for them for the 10th October, at which they delivered Philip and Mary's letter to the Czar. The present prepared for him (sugar and "Hollocke") had not yet arrived, and consequently it was merely announced. The cask of "Hollocke" was afterwards lost through the upsetting of the sleigh ("the Emperor's present was delivered to a gentleman at Vologda" (perhaps Nepeja), "and the sled did overthrow, and the butte of Holloche was lost, which made us all very sorry"). The winter set in very late in 1555, and the weather was milder than it had been within the memory of the oldest inhabitants—consequently the road was very bad in November, and the Englishmen's goods must have remained for a long time at Vologda. Killingworth informs us that the Czar took each of them by the hand, but Lane says that they were permitted to kiss his hand. After the audience, the Englishmen were invited to the Czar's table, at which Malcary, the metropolitan, was likewise present. They were called the naval guests ("gosti korabelinge"), and were placed at a table opposite to the Czar, who sent to each of them, calling him by his Christian name, bread, as well as several dishes and beverages.

After the repast, the Czar caused each of the "korabelinge gosti" to approach him, and handed them drink; on this occasion he admired Killingworth's beautiful beard, which, according to Lane's testimony, was five feet two inches in length, broad, strong, and light-coloured, and placed him before Makary, the metropolitan, who said, " that is a gift of God." It now appears strange that an Englishman's beard should have attracted attention at Moscow. At Herberstein's audience, in 1527, he was asked by the Czar, Vassily Ivanovitch, who had shaved his beard off on account of his second marriage, whether he had ever shaved, " bril li borodu?" Herbertstein understood this, and answered immediately, " bril;"—" yes, I have shaved."

Philip and Mary's letter was well received by the Czar, and Chancellor and Killingworth conferred incessantly together on the necessary measures to be adopted for the establishment of the trade between England and Russia on a solid footing, and obtaining extended commercial privileges; to which end suggestions were made by Alexis Federovitch Arlascheff, now appointed Steward of the Bounds, and still more so by the friendly secretary, Viskowatü. Several committees were held by the latter, at which Russian merchants were also present; and it was considered most advisable to erect warehouses at once at Cholmogorü, Vologda, and Moscow.

It is generally believed, that, in compliance with the petition of Chancellor and Killingworth, in 1555-56, the Czar, Ivan Vassilovitch, confirmed to the English, in a fresh document, the permission, already granted them, to trade with perfect freedom, exempt from duties and taxes; and, moreover, that he conceded to them many personal privileges. No direct proof of this, however, is extant, for I have been unable to discover any original charter granted by the Czar in 1555 or 1556. It is clear, that whatever charter is considered to have been granted to the London Company in 1555, and as such appears in Hakluyt, was written by the English, and can only be regarded as a proposal or idea to that effect. Killingworth says, indeed, in a letter despatched to London by way of Dantzic, on the 27th of November, 1555, through Viscovatü's medium : " We were by divers Italians counselled to take heed whom we did trust to make the copie of the privileges that we would desire to have, for feare it should not be written in the Russie tongue, as we did meane ; so first a Russian did write for us a brevet to the Emperor, the tenour whereof was, that we did desire a stronger privilege, and when the secretary" (that is Viscovatü) " saw it, he did deliver it to his grace" (here the Czar is meant), " and when we came againe, his grace willed us to write our minds, and hee would see it, and so we did ; and his grace is so troubled with preparations to warres, that as yet wee have no answere." Further on he writes : " If wee were dispatched heere of that we tarry for, as I doubt not but we shall shortly (you know what I meane)," he here alludes to the desired privilege, " then as soon as we have made sale, I doe intend to goe to Novogorode and to Plesco, whence all the great number of the best tow flaxe cometh."

The advantages set down in the letter relating to the privilege are important. With reference to free trade, we find : " We grant free licence and power to exercise all kinde of merchandizes freely and quietly without any restraint, imperchment, price, exaction, prest, straight, custome, toll, imposition, or subsidie to be demanded, taxed, or paid, or at any time hereafter to be demanded, taxed, set, levied, or inferred upon them."

CHAPTER V.

SHIPWRECK AND DEATH OF CHANCELLOR—ESCAPE OF THE RUSSIAN AMBASSADOR, NEPEJA, AND HIS ARRIVAL IN ENGLAND.

In accordance with instructions received from the London Company, the Edward Bonaventure, still commanded by John Buckland, during the summer of 1555 returned to England; and if it be true that Willoughby's remains were brought to England, it was probably by this opportunity. In the following spring, at the end of April, 1556, she was despatched to Russia not only with merchandise, but with fresh crews (more properly, candidates for death), for both the vessels, Bona Esperanza and Bona Confidentia. The Philip and Mary, which had likewise returned to England in 1555, accompanied the Edward on her voyage to Russia in 1556, and both the newly-manned vessels were brought to the mouth of the Dwina at the same time.

Although John Buckland was the captain of the Edward in this expedition, Stephen Burrough had orders to proceed to Wardhuus in her, and whilst Buckland continued the voyage Burrough was to undertake a voyage of discovery eastward in the pinnace Searchthrift, which was entrusted to him for this purpose, and at all events to endeavour to reach the river Oby.

In this voyage, which was proposed by Cabot in

connection with the now incorporated and newly-privileged company, Stephen Burrough was accompanied by his younger brother William, who already, when a youth only sixteen years of age, had been with him in the first expedition in 1553, and afterwards became better known than Stephen in the English navy. There were likewise eight other persons in their company, and if Richard Johnson was one of these, he must have started from Russia for London in the winter of 1555-56.

These Burroughs signed their names formerly Abourough. William brought Anthony Jenkinson to Russia in 1566. Stephen and he conveyed Thomas Randolph and his numerous suite to the Dwina in 1568. I have seen instructions in William Burrough's handwriting for James Bassendine (Bassington), James Woodoocke, and Richard Browne, who, in 1569, were to start from the Petschora on a voyage of discovery to the East. Hakluyt erroneously dates the letter the 1st of August, 1588, whereas it should be 1568. That this Burrough led thirteen merchant vessels to the Narva, in 1570, and captured some piratical craft on the way, has already been mentioned. Adelung is likewise wrong, for he says that Christopher Hodson was there. In 1574 and 1575 William Burrough was the company's agent in Russia. He travelled from St. Nicholas' Harbour to Moscow, from thence to Narva, and back to St. Nicholas', and forwarded a map to England, which he dedicated to Queen Elizabeth. In transmitting it, he wrote "everything is placed aright in true latitude and longitude, as, till this time, no man hath done the like." William

Burrough, who had also been at Rochelle in France, was frequently consulted by the Russia Company; for instance, in 1576, with regard to the trade with Narva and Kola, as well as with other places on the Lapland coast; and, moreover, on the best season for dispatching ships to St. Nicholas. When Pet and Jackman undertook their voyage in the direction of Cathay (China), he wrote some instructions for their guidance. In the English Marine Department, he occupied the post of Comptroller of the Navy. Christopher Burrough, Stephen's son, travelled, in 1579-81, with Arthur Edwards and twenty-one others, by way of Astracan (where Edwards died), to Persia, of which he wrote a description, returning to England in 1584. In 1587 he was asked for his opinion of the "Muscovia Company," when some disputes arose between the Moscow agents.

On the 9th of June, Stephen Burrough sailed with the pinnace Searchthrift, for a short distance into Kola Inlet, which he calls the Kola River. Here he repaired his craft, and as after his departure he was obliged by adverse winds to return, he remained there until the 22nd of June, by which time many small craft had assembled near him, which were on their way to the walrus and salmon fisheries in the region of the Petschora. He now sailed out of Kola Bay with them.

Burrough's voyage to Waigat, of which he constructed a chart (I discovered in England a sketch by William Burrough's hand, but certainly very superficial, representing the situation of Waigat, and did not omit to copy it), which has unfortunately been lost since then, is sufficiently known, and I seek not to dwell upon a description of it, but cannot refrain from here saying a word in defence of an honest Russian shipmaster of that time, on whom a very false light has been lately thrown, owing to a mistake made in the German translation, by Erman, of Admiral Lutke's excellent work, through ignorance of the Russian language. Amongst the fishing captains with whom Burrough became acquainted during his stay in Kola Inlet, there was one, by name Gavrila, the son of a priest, who offered himself to him as pilot, endeavoured with Russian good-nature to serve the stranger in all possible ways, and was really of essential service to him. Burrough, in several pages of his journal, does our Gavrila due justice, and Admiral Lutke draws attention to this, for he says that Burrough could not sufficiently proclaim the readiness this Gavrila showed to serve him; but Erman makes out that "Burrough decided on doing so (taking him as pilot), but had no great reason to be pleased with the result of the readiness to oblige shown by this Gavrila and his companions."

Stephen Burrough, who reached not only Waigat, but the coast of Nova Zembla, on the 22nd August, gave up the idea of advancing further, and on the 11th of September found his way to Cholmogorü, having deferred the experiment he had meditated of proceeding to the Oby until the spring of 1557. We shall see why he discontinued his voyage for the time.

Richard Johnson, who must have accompanied the

Burroughs, was in the country of the Samoides at the commencement of 1557, and has described the pretended sorcery which he witnessed amongst these people; he likewise gives some geographical information—for example: "East-north-east of Russia lieth Lampas, which is a place where the Russes, Tartars, and Samoeds meete twice a yeere and make the faire to barter wares for wares; and north-east from Lampas lieth the country of the Samoeds, which be about the river of Pechere. And north-east from the river Pechere lieth Vaygatz. Beyond Vaygatz lyeth a lande called Nova Zembla, which is a great lande; but we sawe no people, and there we had foule enough, and there we sawe white foxes and white bears," &c. From these words he must really have been there.

In July, 1556, four English vessels lay at anchor at the mouth of the Dwina, viz. both those arrived from England in that year, the Edward Bonaventure, and the Philip and Mary—and then the Bona Esperanza and Bona Confidentia, which were brought there by their fresh crews from the Bay of Nokujeff.

On the 2nd of August, 1556, the four vessels just mentioned set sail for England. On board the Edward Bonaventure, commanded by John Buckland, there was, besides Richard Chancellor and his son, the Boyar of Vologda, Ossip Grigorjevitsch Nepeja, as (the first) ambassador from the Czar Ivan Vassilovitch to Philip and Mary, with a suite of sixteen persons (Russians), who took leave of the Czar at Moscow on the 25th of March.

Robert Best, the clerk, accompanied him as his

interpreter. On board the Bona Esperanza, two merchants of Cholmogorü, viz. the before-mentioned chief magistrate, Fofaun Makaroff, and Michael Grigorjeff, together with eight other Russians, took a passage, with a view to commence direct commercial relations with England. The Edward Bonaventure had a cargo of Russian wares, partly on account of Nepeja the ambassador and the Cholmogorü merchants, of the value of twenty thousand, and the Bona Esperanza one of six thousand pounds sterling. In the North Sea the Esperanza, as well as the Confidentia and the Philip and Mary, were driven on the Norwegian coast, near Drontheim, by a storm; the Confidentia, on board of which the whole crew were frozen to death in 1553-54, struck on a rock and foundered with her cargo and ship's company; as to the Esperanza, on board of which Sir Hugh Willoughby and his companions were frozen, and in which ten Russians had now embarked, besides fourteen Englishmen, we have never learnt where she perished after her departure from the Drontheim Fiord—so that we are ignorant of the spot where the first Russian merchants, who had intended to visit England, were swallowed up by the ocean.

The Edward Bonaventure, after beating about for a long time in the North Sea, at last made the Scottish coast, and on the 10th of November anchored in the Bay of Pitsligo, in the northern part of Aberdeenshire, where in the night she parted from her anchors and was wrecked, by which Richard Chancellor, with his son and seven persons (Russians) of

Nepeja the ambassador's suite, who attempted to reach the shore in a boat, were drowned; but the ambassador himself was miraculously saved. John Buckland, too, as well as Robert Best, interpreter to the embassy, escaped a watery grave. Almost the whole of the cargo, and the presents intended by the Czar for the King and Queen, viz. a beautiful hawk, with all its accoutrements for the chase, four live sables, and some costly furs, went to the bottom; and what is now still more to be lamented, is the loss of the information, with regard to Russia, collected by Chancellor and his companions, from June, 1555, until August, 1556.

Thus did the three first vessels dispatched from England in 1553 perish, and both of those whose entire crews were frozen to death in the Bay of Nokujeff, on the Lapland coast, were now, with every soul on board, swallowed up by the waves; only a small number of the persons on board the third, *i. e.* the Edward Bonaventure, being saved.

Probably the vessels which had been frozen up in winter had suffered much, because they were not raised out of the ice. In accordance with Cabot's proposition, they were sheathed in lead before their departure, as a defence against the detrimental action of the salt water; and these were the first ships so sheathed in England; in Spain, however, this mode of preserving them was adopted sooner.

The Philip and Mary wintered in the Port of Drontheim, and long after they had given her up in London for lost, she arrived in the Thames on the 18th of April, 1557.

As in December, 1556, the fate of the Edward Bonaventure was reported to London by letter, and as yet there was no information as to what had become of the other three vessels which had sailed from the mouth of the Dwina together with her, on the 2nd of August, viz. the Bona Esperanza, Bona Confidentia, and Philip and Mary, of which during the winter some intelligence must have reached Cholmogorü, Stephen Burrough, in the spring of 1557, resolved on undertaking a voyage along the coast of Lapland in search of them, and for this reason the second one he had projected to the river Oby, on the other side of Nova Zembla, was suspended.

It must here be observed, that instructions were by no means sent to Stephen Burrough from London to undertake this voyage to the Lapland coast. On the contrary, the directors of the company, at the beginning of May, 1557, wrote to him that he was at all events to carry out his intended voyage to the Oby: " Wee doe perceive that Stephen Burrow is returned from his discoverie with the Searchthrift, and wintereth at Columgoo, and is minded to set forth in the beginning of June next, to seek the river of Obi. We pray God to speede him well, and trust to have him here in England this yeere to bring us good newes. We will that Stephen Burrowe doo proceed on his voiage to discover." It appears as if Burrough, through the experience he had gained in the previous year, had lost all desire to proceed with his navigation to the eastward. In 1560 he commanded one of the three vessels, the Swallow, despatched from the Thames to the Dwina. Arthur Pet was at that time the captain of the Jesus. On this occasion Richard Chancellor's only remaining son Nicholas came out to Russia. Burrough's voyage to the Dwina in 1569 I have already mentioned. In England he was one of the superintendents of shipping in Medway-water, where, amongst other places, is Chatham.

On the 23rd of May, 1557, Stephen Burrough, accompanied by his brother William, with the Searchthrift pinnace, from Cholmogorü, sailed from Cape Svatoi Noss, to which he gave the name of Cape Gallant, keeping always close to the Lapland coast, and on the 28th of June reached Wardhuus Bay, without having either seen or heard anything of the missing vessels. On his homeward voyage, meeting with strong contrary winds, he was obliged to run into a bay at the west end of the Peninsula of Rübatschig, which probably was that of Waida. Here he found a craft from Drontheim, and from its owner, who was a son of the burgomaster there, he learnt the misfortune which had happened to the Bona Confidentia. The former vessel had on board the sails which the waves had thrown on shore, with the masts, in the Drontheim Fiord. He was further told that the Philip and Mary had passed the winter at Drontheim, but had sailed for England in March, where, as we have already seen, she arrived in safety on the 18th of April.

Nepeja, after his shipwreck on the Scottish coast, had to contend with many annoyances, but Robert Best, his interpreter, must here have been of great service to him. When the company on the 3rd of December received intelligence of the disaster, the Queen was immediately informed of it, and she, for her consort was then on the Continent, wrote to the widowed Queen of Scotland, Mary of Lorraine, mother of Mary Stuart, and requested her to give assistance to Nepeja and his companions. With this view Lawrence Hussie, doctor of laws, and George Gilpin, were likewise sent to him from London with a "Talmatsch" or "Speachman." These persons found Nepeja on the 23rd of December already in Edinburgh, where they delivered to Mary, the Scottish Regent, the letter they had brought from Mary, Queen of England. The former ordered a herald, with several commissioners, to be dispatched to Pitsligo Bay, in order to prevent the stranded articles from being carried off; but the assistance came too late, and but a few trifles were saved, most of the articles of value being already gone. Nepeja left Edinburgh on the 14th of February, 1557, in company with both the London gentlemen just mentioned.

He arrived on English ground, at Berwick-upon-Tweed, on the 18th of February, and there he was met by Lord Thomas Wharton, Warden of the East Marches. On the 27th, when at a distance of twelve miles from London, he was received with much pomp by eighty merchants on horseback, and escorted to the house of one of them, situated four miles from that city, at which he passed the night after receiving sundry presents. On the following morning the Lord Viscount Montague, with no less than one hundred and forty members of the Russia Company, with just the same number of servants, arrived there in order to escort him to London, and welcome him in the name of the Queen. On the road a sort of fox-hunt was got up for his amusement. From the city boundary, north of Smithfield, Viscount Montague and the Lord Mayor, Sir Thomas Offley, rode on either side of Nepeja as far as the quarters prepared for him at the house of John Dimmock the merchant.

English historians write that Nepeja was lodged at Denmark House. There was no such house, so I imagine that they mistook Dimmock for Denmark. John Dimmock, a native of the Netherlands, was a member of the Drapers' Company in London, and during the reigns of Henry the Eighth and Edward the Sixth, was frequently employed in missions on the Continent. I have seen a letter from his brother to him, written from Antwerp on the 16th of March, 1538, in which he treated for the purchase of gunpowder, and the firearms of that period called "halfe huckboshes" (arquebuses). In 1548, he, with the ambassador Sir Philip Hobby, were charged with the private enlistment in Friesland of two thousand foot-soldiers, who were to be employed against Scotland; in the preceding year two thousand men had already been enlisted. He took great pleasure in making himself useful to foreign ambassadors in London. In January, 1561, with the permission of Queen Elizabeth, he undertook a journey to Sweden, in order to sell some jewels to King Eric the Fourteenth. On this occasion he had the assurance to intimate to that King the possibility of still carrying into effect his marriage with Elizabeth, the negotiations for which had already been broken off. He caused the King's portrait to be taken by an artist whom he had brought with him, and persuaded the King to send her some presents. Elizabeth, who learnt this through the King's ambassador, Dionysius Beurreus, imprisoned Dimmock as soon as he returned, and wrote to Eric on the 22nd of June, 1561, that Dimmock had received no authority from her so to act. This accounts for the order given by Cecil on the 21st of July, 1561, to the Lord Mayor of London, that all pictures in books containing Elizabeth's and Eric's portraits together should be destroyed. In December, 1565, the Queen wrote again to Eric, and requested him to order that a sum due to Dimmock, then in the debtors' prison, for articles delivered, should be paid to him.

After Philip's return from Flanders, which took place a few days before Nepeja's audience, and consequently not on the 20th of May, as is stated in many places, amongst others in "L'art de Verifier les Dates," Nepeja was invited on the 21st of March to the palace at Westminster, where he and the Queen gave him an audience.

Lord Montague escorted Nepeja on the Thames in a state barge to the landing-place at Westminster, where the bridge has been since built. Here he was received by six lords, who were to attend him to the state chamber in the palace, where the first dignitaries in the kingdom paid him their respects before he was ushered into the royal audience chamber. These were

Nicholas Heath, Archbishop of York, as Chancellor, William Paulet, Marquis of Wiltshire, as Lord High Treasurer, William Paget, Baron de Beaudessert, as Keeper of the Seals, William Howard, Baron of Effingham, as Lord High Admiral, and Thomas Thirleby, Bishop of Ely.

At this audience Nepeja delivered his letter from the Czar, Ivan Vassilovitch, carried on a short conversation, and presented fourscore sable skins. Notwithstanding all my researches, I have neither found the original of this letter, nor even a copy or translation of it. In Philip and Mary's reply, drawn up by Roger Ascham, Latin secretary, it is said of the Czar's letter that it was full of friendly assurances.* "We have received your letters, full of love and friendship, brought to us by your chosen messenger and ambassador Osiph Nepea. We understand from your letters, that out of your liberality you have given and awarded various privileges, liberties, and immunities, to our merchants, and others of our English subjects, who carry on their trade in some parts of your empire." Nepeja's speech was repeated in English and Spanish, in the first language probably by Robert Best. It is likely that the sable skins presented were imported by Chancellor in 1554. Nepeja was escorted back to the city in the same order in which he had set out. Two days afterwards Thomas Thirleby, Bishop of Ely, and Sir William Peter, their Majesties' first secretary, had an interview with Nepeja at his quarters, in order to discuss what was necessary. These two persons are designated

* See Appendix G.

in the following passage in the letter to the Czar:*
" We caused the matters proposed to us in your name by him (Nepeja) to be freely and diligently considered and discussed by certain of our councillors, to whom we committed the business." On the 23rd of April he had his audience of leave-taking; to which he was brought by the lords Talbot (Earl of Shrewsbury) and Lumley; after which he attended, in the presence of their Majesties, accompanied by the Duke of Norfolk (Thomas Howard), as well as by the lords just named, at the banquet of the Order of the Garter. On the 29th of the same month, the members of the Russia Company gave him a banquet at Drapers' Hall, in Throgmorton Street. ("A notable supper garnished with musick, enterludes, and bankets.") When Nepeja's health was drunk, it was stated to him that the company would defray the whole of the expenses of his voyage and of his residence in Scotland and England. The contemporary author of an account of what the Russia Company had done for Nepeja in London, says,—" the like is not in any president" (he means precedent) " or historie to be shewed."

On the 1st of May, Thomas Thirleby and Sir William Peter delivered to him the letter from the King and Queen to the Czar. I have already observed that this letter was composed in Latin by Roger Ascham, and it contains the following passages:† "We hope that the foundation of mutual friendship, thus well and happily begun and established, will be productive of considerable and abundant fruits, not only of fraternal

* See Appendix H. † See Appendix I.

love and firm friendship between you and ourselves and our successors, but also of a bond of perpetual commercial union between our subjects. As good ground for this hope, we are induced to believe that, as God, of his infinite goodness and favour, has in our time opened a road by sea and a navigation previously unknown, He will think fit to preserve and prosper the same to his honour and glory, the increase of the Christian and Catholic religion, and the public advantage of the subjects and kingdoms of both."—" And since your ambassador, Osiph Nepea, who has behaved himself prudently and considerately in his embassy to us, is about to return to you, he will best be enabled to explain to you, as we trust he will do freely, in what disposition we are with reference to the commerce lately opened between our subjects and yours, and the kingdoms and cities under our respective dominion." Thirleby and Peter also consigned to him the presents intended for the Czar. Besides sundry stuffs and cloths, a magnificent suit of armour and a helmet covered with crimson velvet and gilt nails were transmitted (" a notable pair of brigandines, with a murrion covered with crimson velvet and gilt nails"), and a pair of lions were added. Nepeja likewise received several presents for himself, and on the 3rd of May he proceeded to Gravesend in order to embark for Russia on board the ship Primrose.

This was one of the two vessels of which King Edward the Sixth wrote in his Journal on the 6th of July, 1551, that they were launched when he was at Deptford. The Primrose sailed on the 12th of

August, 1553, together with the Leon, and the Moon Pinnace from Portsmouth for the coast of Guinea. This undertaking was projected by Barnes and Garret, a short time after the Cathay expedition reached Russia—the two vessels having been lent to them by the King for the purpose. The enterprise to Guinea here mentioned, which failed through Captain Wyndham's conduct, has been often confounded, even by Strype and Campbell, with that of Willoughby.

Towards the end of Nepeja's stay in London, the members of the Russia Company were not quite satisfied with him. In a postscript, dated the 10th of May, 1557, to a letter previously despatched to the agents at Moscow, they say: " Wee doe not finde the Ambassador nowe at the last so conformable to reason as wee had thought wee shoulde. Hee is very mistrustfull, and thinketh everie man will beguile him; therefore you had neede to take heed how you have to doe with him, or with any such, and to make your bargaines plaine, and to set them downe in writing."

CHAPTER VI.

VOYAGE OF ANTHONY JENKINSON — RAPHAEL BARBERINI IN RUSSIA, WITH A LETTER OF QUEEN ELIZABETH TO THE CZAR IVAN VASSILOVITCH.

NEPEJA was accompanied to Russia by the well-known, active, and enterprising Anthony Jenkinson, who afterwards came several times from England to visit us. Robert Best acted as interpreter. There moreover came a physician, Doctor Standish, an apothecary, and several persons besides, with the intention of following their different professions. Two coopers were to put together casks at the Dwina, for the exportation of tallow, train oil, &c.

On the 10th of May, 1557, when some of the articles saved from the wreck of the Edward Bonaventure arrived in London, the Russian casks (with train oil) were found to be far better than the English ones, of which one hundred and forty, partly in staves, had just been sent off in the vessels which had sailed for the Dwina. This last measure was one of forethought on the part of the Directors, who, it seems, were not certain whether good wood for making casks was to be found in sufficient abundance in Russia.

Seven cable and rope makers, whose master's name was Robert Bunting, came over for the purpose of erecting a rope-walk, and manufacturiug every description of cordage for exportation to England, where it then bore a high price. A furrier, by name Allard, was sent to assist in the selection of furs, and a certain Leonard Brian, in order to examine the yew-trees (*Taxus baccata*) " in Permia or the Petschora region as well as in Ugoria," and ascertain whether the wood was fit for exportation to England.

With regard to this matter, the directors of the Russia Company wrote as follows: " We doe understand that in the country of Permia, or about the river of Pechora, is great quantitie of yewe, and likewise in the country of Ugory, which we be desirous to have knowledge of, because it is a speciall commoditie for our realme; therefore we have sent you a young man, whose name is Leonard Brian, that hath some knowledge in the wood, to shew you in what sorte it must be cut and cloven. So our minde is, if there be any store, and that it be found to be good, that you doe provide a good quantitie against the next yeere for the coming of our shippes. One of the coopers may goe with Leonard Brian to cut and cleve such yewe as he shall like there." The leaves of our Pichta (*Abies sibirica*) so much resemble those of the yew, that it has been called the yew-leaved fir. I may here observe, that in the third expedition to Persia (in 1565–67) the English found many yew-trees at Schamachi, which were there used as wood for cross-bows. Arthur Edwards wrote to London, on the 26th of April, 1565: " You shall understand there is plentie of yew-trees for bow-staves. I caused three horse loads to be bought us for to know the truth, but they were cut out of season this month of April, the sap being in them. Three moneths I never left speaking to the countrymen to bring some. Your agent will send some home for example."

As the yew-tree does not thrive so far north, it must be presumed that the silver fir (*Pinus picea*), which is allied to the Pichta (*Abies sibidica*, Ledeb), must have been mistaken for it, for its leaves bear some resemblance to those of the Taxus. The mistake is probably to be ascribed to our Ambassador Nepeja, who saw the Taxus in England in winter, consequently without fruit, and as he knew the Russian Pichta, he may have called the attention of the company to it. Ten young persons were likewise sent in these vessels as apprentices to learn the trade with Russia: amongst them was Thomas Alcock, who was despatched to England in the course of the following winter by way of Smolensko and Dantzic, but was detained as a prisoner in Poland. He represented that he was on his way to London commissioned to attend to the equipment of a vessel in the following spring, in 1558, with the object of searching for the passage to China; for as the winter was milder, and consequently less drift ice would be encountered in the North Sea, a favourable result might be anticipated. They objected that the English brought many warlike stores to Russia ("thousands of ordinance, as also of harness, swordes, with other munitions of warre, artificers, copper, &c."). He replied, that scarcely a hundred mail shirts had been exported from England to

Russia, and that they were old and merely scoured ("such olde thinges newe scowred as no man in Englande woulde weare"). Alcock had forty altins of Russian money with him, more than half of which had been entrusted to him by the English at Moscow, in order to be distributed amongst their friends in England as tokens of remembrance. He wrote:—"They tooke from mee fourtie altines in Russe money, whereof twentie and more were for tokens." From this it might be supposed that altins were coined as early as 1557, but so far as I know there is not an altin of that period in any collection. The before-mentioned agent, Richard Gray, sent his wife and daughter two Bulgarian coins. On the 26th of December, 1558, Queen Elizabeth wrote to Sigismund, King of Poland, as well as to the Stadtholder of Lithuania, and to the Governor of Wilna, concerning Alcock's journey homewards, requesting that he might be permitted to continue it without hindrance. In January, 1560, he was at Stockholm on his way to Russia, but permission to pass through Poland was denied him.

The nine Russians of Nepeja's suite, who escaped with life in Pitsligo Bay, likewise returned with him to their own country. Their names were—Isaac Ivaschenko, Demetrius, Jermolai, Semen, Jeroffai, Stepan, Luka, Andrew, and Foma.

Notwithstanding the shipwreck which John Buckland had met with in his last voyage in the Edward Bonaventure, he did not decline to assume the command of the Primrose, on board of which were Nepeja and Jenkinson. During this voyage the Primrose was the flag-ship of the fleet, and Jenkinson was her captain; but he was moreover called "Captaine-general of the flote." Besides this vessel, three others sailed at the same time, the John Evangelist, the Anna, and the Trinitie. The commanders of these vessels were Lawrence Roundall, David Philly, and John Robins. The merchandise brought to Russia by the four ships I have already recorded. The Primrose was nearly lost at the commencement of the voyage. It had also been feared that difficulties would be encountered at Wardhuus. Nepeja was, therefore, not a little rejoiced, when on the 12th of July he set his foot on *terra firma*, at the convent of St. Nicholas. He remained there a week with the other persons who had left England with him, and they all, with the exception of Jenkinson, set out for Moscow, where they arrived on the 12th of September, and were admitted on the 14th to an audience, at which they kissed the Czar's right hand. Afterwards, they were invited to dine with him.

Two days later, the Czar sent Dr. Standish, as well as each of the other newly-arrived Englishmen, a horse to ride about the town. On the 18th of September the former received some sable furs: on the 1st of October he again dined with the Czar. On the 11th he received seventy, and the apothecary and the others each thirty roubles. On the 3rd of November, as well as on the 6th and 23rd December, 1557, and on the 6th January and 12th April, 1558, he was likewise invited to the Czar's table.

Jenkinson, who sent the vessels home from the

mouth of the Dwina on the 1st of August, reached Moscow only on the 6th of December, having been detained some time on the road by commercial matters; consequently, he was too late to show himself on this holiday, but on Christmas-day he had an audience of the Czar and dined with him.

Jenkinson had reached Cholmogorü on the 3rd August, 1557, and left it on the 15th, to ascend the Dwina in a small boat. He noticed on the same day, at the junction of the Pinega, the alabaster mountains on each side, as well as the pine-trees lying in the soil ("pine-apple trees lying along within the ground, which by report have lien there since Noe's flood"). Between the Pinega and the Jemetz he observed the mode of collecting tar, pitch, and potash. At Totma, on the Suchana, he describes the difficulties of the voyage in consequence of the numbers of river craft, which were at that time employed in the conveyance of salt from the works on the sea-coast to Vologda. On the road from Cholmogorü to Vologda he did not enter any house; consequently an axe, a tinder-box, and a kettle were articles indispensable to our traveller. On the 1st of December he left Vologda, and travelled in a sledge to Moscow by way of Jaroslavl, Rostov, and Pereslavl. He does not mention that on Christmas-day any other persons who came with him from England dined with the Czar besides himself. On the 6th of January he was present, in a Russian dress, at the blessing of water; but the Czar recognised him, and invited him again to dinner. On Easter Tuesday, the 12th of April, he dined with the Czar, together with Richard Gray, and probably also with Robert Best and Dr. Standish. After the repast he requested permission to set out on his travels to China, which, however, ended at Bokhara.

The motive for Jenkinson's mission to Russia was the following: As Burrough's endeavour to advance in the North Sea further to the east had failed, Jenkinson, who had great experience in travelling, and was highly accomplished, was to exert himself to reach Cathay (China) by land, and this through Bokhara, for it had been heard that caravans often came to that country from China.

In November, 1553, when Chancellor visited the Dwina for the first time, Jenkinson was at Aleppo. We are indebted to him for an interesting description of the powerful army which the Sultan was then leading against Persia, to make war upon the Shah. Of a thousand pages clad in gold cloth, one-half carried arquebuses, and the others Turkish bows and quivers of arrows. "After the great Turk followed six young ladies, mounted upon fine white hacknies, every one of them having two eunuchs on each side, and little bowes in their hands."

The project of Jenkinson pleased the Czar Ivan Vassilovitch, so that, without having been requested to do so by Queen Elizabeth, he not only gave him permission to travel through the territory of Astracan, lately conquered by him, but likewise gave orders to all the chiefs of towns along the Volga to render him assistance. He, moreover, provided the traveller with letters of recommendation to the sovereign of the territory on the other side of the Caspian Sea.

Jenkinson quitted Moscow on the 23rd of April, 1558; and ascended the Moskwa, Oka, and Volga, accompanied by Richard and Robert Johnson as far as Astracan. On this journey Jenkinson noticed much that is interesting. He names the district between Kasan and the Kama to the left of the Volga-Vachen. Muller (S. R. G. vii. 445) says: "This I really cannot explain. It is nevertheless right to remark it, because it may perhaps induce others to make enquiries on the subject." It might well be wondered at that the Historiographer of the "Votaken" did not immediately recognise in this word written by an Englishman, the Vatschine. In another place, where Jenkinson recapitulates his different travels, he writes, Vachin, and thus it is set down likewise in his map of Russia, published in London as early as 1562. Here it is to be seen that the district he meant did not reach the Volga, but lies on either side of the river Vatka. Leaving the Volga, Jenkinson next sailed on the Caspian Sea, on which never before had a Christian banner waved (his was the St. George's cross), and thus advanced as far as Bokhara. There he learnt that the communication with China had been broken off three years previously; he was consequently obliged to alter his plans. On the 2nd of September, 1559, he returned to Moscow, and two days afterwards was admitted to an audience, at which he was suffered to kiss the hand of the Czar, and presented him with a Yak crupper and a Tartar drum; he afterwards dined with him. On the 9th of May, 1560, he arrived at Cholmogorü, and soon afterwards sailed to England, accompanied by Henry Lane. In place of the latter, Thomas Glover became the company's agent at Moscow. He continued to hold the office until 1566, when he broke faith with the company, and obtained special commercial privileges for himself and some others. His son, Sir Thomas Glover, was at a later period ambassador to Constantinople.

In the ensuing year, 1561, Jenkinson visited Moscow for the second time, having Persia again in view. He was, moreover, instructed to send some one, perhaps Richard Johnson, from Cholmogorü, over-land in an easterly direction; for the Russians probably represented that the open sea could be reached in thirty or forty days' journey. Nothing resulted from this trip. The excursions of our Englishmen towards the east extended at that time simply from Cholmogorü, by Pineja to Lamposhna, and as far as the village of Mesen (230 versts), where the Samoiedes held their fair, and then along the Mesen, by Pogorelskaja and Sesapolskaja to Juroma (115 versts), where they purchased elk-hides for England. In a letter, written in Latin, of the 25th of April, to the Czar Ivan Vassilovitch, Queen Elizabeth thanked him for the gracious reception he had already afforded to Jenkinson, and for his furtherance of his object; and begged that he would still consider the same individual, who was now in her service ("nostrum jam famulatum"), worthy of his continual protection, and furnish him with letters of recommendation to Tahmasp, Shah of Persia. A similar letter to the Shah the Queen herself had given him. I have had in my hands the following order with reference to this matter given by the Queen's Keeper of the seals, Sir Nicholas Bacon: "Primo Junii, 1561; To Thomas Cotton, the under Clerk of the Hamper, in the Court of Chancery, ye shall allowe for certene lace myngled with gold and silver, putt to several lettres patents sent by the Queene's Maiestie, as well to the Emperour of Russia as to the Sophie, which lace amounteth in yards to the number of viij after the rate of vj s. viij d. for every yard, and this letter shall be your discharge, N. Bacon." Sir Nicholas was, as is well known, the father of (Lord) Francis Bacon, then four months old. Jenkinson came to the Dwina in the ship Swallow. The company delivered him a locked-up chest containing costly articles, intended partly as presents for the Czar, and his eldest son the Czarovitch Ivan. They comprised jewels, gold stuffs, and scarlet cloths.

Jenkinson reached Moscow on the 20th of August, when Ivan Vassilovitch was preparing to solemnise his marriage with the beautiful Circassian, Marja Temgrukovna, when the gates of the city were closed for three days, and no inhabitant, native or foreigner, was allowed to leave his house. Jenkinson wrote: "The cause thereof unto this day not being known." As he perseveringly refused to trust the Queen's letter out of his hands previously to delivering it himself to the Czar, they endeavoured to thwart him; notwithstanding which the audience took place somewhat later, and he was invited to the Czar's table.

Repeated difficulties were thrown in the way of his journey to Persia, and he had already received a passport for his return to England, when, through Nepeja's mediation, his wishes were at length gratified. On the 15th of March, 1562, he dined with the Czar at the same time as an ambassador from Persia; and the Czar not only provided him with the promised letters of recommendation, but honoured him with sundry commissions.

On the 27th of April he quitted Moscow, in company with the same ambassador, and ascended the Volga as before. Edward Clarke, an Englishman, accompanied him. A peace, concluded a short time before with the Turks, was the cause that Jenkinson's endeavours to establish a commercial intercourse between Persia and England had not altogether the desired result; for Persia at that time received cloths and other goods through the Turks. On the 20th of August, 1563, Jenkinson returned to Moscow, where he delivered into the treasury the precious stones and silk stuffs purchased for the Czar, and presented a report of the execution of his other commissions The Czar gave him to understand that he was perfectly satisfied with what he had done, and intimated his wish to employ him further.

Jenkinson availed himself of the Czar's favour to obtain a new charter; wintered at Moscow; sent Edward Clarke by land to England; and despatched another expedition to Persia on the 10th of May, 1564. This consisted of Thomas Alcock, George Wrenne, and Richard Cheinie. The route by water did not commence this time at Moscow, but at Jaroshlavl. Alcock was murdered not far from Schamachi. Richard Johnson was appointed to the command of the expedition despatched to Persia in 1565 by Glover, the agent; so that Arthur Edwards, who was a man far more adapted to the purpose, was obliged to serve under him. The directors of the company wrote in 1567: " We marveille that Richard Johnson was sent into Persia as chefe, being a man in our opinions unfitt for that chardge, and nothing so fitte as another." Still they desired that he should make a map of the Volga and the Caspian Sea : " We be desirous to have a sea Carde made of the viage of the Caspian sea, with a note in writing of the courses, soundings, marks, dangerous places, variinge of the compasse and latitude of places, quallitie of harbroughes. Will Johnson to make a charde of the Caspian sea, and viage down the Volga." For the expedition of 1565 a craft was built expressly at Jaroslavl, and Edwards proposed that for future expeditions a larger one should be constructed, to command which a shipmaster should be sent from England. Jenkinson quitted Moscow on the 28th of June, embarked at the mouth of the Dwina, again in the ship Swallow, and arrived in London on the 28th of September.

On the 4th of May, 1566, he was again despatched to Russia, and arrived at the Dwina, on the 10th of June, in the ship Harry. Jenkinson wrote to Sir William Cecil from Cholmogorü on the 26th of June, by William Burrough, who was about to return home with the vessels. He dwelt on the various political relations of Russia at that time, as well as on the negotiations with the Czar. Amongst other things he says of him, that he was building a castle two thousand four hundred fathoms in circumference; the stones for which were brought from a distance of five hundred miles, at an expense of twelvepence per cwt. for carriage. This was the castle then built by the Czar at Vologda. Jenkinson sent an elk to Cecil by Burrough ("a strange beast called a loyche, and bred in the country of Casun in Tartarie").

I may here observe that, several times during the first few years after the establishment of the company, the agents at Cholmogorü sent the directors in London reindeers and white bears as curiosities; but after 1559 a special permission from the Czar was necessary for this purpose. One great inducement to the present expedition was the recommendation of the before-mentioned Raphael Barberini, an Italian, who resided at Antwerp, then the emporium of commerce. He was the uncle of the famous Pope Urban the Eighth. In 1564 he succeeded in procuring a letter of recommendation from Queen Elizabeth to the Czar Ivan Vassilovitch; and another, but not so useful to him, he received from Philip the Second, King of Spain and ex-King of England. With these credentials he arrived at Moscow in the summer of that year. A mercantile firm from Antwerp came over at the same time, which was to transfer half the profits to him, if the Czar granted permission for free trade with Russia. This the latter not only did, but assisted him in obtaining similar favours from Frederick the Second, King of Denmark, and Eric the Fourteenth,

King of Sweden. Barberini had scarcely returned to Antwerp in the summer of 1565, when he dispatched a vessel to Narva with salt and silver coin. The English reported this to London, and the directors of the company made a representation to the Queen on the subject. Elizabeth now wrote, on the 20th of April, 1566, to Ivan Vassilovitch, by Jenkinson, that she had recommended Barberini to him as a traveller, and in nowise as a merchant.

This Italian was the youngest son of Carl Barberini. His brother Ivan was learned in the law, resided at Rome, and superintended the education of the sons of his elder brother Anthony, of whom Maphœus, the first-born, arrived at high ecclesiastical dignity, and in 1623 even became Pope, under the name of Urban the Eighth. On the 10th of June, 1564, Raphael wrote from Antwerp to Franz at Rome:* "I will tell you briefly how it is that I am going to Muscovy to make arrangements with its Sovereign. To do this, in the first place, 400 D (?) have been paid me at once in cash, and afterwards I am to have half the profits of the business."

He made this request: † "Do not say that I have gone to Sweden on any other business but my own, as this is what I have written to every one, excepting privately to my own family, in order that no obstacles may be thrown in the way of my project. I shall start at Midsummer."

The rough sketch of the letter from Queen Elizabeth to Ivan Vassilovitch, which was discovered by

* See Appendix K.   † See Appendix L.

me in England, is dated the 20th of June, 1564. Elizabeth says:* "In consequence of Your hearty goodwill towards Us, We gladly, on this occasion, recommend to Your Majesty by these our letters Raphael Barberini, who, although an Italian, is very dear to Us, for certain reasons. We, therefore, beg that he, by Your good favour and pleasure, as well as by Your commands and authority, if necessary, may be courteously treated, as well by Your Majesty as by Your subjects; and that he, with all his goods, may pass safely and freely through the provinces of Your empire, dwell there so long as he may think fit, and depart thence whensoever he and his followers are so inclined."

Lord Montague, who in 1557 received and escorted Nepeja, our ambassador in London, had previously been at Rome, was afterwards at Madrid, and in March, 1564, was sent to the Netherlands by Elizabeth, with Dr. Wotton, the able diplomatist, and the statesman Walter Haddon, for the purpose of regulating commercial matters between England and that country, with the commissioners of the King of Spain. Probably Barberini obtained the letter of recommendation from Queen Elizabeth to Ivan Vassilovitch through Montague. At Moscow Barberini received many marks of attention from the Czar; and when an audience was granted in November to the envoys from Ivan Vassilovitch's Circassian stepfather, as well as to the embassy from the Emperor Ferdinand and Wolfgang, grand-master of the Teutonic Order, (with reference to setting Furstenberg at liberty,) Barberini

* See Appendix M.

was presented to the Czar at the same time, and dined afterwards at the Granotvitaja Palace, together with the persons first named. Having returned to Antwerp in the summer of 1565, he wrote to his brother Franz, on the 21st of July, as follows: * "Having obtained privileges and a safe conduct in the country of the Muscovites for me and my people, I hope that in future I may be enabled to benefit you, because in the first place I have certain information of which few are possessed, and in the next have passports and safe-conducts from the King of Denmark and King of Sweden, matters which I am rejoiced at, and which are of consequence. Not to lose the opportunity, therefore, I despatched on the 11th instant, (July, 1565,) a vessel with X. M. (10,000) D (?) in goods and ready-money, which, please God, will go and return in safety. I hope that I shall progress in the same way, and that God will thus recompense all my family."

On the 8th of September he added to another letter: † "I know not what to say excepting that I am but half alive, trusting that God of his goodness will cause the vessel I have sent to arrive in safety. My hope is in Him."

To his father he also wrote in August: ‡ "Since I know that you must be aware that I have sent a vessel to Narva, I will tell you that I have received a letter from the supercargo. Therefore, if God pleases that she return in safety, I am very certain that I shall double my venture and be satisfied, because I have a cargo of salt there, the first cost of

* See Appendix N.   † See Appendix O.   ‡ See Appendix P.

which was D. 1500. The favour of allowing it to pass was a great one, and that I received from the King of Denmark, at the instance of the Muscovite who gave me letters for the said King greatly in my favour, and others for the King of Sweden, in order that my vessel might pass free."

Russia was then on good terms with Denmark; according to the treaty of friendship of 1562 the Russians were to have factories at Copenhagen and at Wisby in Gothland, and the Danes at Novogorod and Ivangorod. In 1564 Ivan Vassilovitch concluded a peace with Eric the Fourteenth.* "The Muscovite has conceded to me many privileges, immunities, and exemptions, in favour of myself, my ship, and my men, so that I do not pay one penny for anything. Notwithstanding that whosoever goes to that country cannot leave it, he has ordered that my people should be free in everything. I therefore perceive the road open to fortune, and if I desired to serve him, as two Ferrarese who are prisoners there have often told me, I think I should do very well there, setting aside the inconveniences of the country; but I shall not resolve on going thither, unless necessity compels me, because I know that I might never be able to leave the country."

Barberini drew up for his friends a short account of Russia ("Relazione di Moscovia"), which is preserved in the Barberini Library at Rome, and was published in 1658. We are indebted to Barberini for his MS. notes on those articles of commerce which

* See Appendix Q.

he at that time thought worth importing into Russia, from which we have been enabled to ascertain many of the prices. In 1564 the pood of sugar was worth at Moscow 60, alum 55 to 60, and Brazil wood 30 altins; gold thread, 18 dollars the pound; pearls (large and white) 2 roubles per ounce; the dollar 50 dengi.

Barberini describes the sort of armour, horse-trapping, sledge and horse-cloths, and other articles which were to be provided for the Czar. He recommended that Turkey cocks and hens, kidney-beans, cauliflower, and pumpkin seeds, "vini buoni e grandi ma non dolci," thick paper for printing at Moscow (the art of printing had but just been introduced into Russia, and an edition of the "Lives of the Apostles" was then passing through the press), and markasite for the composition of type, should be sent to Russia. Elizabeth wrote to Ivan Vassilovitch by Jenkinson on the 20th of April, 1556:*—

"We understand that Your Majesty holds our letters in such esteem that, out of respect to their contents, You grant more favours to our subjects and even to foreigners, out of courtesy to Us, than We ourselves ask for them. This happened last year, when we recommended to you a certain Italian, named Raphael Barberini, not as a merchant, but as a traveller. But how this Italian has dared to abuse Our recommendation of him in Our letters as well as Your Majesty's goodness and other things which appertain to the intercourse established between Us and Ours, our well-beloved servant, Anthony Jenkinson, will explain to you per-

* See Appendix R.

sonally at greater length, but in Our own words, acquainting you with the resolution We have formed."

The well-known Alba arrived in the Netherlands from Spain in the following year, 1567, and Barberini, who was a knight of the Order of St. Stephen, took service under him, or rather under Vitelli, as a soldier. The letters he wrote at that time to his brother in Rome have been of use in compiling the history of the war then commencing. In 1569 he was sent as ambassador to Queen Elizabeth of England. His nephew, Urban the Eighth, laid the foundation of the celebrity of the Barberini house. Who has not heard of the palace of this family at Rome? The rich library, with its treasury of MSS., now unfortunately closed, was founded by Cardinal Francesco Barberini, great nephew of Raphael. Jenkinson was commissioned to make a representation to the Czar concerning Barberini, and managed to obtain an edict from him, that besides the English privileged company no foreigners should enjoy the advantages of free trade in Russia. It was likewise considered desirable that the privileges previously obtained from the Czar, with reference to the trade from Russia to Bokhara and Persia, should be extended.

Jenkinson reached Moscow on the 23rd of August, and had an audience on the 1st of September. The Czar, who was then building a new fortress at Moscow, a castle at Vologda, and much besides in the Alexandrian suburb, commissioned him to engage a skilful architect in England ("an architecture which can make castiles, townes, and palaces"), and moreover a doctor and an apothecary, as well as practical men who understood the art of discovering gold and silver ("masters such as are cunning (not coming) to seke ought gold and silver"). It seems to me likely that Jenkinson paid London a visit during the winter of 1556-57 to look after these matters. In a letter from Queen Elizabeth of the 18th of May, 1567, she requests Ivan Vassilovitch to fulfil the promise he had made in the foregoing year, to grant the English a fresh charter; and at the same time announces that she had given permissson to the persons required by the Czar to proceed to Russia. In fact, there then came over (in 1567) a doctor (Reynolds), an apothecary (Thomas Carver), an engineer (Humphrey Lock), his assistant (John Finton), "a goldsmythe and goldefiner," or assayer (Thomas Green), and other professional men. Lock wrote to Sir William Cecil on the 4th of March, and on the 20th of May, 1568; and, amongst other things, says: "I cold do for the Emperor such things, and make him such engynes for his warres, that he might thereby subdue any prynce that wold stand against him with devyces, yf I would make manyfest I cold have land and money enoughe; but that goods is evil gotten, that proffyt pressyts (precipitates) a man down into hell." He further explains that he had become acquainted in England with a very profitable contrivance for precipitating salt; but had not availed himself of it, because he feared that others would derive all the advantage.

On the 1st of July, 1568, he wrote, that at the end of May, a doctor, an apothecary, and a surgeon had arrived; "the doctor was jolyvated" (he makes an English word out of jalobatoi) "with 200 roubles, the potycarye with 100, and the surgeon with 50 roubles." On the 19th of May, 1572, Lock wrote to Lord Robert Dudley, Earl of Leicester, that he knew not whether the Czar would go on with his buildings, and that he wished to return to England. The London Company likewise sent three ropemakers: Robert Wilson, Robert Bland, and John Bushell. The first was engaged at £9 per annum, and the others at £5 for the first three, and £6 for the three ensuing years. I am not quite certain whether it was on this occasion that Francis Older (Ouldre) came over, who was to superintend a manufactory of Poldavys, *i. e.* coarse sackcloth, established in Russia.

The Czar Ivan now acquainted Jenkinson that he wished, 1st, to enter into a treaty of friendship with Queen Elizabeth ("which shall be the beginning of further matter to be done"); 2ndly, that she should be kind to his friends, but hostile to his enemies, and he would be the same to hers; 3rdly, that it should be particularly stipulated that she should not become friends with the King of Poland, for Sigismund actually sought to injure both herself and people. The latter, indeed, had lately sent a spy with a letter to the English merchants at Moscow, requesting them to assist those Russians who were favourably disposed towards him, the king, with money and in other ways. The object he proposed to himself by this was, to throw suspicion on the English merchants, to undermine the good understanding which existed between England and Russia, and by these means to annihilate the flourishing trade which was carried on between both nations. It was stipulated, 4thly, that she was to allow persons skilled in ship-building and navigation ("masters which can make shippes and sayle them") to come to Russia; 5thly, that artillery and other warlike stores might be sent there from England; 6thly, that it should be ratified by oath between her and himself that either sovereign might take refuge in the country of the other in case disturbances in their own realm should compel them to do so: this clause was to remain secret; 7thly, that she should send him a person of rank for the purpose of signing the treaty; and lastly, 8thly, that the Czar desired to receive her reply to all this on St. Peter's and St. Paul's day (29th June), 1568. Besides these, Jenkinson received other messages, which he was to deliver verbally. Here the private negotiations with Queen Elizabeth with reference to a marriage must have commenced.

The desired commercial charter was signed on the 22nd of September, 1567. It comprised the permission to carry on trade as far as Kazan and Astracan, to Narva and Dorpat, Bulgaria, and Schamachia. On the Icy and White Seas the harbours were not to be closed against merchants belonging to the company; and possession of the houses of the latter was confirmed to them at Moscow, Vologda, and Cholmogorü. The directors of the company wrote to Russia in 1566 that the route from the mouth of the Dwina to Novogorod and Narva, both by water and land, was to be surveyed with reference to its condition for the conveyance of goods. In consequence of these instructions,

Thomas Southam and John Sparke undertook this not uninteresting journey at the end of July of that year. They started in a coasting craft (lodge) from Cholmogorü to the convent of Solovetz (whose abbot, Philip, had been just named metropolitan of Russia); there received a pilot for the first and most difficult part of the route; sailed past Soroka at the mouth of the Vüg, and there ascended the latter river, as far as its course extended, in three small boats. They found themselves often obliged to track their boats and goods over land, but came at last to Voyets, rowed along the lake of that name (Vüg Lake), ascended that small river as far as practicable, and then proceeded by Telegen to Povenetz. They then embarked on Lake Onega, and rowed up the river Svir to the Lake of Ladoga, and on the Volchov to Novogorod, where they found William Rowley, the agent, just arrived from England by way of Narva, unable to proceed to Moscow because the plague was at Novogorod. The result of Southam and Sparke's surveying trip was the discovery that, between Povonetz and Novogorod, goods might be sent on by water; but, that from Ssumy to Povenetz it would be necessary to convey them by land in winter. At that time much salt, obtained from the White Sea, was conveyed to Novogorod on sledges.

CHAPTER VII.

FIRST ARRIVAL OF RUSSIAN MERCHANTS IN LONDON — THEIR RECEPTION BY QUEEN ELIZABETH — THE CZAR IVAN VASSILOVITCH'S PROPOSAL OF MARRIAGE TO THE QUEEN — NEW CHARTER GRANTED TO THE RUSSIA COMPANY.

IN 1567 Ivan Vassilovitch sent two Muscovite merchants, Stephen Zerdikoff and Fedot Pogneloi, to London, where they (the first who reached that city) arrived in August, and were quartered in the company's house in Seething Lane. They were commissioned to exchange furs for precious stones and other costly articles for the Czar's treasury. They brought a letter from him of the 10th of April, which was written in two languages, Russian and German. The latter is the copy I have discovered. It is the oldest in England from a Russian sovereign. The commencement of the Czar's title is wanting. The part which remains is conceived in the following terms:—" Ruler of Obdoski Condinski, and all the land of Siberia and the north coast, and Lord of the Livonian territory and other places, to Elizabeth, Queen of Engelant, France, and Ireland, and other places. To the gracious and noble Queen, health. We have sent to your country sundry of our merchants, viz. Steffan Fverdiko and Fedota Pogerela, and with them we have sent wares from our treasury, in order that in your kingdom they may purchase sapphires, and rubies, and cloths, such as we require in our treasury. When these merchants arrive in your kingdom, we pray you to allow them to pass free with the wares which they take to your kingdom, as well as with those which they purchase from your subjects for our treasury, &c. Given under our hand at our palace at Moscow, in the year 7075 from the creation of the world, on the 10th of April, in the 34th year of our age, in the 20th of our reign over Russia, the 15th of that over Kasan, and the 13th of that over Astracan." The seal is well preserved.

Queen Elizabeth received our Muscovite merchants at Oatlands, her country house, on which occasion Henry Lane undertook the office of interpreter. In May, 1568, they had their audience of leave-taking at Greenwich. Elizabeth gave them a letter in Latin, dated the 9th of May, to the Czar, spoke a few words to them, and they kissed her hand kneeling.

Stephen Tverdikoff was at an earlier period in the Netherlands, and had then visited Simon von Salingen and Cornelius de Meyer, at Antwerp. Both these persons sailed from the Lapland coast, in 1566, to the mouth of the Onega, and travelled from thence, dressed as Russians, by way of Kargopol to Moscow, whence they applied to their acquaintance, Tverdikoff, for the purpose of availing themselves of his counsel as to the best mode of laying before the Czar their complaint on the subject of a murder perpetrated on one of their countrymen. Our Muscovite merchants happened to be in London when the first Exchange was built, under the auspices of Sir Thomas Gresham, who then (in 1567-68) resided much in London. Soon after the taking of Narva, in 1558, Englishmen, not employed by the Russia Company, began to send out goods. This was done under the pretence that at the time the original charter was granted, Narva did not belong to Russia, but, in reality, before Chancellor's voyage, to the Hanse Towns. In 1566 the company obtained an Act of Parliament, according to which only members of the company, whose number at that time amounted to four hundred, could trade with that place. It was now entitled, "Fellowship of English Merchants for Discovery of New Trades." Christopher was sent to Narva with goods, and was to erect a factory there on account of the company. Notwithstanding this, several Englishmen continued to trade privately with Narva.

Sigismund, King of Poland, did all that was possible to throw obstacles in the way of the communication between England and Russia. I have in my possession copies of several letters from him to Queen Elizabeth, in the years 1567 and 1568, in which he complains of this commercial intercourse, that by means of it Russia was supplied not only with all necessary implements for carrying on war, but, what was still worse, received people who there spread useful knowledge, and taught every description of engineering.

On the 13th of July, 1567, he wrote as follows :*—
"But so much the less can We permit of free navigation to Muscovy, that your Highness sees it prohibited

* See Appendix S.

by us not only for very weighty reasons of our own, but as affecting religion and the whole Christian commonwealth. The enemy, as we have said, is instructed by intercourse; he is taught, which is of more consequence, the use of arms only just now introduced into that barbarous country; he is taught (which indeed we think likely to be productive of still more serious consequences) by the artificers themselves, so that, even if nothing else should be imported there, still by the labour of those artificers with whom he is freely supplied, whilst the navigation remains open as it is now, everything which can be used in war, and of which he has hitherto been ignorant, will be manufactured in that barbarous empire." Again, on the 3rd March, 1568:*—" For, owing to the navigation which has been thus recently opened, we see the Muscovite, who is not only the temporary enemy of our kingdom, but the hereditary one of all free nations, well instructed and armed. We see him provided not only with arms, wares, ships, and other articles, the introduction of which, although they are unimportant in themselves, might be more easily and effectually prevented; but also with other things of much greater consequence, which can in no way be sufficiently guarded against, and which are of much greater use to the enemy, I mean, with the very artificers who do not cease to manufacture arms, weapons, and other articles never before seen or heard of by the enemy in that barbarous country. And moreover, what is worthy of still more serious consideration, he is made acquainted with our

* See Appendix T.

most secret counsels, to be used hereafter to our destruction. We do not therefore think it can really be expected that we should suffer navigation to be thus rendered free."

Hakluyt has published a letter from Sigismund of this period, but dates it erroneously in 1559. It contains the following passage:—" We know the Moscovite dayly to grow mightier by the increase of such things as be brought to the Narve, while not onely wares, but also weapons, hitherto unknowen to him, and artificers and arts, be brought unto him, by meane whereof he maketh himself strong to vanquish all others. We seemed hitherto to vanquish him onely in this, that he was rude of arts and ignorant of policies. If so be that this navigation to the Narve continue, what shall be unknowen to him? The Moscovite, with those things that be brought to the Narve, and made more perfect in warlike affaires with engines of warre and shippes, will slay or make bound all that shall withstand him: which God defend."

For the purpose of putting a stop to the trade carried on at Narva by Englishmen who did not belong to the privileged company, the directors sent Lawrence Manley there in the autumn of 1567, and the Queen gave him a short letter to the Czar, dated the 14th of October. Manley was accompanied by Nicholas Proctor, who was afterwards agent at Moscow; and it is worthy of remark that the former was despatched before Jenkinson had returned to London with the Czar's letter and commissions. Three months later George Middleton, a gentleman, was despatched to Moscow, and took with him a comprehensive letter from the Queen, dated the 10th of February, 1568. In this letter the Queen alludes, but very briefly, to the epistle of September, 1567, which she had received from the Czar by Jenkinson, saying that it had given her the greatest pleasure, and that she most thankfully acknowledged the good-will he displayed towards herself and subjects. On the other hand Elizabeth enters into the following details:*—" Amongst other commissions, George Middleton is especially enjoined to treat at once with your Majesty for the apprehension, and as speedily as possible, of certain Englishmen at Narva (Thomas Glover, Ralph Rutter, James Watson, and Christopher Bennet), who, in open contempt of Us, seriously defrauding Our subjects, and not slightly wronging even your Majesty, have behaved in the most faithless, insulting, and wicked manner to us all. They, as We have heard, have, without the knowledge of their masters, who are here in England, contracted marriages with Polish women; and if the best mode of arresting them is not maturely considered, it is to be feared that they will take refuge in Poland."

It was, moreover, announced that in the spring an ambassador, with some respectable merchants, should be despatched to Moscow, in order to treat of commercial and other necessary matters. Ivan Vassilovitch asked Middleton whether he knew anything of Jenkinson's embassy; and as he did not receive a satisfactory reply, he considered it wrong that the Queen, to whom he had sent by Jenkinson a verbal communication and

* See Appendix U.

a proposal for a close alliance, should slight all his advances, and send people, and write to him, simply on mercantile affairs. As they were apprised in London that neither Manley nor Middleton had been enabled to arrange anything, and that they were viewed with suspicion, Thomas Randolph, an experienced diplomatist, was despatched to Moscow in June of the same year. He was accompanied by George Turberville, his secretary; Thomas Banister and Jeffrey Ducket, who desired to travel to Persia; James Bassendine, James Woodcock, and Richard Browne, who were to start from Petschora on a voyage of discovery to the eastward of Waigats, and several other persons, all of whom arrived at Rose Island, at the mouth of the Dwina, on the 3rd of August.

Thomas Randolph, born at Badlesmere, in the county of Kent, studied at Christchurch College, Oxford; was afterwards principal of Pembroke College; and in 1553, at the commencement of Mary's reign, went to France. From 1560 he was employed as Queen Elizabeth's active agent in Scotland in matters concerning Mary Stuart, and after he had been in Russia was dispatched again to Scotland by her. He had at that time the title of a Director of Posts (Post-director). In 1573 he was sent to France. He died on the 8th of June, 1590, and was buried in the Church at St. Peter's Hill, Paul's Wharf. I have discovered a great number of his letters in England. His widow, Ursula, retained possession of Quinborough Castle.

George Turberville was the youngest son of Nicholas Turberville, of Whitechurch, in Dorsetshire. He received the first part of his education at a school at Winchester; in 1561 became Fellow of New College at Oxford; and subsequently followed the profession of an advocate in London. He passed for a poet, and when in Russia amused himself with writing in verse to his friends in England—Edward Ducie, Spencer, and Palmer. He referred the latter to Herberstein's book on Russia, but states, by mistake, that this author was sent to Russia by the King of Poland.

Randolph visited the convent of St. Nicholas, where they brought him bread and salt, as well as fish of different kinds, and a black sheep with a white face. In passing through Vologda, Randolph makes mention of the fortress which the Czar had built of stone and brick ("the walls faire and hie"): at Jaroslavl, he mentions the craft built by the English in the Volga in 1565 of about thirty tons' burthen, in order to navigate the river ("which there was never seen before"); with the entire equipment, it had not cost more than a hundred marks.

Randolph, Banister, and Ducket reached Moscow on the 16th of October, and were lodged in the house built for ambassadors, but no one was allowed to approach them. Dr. Reynolds, however, and some English professional men, visited Randolph clandestinely. The latter read a letter from the Queen, dated the 12th of June, which in nowise corresponded with the expectations of the Czar, for he had entrusted Jenkinson with an important private communication to Elizabeth.

The Queen says merely that she had received the

Czar's epistle of September, 1567, sent by Jenkinson, and that the good-will which he therein expressed towards her subjects and herself, called for her own and her successor's cordial thanks, and that she now sent Randolph, because the Czar had desired that an envoy plenipotentiary should be despatched by her to Moscow. I have a copy of the "full powers" given to Randolph. Banister and Ducket had likewise a short letter from the Queen to the Czar, and "full powers" as ambassadors to the Shah of Persia.

Randolph declined making any preliminary statement to the Boyar Prince Afanassy Ivanovitch Väsemsky (Governor of Vologda) and the Secretary Peter Grigorjevitch, with reference to his embassy, and the audience was postponed in consequence; at length came a letter to Moscow from Queen Elizabeth, dated the 16th of September, 1568, by way of Narva, in which the commissions entrusted to Randolph were treated of separately. When she despatched this explanation, the Queen wrote to the magistrates of Narva, saying, that she had learned with surprise that Manley and Middleton were detained there, and demanded that the letter which she now sent to Ivan Vassilovitch should be forwarded without delay.

The following is a copy of this letter to Narva, written at Windsor, on the 16th of September, 1568:*—" To the magnificent and illustrious supreme Magistrates of the Emporium of Narva, under the most potent Emperor of Russia, &c., and Our very dear friends. Magnificent, illustrious, and very dear

* See Appendix W.

friends: We have this year sent two ambassadors, Laurence Manley and George Middleton, Our well-beloved servants, with letters to His Imperial Majesty of Russia, and have heard that permission to pass through your Jurisdiction to your Emperor has been denied our ambassador George Middleton. This is a matter which excites the greater surprise in Us, the more so as We are certain that you cannot be unaware of the friendly intercourse existing, and the numerous offices of mutual kindness which are being amicably and courteously interchanged between your Prince and Us, and between the subjects of both, at this time. But as We now desire certain matters of great moment to be communicated to your Emperor, which it will interest His Majesty to hear, We, in the first place, request that, out of obedience to your Prince, and, in the second place, beg, out of the courtesy We expect you will show Us, that you will take care that these Our letters which we enclose in ours to you, be conveyed to His Majesty as speedily as possible. We therefore trust that We shall hear (and, indeed, We shall diligently endeavour to ascertain the fact), that in this part of your duty you have been serviceable Magistrates to your Prince, and to Us complaisant and obliging friends. By so doing you will be enabled to merit approbation from your Prince and thanks from Us. This will be proved to you on Our part, when a suitable opportunity presents itself. Farewell."

Even the fresh letter, however, sent to be forwarded with that here quoted did not satisfy Ivan Vassilovitch, for it simply referred to the affairs of the merchants, and to the irregularities at Narva. The Queen therein expressed her surprise that Ivan Vassilovitch should have conferred special commercial privileges on former agents and clerks of the company; on Glover, Rutter, Bennet, and Chappell. These Englishmen were connected with Jacob de la Folia, and other Dutchmen. Queen Elizabeth's letter, as well as those from the directors of the company to Randolph and Middleton, were sent to Narva, to Andrew Atherton to be forwarded. That for Randolph was delivered by Atherton to Thomas Green, the assayer, who happened to be at Narva at the time. This was the cause of annoyance to both, for Atherton, who had likewise forwarded to London letters which had reached him from Moscow, was thrown into prison, with his servant and Green. At Narva, there was at that time Gregory Stephanovitch Ssobakin, Steward of the Bounds, whose niece, Martha Vassiljevna, was two years afterwards selected by the Czar out of a number of beautiful women, to become his third consort.

The result of the letter from the Queen was, that Randolph, Banister, and Ducket, had their audience on the 9th of February, 1569, at which they presented the Czar with a quantity of silver plate, at the same time that they stated their wishes. A few days afterwards, Randolph was sent for in the evening by Ivan Vassilovitch, who conversed with him for three hours; but it must not be supposed that at this private audience important affairs were settled, for it probably only related to the marriage project. I have seen a letter from Randolph, in which he says with reference to it: "I had private tawlke with his Maiestie at good lengethe of maynie matters, and chieffeste point of my legation. Much hathe byne said of other parte, but no resolution taken in anye thinge, that yet I have in hande." Randolph was sent for by Ivan Vassilovitch at the late hour in question, because the latter was to set out from Moscow on the following day for the Alexandrian suburb, and on his return, in April, Randolph had again several interviews with him. A letter from Randolph to the Czar, in which he complains of Glover, Rutter, Bennet, and others, is dated the 12th of April, and it was on the following day that Ivan Vassilovitch again quitted Moscow. Randolph wrote to him and to the council again on the 7th of May, complaining now especially of Bennet, who had had the impudence to give out at Narva that the letters, sent by Randolph by this route to England, contained improper expressions directed against the Czar. Randolph's letters, sent to Narva to be forwarded to England, had, as it happened, been given to Bennet to translate. In June, Randolph, Banister, and Ducket, received an order to follow the Czar to Vologda. Here the new charter desired by the English was granted, and on the 20th of June ratified. On the 24th of June Randolph had his leave-taking audience, and on his return home was to be accompanied by the noble Andrew Grigorjevitsch Ssavin, as ambassador to Queen Elizabeth, the Djak Ssemen Ssevastjanoff being appointed his secretary. Daniel Sylvester, one of the clerks, went as interpreter, and Thomas Glover for the purpose of settling the trade accounts. At the end of July they embarked at Rose Island, and arrived in London in September.

According to the privileges obtained by Randolph, all the English who were in Russia were to depend on the enactment of Ivan Vassilovitch, dated four years before, and by no means on the exterior jurisdiction. The English factory at Moscow was situated on the Varvarka, behind the Caravanserai, near the church of St. Maximus, at the so-named Juschkov court-yard. Now, although the Varvarka belonged to another jurisdiction, the English house was not placed under it. In like manner such houses as they might have in the towns included in the "temschtschina" jurisdiction, or which they might build, were to be comprehended within the chamberlain's jurisdiction. In a letter, of which I have a copy, Banister wrote to London as follows:—"So that being of oppris nay no man of Esemsekye dare meddle with the English." In the manuscript English translation of the charter, there is likewise the following sentence:—"Their other houses in our townes of the Sempskyes." Hakluyt, however, sets down by mistake—"houses in the towne of Senopski." Karamsin, who read this in Hakluyt, and could not guess that Senopski stood for Semski, and towne for townes, supposed that a distinct town, unknown to him, and called Senopski, was meant. In the manuscript of Randolph's charter which I have seen, it stands thus:—"We have graunted them the said house at St. Maxim's free." Hakluyt, however, has changed this into—"at St. Maxim's in the halfe free," which again is an unpardonable error.

The Company in London had already (in 1557) become acquainted through Nepeja, and by means of his interpreter, Robert Best, with the existence of iron ore and of the "Uklad" forges to the north-east of Vologda (as well as at Tula). On Nepeja's return home, the directors expressed a wish to receive samples of this "uklad" (a particular kind of steel). In 1566-67, Jenkinson was commissioned to solicit the Czar's permission for the English trading Company in Russia to establish iron works, and now this clause was inserted in its charter. At Vütschegda, where the chief town Ssolvütschegodsk, in the government of Vologda, now stands, the English were allowed to build for themselves and to erect iron foundries, and to supply fuel for these extensive woodlands were likewise assigned. Hakluyt has it—"We have graunted to the English merchants leave to buy them a house at Wichida;" but in the MS. it is "leave to build them a house." In a letter from Banister and Ducket, the merchants, dated the 25th of June, I found this:—"He hath given the company a mine of iron, with wood and ground to make the same six miles compasse, lying hard by the water-side, and is like to prove a great commoditie both to the company and to our country." The principal workmen were to be sent out from England to carry on the works, and instruct the Russians in the art, for in their country at that time all iron was still smelted with charcoal; and it was only half a century later that stone-coal, or rather coke, was employed for the purpose. The iron prepared at Vütschegda was partly to be disposed of for home consumption, and partly to be exported to England.

The English merchants likewise received permission to smelt down foreign dollars, and to stamp them anew as current coin. The charter granted to Glover, Rutter, Bennet, and Chappell, in 1568, was annulled, and only those Englishmen in the service of the company were to be allowed to trade in Russia itself, and through that country with Persia. Nevertheless, it was stipulated that articles of high value brought from England, as well as from Persia, should be first exhibited at the Czar's treasury, in order that he might have a prior choice; the English were, moreover, bound to execute his commissions. They were likewise permitted to erect a building for forging bolts, at Vologda, close to their house, on the land granted to them for the purpose. The Czar likewise ordered a space to be allotted to them at Narva, on which to build a house.

It is time that I should also speak of the English establishment at the mouth of the Dwina, which has been altogether overlooked by our geographers and historians, and which was situated on Rose Island.

The easternmost corner of the south side of Dwina Bay, in the White Sea, east of Nenoksa, where Stephen Burrough and Chancellor first set foot on Russian soil, was at first the anchorage for English shipping, and was called the Roadstead or Bay (also harbour) of St. Nicholas.

The southernmost of the four mouths of the Dwina, on Reineke's map, called that of St. Nicholas, was then termed the Korelian. Between this one and the next, which is further to the north, and still, as then, called that of Pudoshem, there is an island named on the map I have just mentioned, Jagrü, but at the commencement of the seventeenth century Jagornü, probably from jakor, an anchor, simply because here, after 1553, vessels were wont to anchor.

The southern mouth is called the Korelian, because it faces Korelia; that of Pudoshem had its name from the Pudoshem Islands lying opposite to it (formerly also called Podushemje; Sauvage, the Frenchman, wrote it, in 1586, Poudes James); the Murman mouth is named after the Murman Sea (the North Sea), and is the northernmost, considering its position with reference to that of Bereso, which is used for large vessels. We learn from Stephen Burrough that the bay is called after it Beresova Guba (Birch Bay).

This island received the name of Rose Island from the quantities of wild roses which there grew luxuriantly. Its south shore is separated from the main land, on which is the monastery of St. Nicholas, merely by the narrow southernmost embouchure of the Dwina, which formerly, as is to be seen in old documents, was called Molokurje.

On this island, where "Damascus and red rose, violet and wild rosemary" grew, and where there was also a pine and birch wood, the English established themselves, opposite to the convent of St. Nicholas and close to a spring of excellent water. Before they did so, they had intended building a house in Bereso

Bay, but it was not to cost more than three roubles. Stephen Burrough sounded the Bereso bar on the 29th of May, 1557, and found thirteen feet when the tide was at its lowest. Gray wrote on the 19th of February, 1559, from Cholmogorü to Lane, at Moscow :—"I doe intend to set up an house at Boroseva over against the place whereas the shippes shall ride; it shall not cost above three roubles, and yet if we will there shall be two warme roomes in it."

At Rose Island the goods taken out of the vessels arriving from England were placed in lighters, in order to be conveyed up the Malokurje and Dwina to Cholmogorü, and then on to Vologda. Similar craft brought Russian produce in the same way down the Dwina to the vessels at the Island for the purpose of being shipped for England, whence it was sometimes transmitted to the south of Europe.

Of the six vessels sent from the Thames to Rose Island, in 1567, only the three smallest, according to the instructions given by the directors of the company, were to be loaded with goods for London, and the remainder with wax and tallow for "Byskeye," "Gallyssia" (in Spain), "Lysheborne" (in Portugal), and Rome. For the latter city likewise yarn and a quantity of flax and hemp were sent on trial ("for the flax hathe as good a vent there as here, and a better all this last yeare"). The directors wrote that in the vessels intended to be sent to the south, cables (not above ten-inch), bales of flax, packages of furs, yarn, &c., as well as other light articles for England, might be placed on the top of the rest of the cargo, so as to be easily taken out at Harwich (Harwedge), or in the Downs, and the vessels then continue their voyage. Then (in 1567) the prices of Russian produce in London were as follows:—Wax, £3 14s. to £4 the cwt.; tallow, 18s.; flax, 28s. to 30s.; hemp, 12s.; tarred ropes, prepared by the English at Vologda, 18s. (England had previously imported her cordage from Dantzic); yarn, 11d. per lb.; train oil, £10 per ton; elk-hides, 6s. 8d. each; hides for tanners, 3s. 4d. It is remarkable that a quantity of Russian wool was then ordered on trial, as it was considered well adapted for working into hats and felt. The directors of the company wrote:—"There is a certayne kind of woll verie good in those parts for hats and ffelts. The Tartarians are accustomed to make their cloaks thereof, yt is much like the Estrich wooll. We praye you to send us some thereof for a prooffe, ffor we have more perfeet ffelts made here in London at this present than any are made in Spaigne, and in great quantitie also." I will here, moreover, observe that at that time considerable quantities of salt were brought from England to Rose Island as well as to Naroni. Even at the Dwina, where there were salt pits, the sale of a pood produced "six Dingots."

At Rose Island there was no Custom House, the trade was quite free, and everything was imported and exported *ad libitum*. Here, in the English house, not only the English engaged in trade, who were arriving, departing, and passing by, but likewise the ambassadors, were lodged and entertained. Here Southam and Sparke spent a day in 1556 (on the 13th of July), when on their way from Cholmogorü to Novogorod.

It was from this place that, in 1568, Randolph visited the monastery of St. Nicholas, and that he, as well as Banister and Ducket, wrote to Sir William Cecil on the 12th of August, 1568, by " William, of Burrowe;" here, likewise, the same Burrowe gave his instructions to James Bassendine for the projected expedition from Petschoram to the East.

The dispatch from the Czar Ivan Vassilovitch delivered by the Ambassador Ssavin to Queen Elizabeth, was dated from Vologda, the 20th of June, 1569. I discovered it in the British Museum. It is the oldest Russian letter from the Czar, in England, and possesses on this account a certain degree of interest. The place where it was folded has been much damaged by fire, so much so, that the letter is separated into two pieces. No one appears to have examined the contents until now; in the catalogue of the Cottonian Library (Nero, book xi. 90) it is merely stated to be "two papers, Russian."

Unfortunately it is exactly that spot in the letter where the Czar gives vent to his displeasure that his own affairs should be neglected for commercial matters, that has been injured by fire. Here he stated that the sovereign's business should always take precedence of private interests. In a contemporary English translation of the letter, there is this passage:—" They (Manley and Middleton) would not come to our near and privie counsaile, and would make them privie of none of theire affaires; all that they saide was of marchant affaires, and settinge our highest affaires aside, as it is the use of all countries that princes' affaires should be first ended, and after that to seek a gaine."

Together with the Russian letter Ssavin delivered to Queen Elizabeth a Latin and Italian translation of it. In her letter of the 18th of May, 1570, delivered by Ssavin to the Czar, she says: "Both which tongues (the romayne and the italian) wee doe well understand."

Ssavin spared no trouble in procuring a document establishing a treaty of friendship between Ivan Vassilovitch and Elizabeth. On the 6th of May he handed in a note requesting that it might be drawn up in the Russian language (because the Czar understood no other), word for word according to his wish, signed by the Queen with her seal affixed, and likewise that Elizabeth should ratify it in his presence with an oath. He, moreover, requested that the Queen should, on her side, send an ambassador with him, when Ivan Vassilovitch might have a similar document drawn up. He further expressed a wish that Anthony Jenkinson might likewise be dispatched to Russia, for it was through him that this matter was first brought on the tapis.

CHAPTER VIII.

TREACHERY AND PUNISHMENT OF DOCTOR BOMEL—DISSATISFACTION OF THE CZAR AT THE CONDUCT OF THE ENGLISH—SUSPENSION OF THE RUSSIA COMPANY'S CHARTER — MOSCOW BURNT BY THE TARTARS—ENGLISH HOUSE IN THE VARVARKA DESTROYED — ROBERT BEST AND ANTHONY JENKINSON DISPATCHED FROM ENGLAND WITH LETTERS TO THE CZAR.

THE Russian Ambassador, Ssavin, returned to Moscow in the summer of 1570, with Ssevastianoff, Sylvester, and Glover. It had been discovered in London that the latter was more than four thousand roubles in debt to the company, which sum he was now to pay to Nicholas Proctor, the agent at Moscow. In consequence of the intercession made for him by Ivan Vassilovitch in his letter, Glover was treated with more forbearance by the directors of the company than would otherwise have been the case.

The document containing the treaty is of the 18th of May. Sylvester had already translated it into Russian, in London, by Sir William Garrard's desire. As it is tolerably well preserved in the archives at Moscow, I need not dwell upon it at greater length. I merely recollect at this moment that Elizabeth assured the Czar Ivan Vassilovitch, who had for the second time become a widower, on the 1st of September, 1569, that "he would be very well received in England with his noble consort and his dear children." I discovered in England another sketch of this document, with the following passage:—"We have thought good in some secret manner to send your highness for a manifest and certain token of our good will to your highnes estate and suretye this our secret lettre, whereunto non are privie beside ourselfe, but our most secret councell."

Ssavin brought with him from England a man who did much mischief in Russia, Doctor Elisæus Bomel. He was born at Wesel, in Westphalia, had studied medicine at Cambridge, and passed for a skilful astrologer. People in London considered him almost a sorcerer, and he had likewise some adherents amongst the great. Archbishop Matthew Parker threw him into the Queen's Bench prison, and he was about to be released, on condition that he should leave England immediately, when, on the 3rd of April, 1570, he wrote to the same archbishop, informing him that he could indicate means by which a great evil which threatened England might be averted. Parker wrote on the same day to Cecil, to whom Dr. Bomel likewise addressed himself on the 7th of April, sending him a fragment of his treatise, "De Utilitate Astrologiæ," in which he sought to demonstrate from history that every five hundred years great changes took place in a kingdom; at the same time he reminded him that just this period of time had elapsed since the Norman invasion. It was evidently Bomel's design to alarm the Government at that troubled period, and make himself of importance.

At the beginning of May, Bomel announced to

Sir William Cecil that the Russian Ambassador, then in London (consequently Ssavin), had sent to him in prison an invitation to betake himself to Russia, where he would receive good pay. Bomel requested Cecil not to throw any obstacle in the way of this project, for on the following Sunday Ssavin intended to solicit the Queen's leave to depart He, at the same time, promised Sir William that he would keep him punctually informed of all that passed in Russia, as well as send him annually thence some small presents ("munusculæ grati animi significationes"). Probably they were glad to get rid of Bomel, and, unfortunately, he really did accompany Ssavin, the ambassador, when he returned to Russia.

Dr. Bomel was much about the person of Ivan Vassilovitch, not only at Moscow but in the Alexandrian suburb, and at Vologda. It is a mistake to suppose, with Karamsin, that he was the first who suggested to the Czar the idea of a marriage with Elizabeth, for he merely urged him to it anew by his astrological mystifications and calculations.

The following is the original letter which I have seen, written by Bomel to Cecil, from the Queen's Bench prison : * " Illustrious Lord—In about a month hence I shall be enabled through your magnificence to devote my services and assistance to Her Royal Majesty, and point out a way whereby these intestine evils may be healed, without any effusion of blood. A short time will show whether my deeds as well as my suggestion do not please your magnificence. As, therefore,

* See Appendix X.

the Russian Ambassador (*i. e.* Ssavin) sends messengers to me daily, and does not expect to obtain my services without a large stipend, and I would not resolve on doing anything either in this matter or in others of my own accord, without first obtaining the leave and counsel of your magnificence, I earnestly entreat that you will plainly acquaint my servant" (he at first wrote my wife), "who is well educated, with your intention, before the ambassador on Sunday next presents my humble supplications to the Queen, explains the cause of my detention in this filthy dungeon, and obtains a free exit for me from this island to Russia. You cannot do me a greater favour than this, and you will confer such a perpetual obligation on me, that if Her Royal Majesty desires to make use of my services, you will always have me ready to come when called upon. Truly if I am permitted to depart hence, I shall not only make you acquainted by my letters with the customs of the Muscovites and their neighbours, their mode of government, the character of their climate, the position of the country, and such other things as are worthy of being noted; but you will also receive from me annually such small presents of the produce of that extensive region as are proofs of a grateful mind. Lastly, if Her Royal Majesty has no desire to avail herself of my art, I earnestly entreat your magnificence that, together with the ambassador, you will stand my friend, intercede for me with our Most Gracious Queen, and be the cause of Her Royal Majesty's freeing me from these bonds. I doubt not that you will do this out of your wonted humanity and your attachment to the learned.

Farewell your magnificence. I beg that you will recollect Bomel. From the Royal prison—addressed to your magnificence by Elija Bomel, your most attached physician." It is addressed: "To the right honourable Syr Wylliame Cecille, Knight, principall secretarie to the Queene's most excellent Maiestie these."

By his artful and interested persuasions, Bomel certainly induced Ivan Vassilovitch to commit several rash acts which, had it not been for him, would not have taken place. His fearful end he must have brought upon himself, principally by engaging in a conspiracy with other persons in favour of the Kings of Poland and Sweden. After having been put to the torture, he was bound to a stake and thrown on the fire; then as he was being carried off to the Kremlin in a sledge, in order to be cast into a grave, Jerome Horsey observed that life was still in him, and that he opened his eyes and uttered the name of Christ. His widow, Jane, *née* Ricards, returned with Sir Jerome Bowes to England, in 1583. This same Horsey, who had known Bomel personally at Moscow, wrote of him as follows:—"He had deluded the Emperor, makinge him believe the Queen of England was younge, and that yt was very favourable for him to marry her;" and likewise, "he lived in great favour and pompe; a skilful mathematician, a wicked man, and practiser of much mischieff; most of the Nobles wear glad of his dispatch, for he knew much by them. He had conveyed great riches and treasures out of the country by way of England to Waesell, in Waestvallia, where he was bourn, though brought up in Cambridge, an enymie alwaies to our nation." Strype says of Dr. Bomel:—"He was a physician of great fame, pretending to be skilled much in art, magic, and astrology, as well as physic, perhaps the son of Henricus Bomelius, a preacher of God's word at Wezel."

When his treacherous conduct had been discovered through the correspondence carried on by him in Latin and Greek as well as in cypher, he strongly asserted his innocence, relying upon some friends who, together with the Czarovitch Ivan, were appointed to examine his papers; but the rack extorted a confession from him. "Upon the racke his arms drawen back, disjointed, and his leggs stretched from his middell loyns, his back and bodie cutt with wyre whipps, confessed much and many things more than was written or willinge the Emperor should knowe. The Emperor sent word they should rost him. Taken from the pudkie and bound to a wooden povel or spitt, his bloody cutt back and body rosted and scorched till they thought no liff in him. Cast into a slead, brought throw the castell. I prest amonge many others to see him. Cast up his eys naminge Christ. Cast into a dungeon and died there." This is Horsey's account, and consequently, Karamsin is not altogether correct when he says that he was publicly burnt.

Ivan Vassilovitch was by no means contented with the arrangement effected by Ssavin in London, and the latter sought to justify himself by stating in writing that he had not been properly treated in England. Although Ssavin died soon afterwards, this letter still remained as a document which might be used in a manner unfavourable to the English merchants.

Daniel Sylvester, the interpreter, who had been in London with Ssavin, was now dispatched with a letter from the Czar to Queen Elizabeth, dated the 24th of October, 1570. This dispatch contains a concise historical retrospect of the intercourse existing with England up to that time, but it is not correct. It states, for instance, that Chancellor visited Russia three times. The Czar complains that the private commission entrusted to Jenkinson, was not properly executed by him, although he had exacted an oath from him as well as from Ralph Rutter, who acted as interpreter on the occasion. He likewise intimated that he was displeased with Randolph, because he would make no preliminary communication either to Prince Väsemky or to any one else, whether he had any report to make relative to the private commission in question; that Ssavin was not so well received in London as he ought to have been; that Elizabeth reigned like a woman without energy, and yielded the guidance of affairs to merchants; that no attention had been paid either to the wishes expressed by him, or to the commissions he had given, but that commercial matters alone had been discussed: and he now commanded that not only the charter granted at Randolph's request, but all preceding ones, should be forthwith suspended. He at the same time declared, that under these circumstances he now relinquished all views he had entertained with regard to England.

The English translation of the dispatch of the 24th of October, 1570, is partly as follows:—"You have set aside those (our) great affairs, and your councell doth deale with our ambassadour about marchaunts affaires, and your marchaunts (viz. those of the Russia Company) did rule all our busines, and wee had thought that you had been ruler over your lande and had sought honor to your self and profitt to your countrie, and, therefore, wee did pretend those weightie affaires between you and us. But now wee perceive that there be other men that doe rule, and not men but bowres and marchaunts, the which seeke not the wealth and honour of our maiesties, but they seeke their own proffitt of marchaundize. And you flowe in your maydenlie estate like a maide, and whosoever was trusted in our affaires and did deceave us, it were not meete that you should credditt them. And now seeinge it is so, wee doe sett aside these affaires and those bourishe marchaunts that have been the occasion that the pretended welths and honors of our maiesties hath not come passe but doe seeke their owne wealthes, they shall see what traffique they shall have here. All those priviledges which wee have given afforetime shall be from this daie of none effect."

During the difficult period, from 1567 to 1571, William Rowley was the company's agent at Moscow. The management of the cloth trade was very properly entrusted to him, for he had been apprenticed to it for seven years, and had made himself acquainted with the colours and textures of cloth both in Holland and Germany.

Previously to Sylvester's arrival in England, the Queen, in consequence of a report received by the directors of the Russia Company, that their privileges had been abolished, had dispatched the before-mentioned Robert Best, a man well versed in the Russian language, and in some measure known to the Czar Ivan Vassilovitch, with a letter to the Czar, dated the 24th of January, 1571; and he proceeded by way of Sweden. Queen Elizabeth wrote to John, the third King of Sweden, on the 24th of January, 1571, that the Czar Ivan Vassilovitch had entirely, without grounds, confiscated the whole of the property of the English in Russia ("vinctis manibus sub aresto custodiantur"); and thus the company, in consequence, sent this messenger (Best, who, however, was not named), in order to discuss the matter with the Czar (who is here entitled Dux). She said, moreover, that the merchants intended to export all such goods as they might have in Russia in the ensuing spring, in order that for the future they might not be exposed to similar vexations. She therefore requested the King to permit the messenger (Best) to pass without hindrance through Sweden, and return in like manner; and, moreover, that the vessels of the English merchants might be suffered to pass by that country unharmed. In her letter to the Czar, Elizabeth assured him that Ssavin had been received and treated in England with all honour ("nihil nec nostra nec aliorum opinione fieri potuerit honorificantius"), and requested that the exercise of free trade might be permitted to her subjects as it had been previously.

Best arrived in Russia at a calamitous period: a fearful famine prevailed, and, moreover, the plague raged in a frightful manner. Still all these evils did not seem sufficient, for, on Ascension Day (the 24th of

May, 1571,) the Khan Dewlet Girei advanced towards Moscow with a mighty horde of Tartars, and the result was, that these barbarians, having set fire to several houses in the suburbs, in a few hours the imperial city was so completely reduced to ashes, that, as an Englishman wrote, not a post was left to which a horse could be fastened. One hundred thousand men, not only citizens, but fugitives from the surrounding country, were partly burnt, partly smothered in the stone churches and in cellars, and partly drowned in the Moskwa. Jenkinson mentions, in his letter of the 8th of August, 1571, the same thing that was written on the 20th of June, 1570, by some one in King Sigismund's embassy to a friend abroad, that in some places in Russia hunger compelled the people to have recourse to human flesh in their despair, in order to appease its pangs. Jenkinson remarks that the plague at this period carried off about three hundred thousand persons; and that by the incursions of the Tartars under Dewlet Girei, Russia was deprived of about an equal number of her inhabitants.

Daniel Sylvester must have given an account in England of the great famine in Russia at the end of 1570, for, in the following year, 1571, the Russia Company shipped corn to Rose Island. I have already observed that the vessel, the Magdalene, on board of which came Richard Uscombe, was laden therewith, but, under the then existing circumstances, the corn could not be sold; and it was not until 1572, that at Staritz Jenkinson obtained permission from the Czar for this to be done, when its sale was allowed altogether duty free. The house of the English in the Varvarka was destroyed by the fire we have named above; and in the beer-cellar attached to it, thirty persons, including the inhabitants and their acquaintances, and strangers who had taken refuge there as the fire approached, perished. Amongst them were the following Englishmen: Thomas Southam, who, in 1566, made the journey from the Dwina to Novogorod, and two other clerks; Thomas Field (not Tofild, as Uscomb copied the name), and John Waverley; Thomas Carver, the apothecary, who arrived at Moscow either in 1567 or 1568; also Thomas Chafin, one of the principal workmen; the widow of Thomas Green, the goldsmith and assayer, with both her children, and two children of Ralph Rutter, though the latter himself, with his wife, as well as John Brown and John Clarke, were, wonderful to relate, preserved alive. Thomas Glover, the former agent, and William Rowley, who then occupied that post, in order to escape from the heat as well as from the foul air in the beer-cellar, hazarded an attempt to quit it and reach another, and, although blinded by the smoke, they attained their object, and saved themselves; but a boy who followed them on foot was caught by the flames. In this second cellar was also John Sparke, who, in 1566, had made the journey to Novogorod with Southam, and, in 1568-69, was one of the four who composed the expedition led by Arthur Edwards to Persia.

Thomas Glover, who, as we have seen, found great difficulty in escaping from the fire with his life, betook himself to Narva, and thence, on the 2nd of July, 1571, he sent a description of the misfortune which had befallen the company's house to Sir William Gerrard, the oldest of the directors (he died in 1571), as a supplement to a letter which he had sent by his servant John Hunt, who was to communicate the details by word of mouth. He likewise wrote about this catastrophe to Sir William Cecil, who, unknown to him, had borne the title of Baron of Burghley since the 13th of February. Sir William Gerrard sent Hunt, immediately on his arrival in London, on the 17th of August, to Lord Burghley with the letter addressed to him, and likewise delivered to him the intelligence received from Glover. Another and shorter description of the conflagration appears to me to have reached London by means of Nicholas Proctor, afterwards chief agent at Moscow, because he writes that he had quitted that city eight hours before the gates were closed and the fire broke out, and that he hurried by way of Pereslavl and Rostov to Jeroslavl. Now we find Proctor soon afterwards, at the end of July, at Rose Island, where he made the same communication with reference to the catastrophe to Richard Uscombe, who had arrived from England at the same time as Jenkinson, as the former wrote to his friend Henry Lane on the 5th of August, and agrees in substance with that account. It is, for instance, stated by both that altogether five-and-twenty persons perished in the company's house, whereas Glover says that there were thirty.

John Stow, the well-known historiographer of England, and particularly of London, who was at that time occupied with a new edition of his "Englishe Chronicles," copied both the above-mentioned accounts when they reached him, although not correctly, and thus they were very improperly amalgamated. Stow, also, erroneously gives the name of William to Glover where the latter speaks of himself, whereas it was Thomas. Stow's MS. is preserved in the British Museum with a note outside, "in Stow's hand-writing." Of the leaf which contains the account, a highly-faulty and imperfect copy was made for Count Rumänzoff, which was superscribed, "Destruction of Moscow, by John Stow." Hence it was that Herr Adelung, as I just find, was led to suppose that Stow was the author of the description, and that in 1571 he was occupied with commercial matters at Moscow, where he was an eyewitness of the conflagration, and described this fearful catastrophe. To the copy in question is attached another of a translation, made by Jerome Horsey, of a letter written by Theodore Ivanovitch to Elizabeth (and delivered by Dr. Fletcher) in April, 7097, *i.e.* 1589. This latter translation of an Imperial letter is considered by Herr Adelung to be the conclusion of Stow's supposed description of the conflagration of Moscow, which took place on the 24th of May, 1571. The loss of property sustained by the English Company was very considerable, for it was calculated by William Rowley, the agent at that time, to amount to ten thousand roubles.

Ivan Vassilovitch, on the approach of the Tartars, proceeded to Jaroslavl from Serpuchov, on the other side of the Oka, by way of Pereslavl, and without touching at Moscow. There he was also on the road from the capital to Vologda, where, in 1566, he had constructed a strong fortress, containing a treasure-chamber made of stone, and whence he could proceed to Rose Island in the spacious craft built for him, in order to embark either for the isolated monastery of Ssolovetz or, in case of the worst, to England. He afterwards resided at the Alexandrian suburb, situated between Moscow and Jaroslavl, now the chief town, Alexandroff, in the government of Vladimir. Thence he replied to the letter from Queen Elizabeth, of the 24th of January, received through Robert Best, promising to renew the charter as soon as Jenkinson brought him satisfactory intelligence with respect to the private commission entrusted to him. In a postscript to this letter, Ivan Vassilovitch says that he had just been made acquainted with Jenkinson's arrival in the Dwina. Best had been commissioned to solicit from Ivan Vassilovitch the release of Thomas Green and Ralph Rutter, who, according to Randolph's information, he supposed, had been cast into prison. Green was already dead; and with regard to Rutter, who was at liberty, and who was expected in England, in order to submit his accounts to the company, Ivan Vassilovitch declared that he should suffer him to depart in compliance with the stipulation in question. On the 2nd of June, 1571, Elizabeth wrote once more by Jenkinson with reference to Green's release.

Jenkinson had arrived at Rose Island on the 26th of July, accompanied by Daniel Sylvester the interpreter, and remained there some days. He made the voyage again on board the ship Swallow, which had been accompanied from the Thames by the Harry. Nicholas Proctor, who had arrived at Rose Island from Moscow shortly before Jenkinson's arrival there, informed him that Ivan Vassilovitch was highly dipleased with him, whereupon Jenkinson dispatched Sylvester to the Czar, soliciting instructions. The Queen had delivered to the former, besides the principal letter for Ivan Vassilovitch, a very short one, which he was to send on to announce his arrival. Of this letter I discovered two rough sketches at Cambridge. On account of the plague quarantine, Sylvester made just as little progress on his way to the Czar as a second messenger did who was dispatched after him; but we have seen, that as early as August intelligence of his arrival at Rose Island had already reached the village where Ivan Vassilovitch was then engaged in his memorable search for a bride (" lit. bridal show"), and where, on the 28th of October, he married the lovely Martha Vassilgevna Ssobakina, who was selected out of so many there assembled. This "flos florum," however, withered away suddenly, and but seventeen days had elapsed after the nuptials when she died. A week after the ceremony, the Czarovitch Ivan had espoused Jevdokija Bogdanovna Ssaburova, who was selected for him at this time by his father. The widowed Ivan Vassilovitch betook himself to Novogorod, which had not long before been visited by him with so much difficulty. He arrived there on the 24th of December, and quitted it again on the 18th of January, 1572; and on his return to the village, he permitted Jenkinson to come there from Cholmogorü.

Jenkinson must have remained a long time at the latter place, on account of the still-spreading pestilence; and it was only on the 23rd of March, 1572, that he had an audience of IvanVassilovitch, at the Alexandrian suburb. In the letter which he delivered from Queen Elizabeth, she replied (on the 2nd of June, 1571) to all the points separately set forth in the Czar's dispatch of the 24th of October, 1570. Of this interesting epistle I found a copy in the public library at Cambridge; and it is remarkable, that the error which exists in the Czar's letter of the 24th of October, 1570, with reference to Chancellor's third voyage to Russia, should be repeated in it without observation. It is as follows :—
"Scribit deinde Serenitas Vestra eundem Ricardum Chansler iterum et tertio missum et semper quidem honorifice tractatum et dimissum incolumem." With regard to the private commission, the passage runs thus —Jenkinson has on his side rightly fulfilled his mission —" Eum ad vos hactenus non remissimus quod eius opera adversus hostes terra marique utebamur." Manley's conduct Elizabeth would enquire into, but Middleton ("Quem probum virum cognovimus") could not have been properly understood.

Randolph had received orders from her to deliver her letter into the Czar's own hands, before he spoke about the contents with the council; and she thought that Ssavin's report in this case ought to have been satisfactory. In reply to the allusion to her mode of government, she wrote: * " He (Jenkinson) will most truly acquaint your Grace that no merchants govern our state and affairs, but that we ourselves preside over the dispatch of business, as it behoves a virgin and a queen, appointed by the great and good God. In no nation are the people more obedient to their prince than our subjects are to us. This being the gift of the great and good God, to Him we tender our most humble and grateful thanks." She hoped that the charter would be renewed, and reminds the Czar of William Burroughs' capture of Polish corsairs, near Narva, in 1570, and remarked that England might frequently be of great use to Russia. " Res omnis generis in vestrum imperium subditi nostri exportaverunt ad conciliandam vestram benevolentiam, quas nos ad alios nullos orbi terræ principes exportari sinimus." This is an allusion to warlike matters. " Et vero possumus vobis confirmare multos principes ad nos scripsisse," (she means in particular the Emperor Ferdinand and Sigisimund King of Poland,) " ut vestram amicitiam deponeremus, nos tamen nullis literis adduci potuimus quin constanter in amicitia permaneremus." After the formal audience, Ivan Vassilovitch detained Jenkinson for some time with him, when, besides one secretary, only Sylvester the interpreter was present; and the Czar detailed the reasons he had for his displeasure. Besides Manley and Middleton, he likewise named Edward Goodman as one of the messengers who had arrived at Narva, and with whom he was dissatisfied. But I have

* See Appendix Y.

nowhere found that Goodman received a commission from the Queen, or from the directors of the company. Jenkinson took considerable pains in justifying Randolph's conduct; enlarged on the advantages which England had procured for Russia, and solicited the renewal of the privileges which had been suspended. As Ivan Vassilovitch had a journey in view at that time, he requested Jenkinson to wait at Tver until its conclusion; and on the 8th of May he was summoned to an audience at Staritza.

At this audience, which took place at Staritza, in the present government of Tver, on the 13th of the same month (1572), Vassilovitch set forth in substance what he had already written to the Queen by Sylvester. He moreover added, that he was now satisfied with the explanations given by Jenkinson, and with his mission, and would renew the privileges; and repeated on this occasion, that he abided by his former plan with reference to England.

As Ivan Vassilovitch at this audience alluded to the bad conduct of several Englishmen in Russia, I will here observe, that five years previously the directors of the company had much blamed the mode of living of those of their countrymen who had been appointed to the trading establishments at Moscow, Vologda, and Cholmogorü. They wrote, on the 18th of April, 1567, to their agent, William Howley, animadverting upon certain irregularities and abuses: for instance, great use of wine ("typling"), debauchery, hound and bear keeping, coursing ("they ride when we goe afoote"), useless expenditure in dress ("in velvets and silke"), &c. A uniform dress was prescribed, and the price of one portion of it fixed, viz. for the furs. The "pelch of furres," which was to last for three years, stands on the list at one rouble.

CHAPTER IX.

NEGOTIATIONS OF DANIEL SYLVESTER—FREEDOM OF TRADE RESTORED TO THE RUSSSIA COMPANY—ENGLISH DEPÔT AT ROSE ISLAND.

On the 14th of May, 1572, Jenkinson received from the Czar a decisive answer to all his requests, a letter to the Queen, and the promise that the charter should be sent after him to Cholmogorü, and that Ralph Rutter, whose presence was required in England, should be ordered to join him there. He must, nevertheless, have embarked at the end of July at Rose Island without the charter, and without Rutter; and on the 10th of September he landed on the coast of Norfolk, after a long voyage in which he had encountered many dangers. Although he had been one whole year in Russia he had not seen Moscow, which had been reduced to ashes some months before his arrival.

Elizabeth replied from Windsor on the 20th of October of the same year, to the letter delivered to her by Jenkinson of the 14th of May, 1572. She said that Ivan Vassilovitch had done so much that nothing more could be desired ("nihil uberius fieri potuerit, nec in amicitiâ honorificentius"). She recommended the merchants appertaining to the company, who were still in Russia, to his further protection, especially the new agent, Nicholas Proctor, and Banister and Ducket, who were expected on their return from Persia. The former, however, had already there met his death. She requested him not to give an audience to Glover, Rutter, and others, who no longer belonged to the company, but to send them back to England by Proctor. Sylvester brought this letter from the Queen to Moscow.

The attention which Queen Elizabeth paid to the affairs of the Russia Company is remarkable. If the latter wished to obtain anything from Ivan Vassilovitch, the directors were accustomed to deliver a memorandum of it to Sir William Cecil (Lord Burghley), in 1571, and he laid the matter before the Queen. In the present instance, the company's request was transmitted by Alderman Lionell Ducket, on the 18th of October, to Lord Burghley, by Daniel Sylvester, to whom the progress and position of the affair were known. Ducket requested Sylvester to give him an English translation of the royal letter, because he did not understand Latin; and at Moscow there was now scarcely any one capable of translating properly from Latin into Russian. This, then, was the reason why Sylvester himself was dispatched to Moscow with Elizabeth's letter.

On the 15th of April, 1573, Ivan Vassilovitch wrote by Sylvester to Elizabeth, that, in accordance with her wishes he had conceded perfect freedom of trade to Proctor and the other Englishmen belonging to the privileged company; but that Glover, Rutter, and other persons who had attempted to compete with it, had been banished the country.

On the 28th of July, 1573, the Queen returned her thanks, and recommended William Merritt, the company's new agent, to the Czar. She had heard from Sylvester that the company's property at Novogorod had been confiscated, because it had been reported that many Englishmen were employed by John the Third, King of Sweden, in fighting against Russia, whereupon she gave the Czar to understand that they must be Scotch. Andrew Atherton was appointed factor, probably at Novogorod.

On the 27th of October, 1573, and on the 26th of May, 1574, Elizabeth wrote again to Ivan Vassilovitch, on the former occasion by Sylvester. She had learnt that Ducket's caravan had been plundered on its return from Persia, by way of the Caspian Sea, and that several persons had been slain in the attack, as well as others wounded. She requested that compensation should be awarded, and at the same time announced, that now that the company had recovered the favour of the Czar, and obtained the removal of Glover and other persons who interfered with them, it intended sending many vessels to Russia yearly, and that William Burrough, whom she, the Queen, recommended to the Czar, had been appointed its chief agent.

In 1574, several Englishmen were likewise sent by the company to the Lapland coast, for the purpose of carrying on a trade by barter; and they wintered there, viz.: Roger Leeche, James Alday, Christopher

Colt, and Adam Tunstall, a cooper; they had also a boy with them. From 1565, the Lapland coast had been frequented by traders from Antwerp; and in 1570 the Korelian Sea was, for the first time, visited by them. At that time also arrived Italian artists and handicraftsmen, in Dutch vessels, at the Solovetz monastery, and thence proceeded to Lake Onega, in order to travel on to Moscow.

Ivan Vassilovitch replied on the 20th of August, 1574, by Sylvester, complaining of the conduct of several Englishmen in Russia, and that others had taken service with the King of Sweden; and touching anew on the non-fulfilment of the private commission entrusted by him to Jenkinson in 1567, and of the wish he therein expressed.

On the 9th of May, 1575, Elizabeth answered him by Sylvester, whom she furnished with ample instructions. The Queen lamented that Englishmen should have conducted themselves so ill in Russia, but hoped that they were such as did not belong to the trading company. She repeated that the so-called Englishmen in the Swedish service were probably Scotch, and consequently not under her control. The affair to which the private commission referred, she considered settled since Jenkinson's last mission. The proposed oath relative to the treaty she had not taken, in order that surprise might not be excited; and she further observed that any intimation with regard to her seeking an asylum in Russia would have much displeased her subjects.

On the 29th of November, 1575, Sylvester had an

audience of Ivan Vassilovitch at the house of one of his retinue, built by him in 1560, outside the Kremlin, on the other side of the Neglina, near the Vsdvüshenka, and where originally stood the house of his father-in-law, the Circassian Prince Michailo Zemgrukovitch, which was burnt to the ground in 1564. This audience is memorable in Russian history, because it appears that on this occasion Ivan Vassilovitch appointed the Tartar Khan Ssain Bulat to the Regency of the realm (in 1573), under the title of Grand Prince of the whole of Russia, whilst he called himself only Lord and Prince of Moscow. The Khan, it seems, had but two years before (in 1573) been baptized, under the name of Simeon.

Ivan Vassilovitch frequently expressed to Sylvester who understood Russian well, the dissatisfaction he felt that Elizabeth had not agreed to all the clauses which he wished the treaty to contain. He foresaw what had now come to pass, when, in 1567, he entrusted Jenkinson (whom he himself conducted to his apartment by a secret passage) with a private communication to that Queen. The reins of government held by him until then had just been delivered over by him into the hands of a stranger, who was neither a Russian nor a member of his royal house; he (Ivan), however, retaining the State Treasury in his keeping. The stranger here meant was no other than the above-mentioned Tartar Khan Simeon Bekbulatovitch. We have hitherto been ignorant of the exact period when Ivan Vassilovitch appointed Simeon Bekbulatovitch Regent of Russia. As we are now cognizant of an Ukase issued in Ivan's name as Czar, dated the 1st of December, 1575, we may conclude that the Regency of the Grand Prince Simeon must have commenced just at this time, on the last day of November, or the first of December. In "Willebrand's Chronicle" the year is consequently stated correctly; he says: "In 1575 the Czar, Ivan Basilovitz, made over the government of his empire to a Tartar Prince, who was taken prisoner at the capture of Kasan, whose name was Simeon."

Jerome Horsey, one of the English clerks then at Moscow, mentions that Simeon's appointment was chiefly to be considered as a financial speculation. It has likewise been so described by Dr. Fletcher, whose little work on Russia, be it here said, was collected almost entirely from Horsey's notes, so that Fletcher stands in about the same position with reference to Horsey as Paolo Giovio did to our Demetrius Gerasimoff, and as in a lesser degree Dr. Faber did to Vassily Vlassy the interpreter. Horsey says: Ivan Vassilovitch has crowned Simeon, but without solemnity and without the consent of his council ("crowns him, but with noe solempnitie nor consent of peers"). He farther relates that Ivan bowed himself to the earth before Simeon, and ordered the highest ecclesiastics, the nobility, and the officers to do the same. ("He sitts in Majestie. The old Emperor Ivan comes and prostrates himself, causeth his metrepolletts, bishops, prins, noblemen, and officers to do the like.") It is remarkable that Horsey, too, who frequented the house of Simeon's father-in-law, Prince Ivan Fedorovitsch

Metisslavsky, should call Simeon a son of the Khan of Kasan. Just at the time of Simeon's installation, on the 1st of December, 1575, an embassy from the Emperor Maximilian the Third arrived at Orscha on the frontier of the empire, consisting of Hans Kobenzl von Prosseg, and Daniel Prinz of Buchan. This must have been very disagreeable to the Prince of Moscow, for he naturally would not be desirous that the German Emperor should in this way become acquainted with his quasi-abdication. He certainly would have shown Kobenzl and Prinz the way back again, if he had had a good pretext; but their mission was accredited by a letter from the Emperor, dated the 25th of September, and they were the bearers of his cypher, with a crown set with diamonds of very high value.

The Boyar Nikita Romanovitch, Jurgeff Romanoff, then Governor of Tver, and Vassily Andregevitsch Ssitsky Jaroslavsky, Governor of Moshaisk, together with the Secretary Andrew Jakovlevitch Schtschelkaloff, were dispatched to meet the ambassadors, who had been conducted so far as Dorogobush. They handed the envoys a letter, in which they were requested by Ivan Vassilovitch, under his usual title of Czar, to remain there a short time, as he could not receive them immediately, on account of some travels he had just commenced (Kobenzl was told that they were pilgrimages during Lent); but that he would do so as soon as possible, not at Moscow, but at Moshaisk. Full three-and-fifty days were the ambassadors obliged to remain at Dorogobush, during which time showy furniture, of many different descriptions, was procured at Moshaisk at the Czar's expense, for the purpose of receiving and entertaining the guests magnificently. Notwithstanding all precautions, however, something with reference to the abdication reached their ears, for they had heard that Simeon had been crowned by the Metropolitan. Kobenzl writes: "Paulo ante nostrum adventum quadraginta circiter nobiles qui in caput ipsius (Johannis) iterum conspirarent, capite plexit, et ob unprobitatem subditorum imperio sese abdicans summam rerum Simeoni Czari Cazanensis filio" (thus again son of the Khan of Kasan) "tradidit, et diadema quoque ipsi, uti ex quorundam sermone intelleximus, per Metropolitam imposuit." Kobenzl's account of his embassy, which was composed in Illyrian, and translated into Italian, and also into Latin, has been repeatedly ascribed in Italy to the wrong author, for there it was supposed to have been written by Philip Prenistain who had been in Russia. But as in the account itself it appeared that the author's name was John or Hans, an apocryphal John Prenistain (Pernstain) was created. This error of the Italians has likewise remained uncorrected by Turgenieff; and Adelung is wrong in blaming Karamsin, for what he himself says with reference to John Pernstein and Philip Prenistain, is incorrect. He might easily have discovered his mistake had he compared the Italian MS., thus improperly endorsed and dated in the Rumanzoff Museum, with Kobenzl's Latin account, copied at Vienna by Wichman; Adelung supposing, likewise, that Kobenzl and Prins had been at Moscow.

The whole business of the embassy was dispatched

at Moshaisk in great haste, between the 24th and 29th of January, 1576, and Ivan Vassilovitch did not afterwards invite the envoys to Moscow. Prinz, who has also left behind him in Russia an account of the mission, must have remained at Dorpat until May, for Prince Sachary Ivanovitch Ssugorsky (Governor of Belosersk) and the Secretary Andrew Arzübascheff who were dispatched with him to the Emperor Maximilian the Second. At all events, the reception and entertainment of these ambassadors at Moshaisk were very brilliant. Kobenzl declares, on his knightly honour, that neither in Rome nor in Spain did he meet with a better reception, when he was sent thither by the Emperor. It is remarkable that neither Kobenzl nor Prinz made any complaint that they had not been invited to Moscow; indeed, they rather appear to desire that this should be taken no notice of. Ivan Vassilovitch transmitted to the ambassadors rich presents for the Emperor, and requested him to say, that he would feel obliged by Maximilian "sending him a good gunner and armourer."

Sylvester had his *congé* on the 29th of January, 1576, and, in my opinion, this took place, not at Moscow, but at Moshaisk. On the same day that the above-named envoys, from the Emperor Maximilian the Second, received their dismissal at the latter place, Ivan Vassilovitch again conversed with Sylvester about his abdication, but observed that he could resume the government as soon as he wished. He mentioned the closer alliance he had entered into just then, through Kobenzl and Prinz, with the Emperor Maximilian, and once more repeated his expressions of dissatisfaction with Queen Elizabeth, on account of the indifference she had shown to his former request.

As we know with certainty, through Kobenzl and Prinz, that Ivan Vassilovitch was at Moshaisk on the 29th of January, 1576, Sylvester's audience of leave-taking must have occurred there. The several copies I have seen of the account of this audience state it to have been "in his town of *Moscovia;*" but this latter word must have been substituted by the copyists for *Moshaisko*, for, on the 29th of November, 1575, Sylvester wrote, "in his cittye of *Musco*" (not *Moscovia*), "and house of oprisbeno." In these copies there are, likewise, other errors. Ivan Vassilovitch had the following conversation with Sylvester with reference to his abdication: "Allthough we manyfessted to thyne aparance to have enthronissed another in themperyall dignitye, and thereunto have enthrowled both us and ours, yet not so muche and the same not so farr resyned, but that at our pleasure we can take the dignitye unto us againe, and will yet do thearin as God shall instructe us, for that the same is not confirmed unto him by order of coronation we by consent elected but for our pleasure." Here, consequently, Ivan Vassilovitch himself explains that Simeon Bekbulatovitch had not been crowned. He further said to Sylvester: "Behold" (probably it stood in the original—We hold) "also seven crownes" (for Turgeniev, the copyists have here put provinces,) "yet in our possession, with the cepter and the rest of the stately ornaments apertaynynge unto thempyre, withall the treasures belonginge to eache." At the coronation of Theodore Ivanovitch, which took place in 1584, seven crowns were really seen.

Both Kobenzl and Prinz relate that Ivan Vassilovitch (who then, nevertheless, was only Prince of Moscow) wore a crown at their audience at Moshaisk. The former compared them to the pope's crowns. Near the Czarovitch Ivan also stood a crown; Ivan Vassilovitch held in his left hand a sceptre, and the Czarovitch his father's staff. During meal-time, both these crowns stood on a bench near the table. Until now, it had not been made public that Kobenzl and Prinz were in Russia at the time of the regency of the Grand Prince Simeon Bekbulatovitch; but this appears from what Ivan Vassilovitch said to Sylvester on the 29th of November, 1575, and the 29th of January, 1576. Horsey, who was then at Moscow, mentions, indeed, that the Grand Prince Simeon was obliged to receive all ambassadors arriving at Moscow, and that some of these had refused to appear before him ("all ambassadors to resort before him, which some refused"), but this may merely relate to ambassadors from Asia. Of the Imperial Embassy Horsey saw nothing. We have one Ukase of the Grand Prince Simeon's, of January, 1576, consequently this was probably issued before Kobenzl and Prinz's, as well as before Sylvester's, appearance at Moshaisk.

Hence it must be supposed that, although Ivan Vassilovitch had assumed the title of Prince of Moscow, he laid it down and resumed his own for the purpose of receiving the ambassadors from the Emperor Maximilian, and on the same account prevented their reception from taking place at Moscow. He resumed the reins of government at the commencement of the year 7085, for we have an Ukase from him as Czar, dated the 2nd of September, 1576. Willebrand therefore says correctly, " In 1576 the Grand Prince again assumed the government, and sent the temporary Emperor to his estates at Torsik (Torshok), bestowing upon him, likewise, the principality of Otufee (Tver)." Margeret, on the contrary, is wrong in saying that Simeon's government lasted two full years. Horsey writes, with reference to Ivan Vassilovitch's abdication, " The device of his own head might have sett him clear beside the saddell, if yt had continewed but a little longer, yt is happie he is become invested again in statu quo prius." Fletcher naturally says the same, although expressed in a different manner.

Judging, therefore, from the writers we have quoted, Simeon's regency lasted from the beginning of December, 1575, until September, 1576 (the beginning of the year 7085), consequently nine months. We know that Simeon Bekbulatovitch now received the title of Grand Prince of Tver, which Theodore Ivanovitch afterwards took from him; we know also that he became blind; that the first pretender Demetrius, sent him (on the 29th of March, 1606) to the convent of St. Ciril, at Belosero, where he took the name of Stephen; that the Czar Vassily Ivanovitsch Schinsky, on the 29th of May of the same year (1606), ordered him to be conveyed to the Ssolovetz convent; that at his request Prince Demetrius Michailovitch Posharsky, on the 25th of June, 1612, took care that he should be conveyed back to the convent of St. Ciril; and, lastly, that on the 5th of January, 1616, he died, and was buried in the convent of St. Simon, at Moscow, as was also his consort Anastasia, who had died as a nun on the 7th of June, 1607, under the name of Alexandra. Ivan Vassilovitch acquainted Sylvester that he was negotiating, through Kobenzl and Prinz, with the Emperor Maximilian the Second, a treaty similar to that desired with Elizabeth, and again repeated his expressions of displeasure with regard to the way in which the Queen had received his proposal, observing that she ought to lay aside all arrogance. He alluded to the benefits which he had bestowed upon the English in Russia, specially adducing the permission which he had given for the preparation of ropes in Russia for the English fleet and mercantile marine; and concluded with an intimation that he had conceded more favours to Elizabeth than she had given him proofs of friendship. The Czarovitch, as well as Kobenzl and Prinz, were present at this audience given to Sylvester.

On the 1st of July, 1576, Sylvester arrived at Rose Island with a fresh dispatch from Queen Elizabeth, and proceeded to Cholmogorü, where, on the 15th of the same month, whilst he was making preparations for journeying onwards, he was killed by lightning at the English factory. All his papers, and with them the Queen's epistle, were destroyed by fire, as well as the factory itself. Sylvester was in the upper story of the quarters assigned to him. The tailor had just fitted a dress on him (a new yellow satten jackett or japone") for his journey to the Czar's, and had scarcely gone down stairs, when a flash of lightning struck Sylvester, his boy, and a dog belonging to him, ("pearcing down the collar of the inside of his newe coate, owt the right side of his body not outwardly seen, burnt his deeske, lettres, howse, all at instant"). When Ivan Vassilovitch received intelligence of this occurrence, he was much grieved, and exclaimed, "God's will be done!" Thus ended the negotiation carried on through Daniel Sylvester.

I here break off my survey of the earliest intercourse existing between Russia and England, which embraces a space of more than four lustres, although the succeeding period offers much that is interesting. Of this I select, as an example, from a MS. of Jerome Horsey's, (who arrived at Moscow as a commercial clerk in 1572, and succeeded in ingratiating himself at the court of the Czar Ivan Vassilovitch, as well as with Theodore Ivanovitch, and Boris Theodorovitch Godunoff,) that the Czarina Irenia Fedorovna (Godunoff's sister), who was married to Theodore Ivanovitch in 1580, had been several times *enceinte*, before the year 1592, when she was so, for the first time, of a daughter, who died early. In Horsey's account of his return to England, in 1585-86, undertaken at the request of Theodore Ivanovitch, is the following note: "I spent a good time inquiringe of the learned physicions of Oxford, Cambridge, and London, their opinions and directions concerning the Emporis Irenia in some difficult matters, relating to conception and procuration of children; she had been married seaven years" (in 1586 it was only six years), "and often conceeved, with some other marriage matters, wherein I was charged with secraecie." Horsey made use of the Russian characters (in the word conception, however, he placed a p for a π), in order to render his journal unintelligible to such inquisitive persons as might turn over its leaves.

Horsey, on this occasion, acquainted Queen Elizabeth that he was commissioned by the Czar Theodore Ivanovitch to beg that she would have a good English midwife procured for his consort Irenia Fedorovna; in consequence of which, one was selected, and dispatched to Russia with Horsey. The following is the rough sketch found by me at Cambridge of the letter dispatched by Queen Elizabeth to the Czarina, viz.:*—
"Elizabeth, &c. To the Most Gracious Orine (Irene), Empress of Russia. Most Gracious and Powerful Princess, and dearest friend and sister. The extraordinary report which has frequently reached Us of your exemplary prudence, most rare virtues and manners, truly worthy of such a Princess, which has been verbally confirmed by our physician, that worthy man Dr. Jacobs, induces Us to love Your Highness with the true affection of Our soul, and ardently to wish you all possible happiness and prosperity, so that We cannot but be solicitous for your health and safety. Therefore, We have not only sent you (as you lovingly requested us) an experienced and skilful midwife to assuage the pains of childbirth by her science, but We also send you with her the aforesaid Doctor Jacob our

* See Appendix Z

physician who has been wont to take care of our health (a man previously known to you, full of faith in the medical art in which he excels), in order that he may superintend the operations of the midwife, and faithfully tend your health. We earnestly desire to be of service to Your Highness, not in this alone but in all other matters; and it will always give great pleasure to Our sisterly mind to gratify you. May the great and good God, &c. Given at our Royal Palace at Greenwich, on the 24th March, in the year of Our Lord 1585" (*i. e.* 1586) "and in the 27th of Our reign."

It appears to me that, in translating this Epistle into Russian, the passage relating to the midwife has been purposely omitted. It barely mentions Dr. Robert Jacob, who then came to Russia for the second time. Probably this was done at Godunoff's instigation, as the arrival of a skilful midwife for his sister, the Czarina, was disagreeable to him. The midwife was not permitted to reach Moscow, for she was detained at Vologda. In a letter which I have seen, addressed by the directors of the Russia Company to Lord Burghley, it is stated that the Czarina Irenia Fedorovna was not made acquainted that a midwife had been sent to Russia for her by Queen Elizabeth ("nor was the Empresse made privie of any suche woman commended from her Maiestie: the Empress never knew of her"). After the midwife had remained more than a year at Vologda, she was obliged to return to London, in the autumn of 1587, in a vessel which sailed from Rose Island, leaving her business altogether unperformed. As she supposed that Horsey was to blame for her not having reached the Czarina at Moscow, she brought a complaint against him before Queen Elizabeth. Horsey had already been sent by Ivan Vassilovitch, in 1580, by way of Livonia, to England, entrusted with an important commission— the purchase of all sorts of military stores, at that time very necessary.

The Czar's letter to Queen Elizabeth, and his instructions to Horsey, were carefully concealed by the Secretary Savva (or Saveli) Froloff in the secret compartment of a wooden brandy flask of rough exterior; and this was suspended by Horsey under his horse's mane. He arrived in safety in London. Queen Elizabeth observed that the Czar's letter smelt of brandy. She ordered that all the stores that Ivan Vassilovitch required should be dispatched, and in the following summer of 1581, Horsey sailed with no fewer than thirteen large vessels, which conveyed to Rose Island saltpetre, sulphur, powder, lead, and copper, amounting in value to nine thousand pounds sterling.

At the North Cape he had an engagement with some Danish vessels, of which he sent in his report to the Czar at the Alexandrian suburb, and was honoured with his thanks. On this occasion, Dr. Robert Jacob came for the first time to Moscow with Horsey. The Russia Company gave the former a hundred roubles at his departure, and maintained him at its cost until December, when Ivan Vassilovitch awarded him a salary. Dr. Jacob afterwards gave not a little offence to the company by sending a large quantity of wax to

England on his own account, whereby they suffered great loss. His brother died in Russia, and he returned to England after Ivan Vassilovitch's decease, in 1584, in company with Sir Jerome Bowes, Fincham, the apothecary, and the widow Bomel.

In 1586 Horsey brought articles of many different kinds to Moscow, whereby he gave no small pleasure to the Czar, and still more to Godunoff. Amongst them were two lions, twelve dogs ("mastive dogs, grey and blood hounds"), gilt armour, halberds, pistols, organs and virginals, jewels, gold chains, and pearls, together with white, red, and scarlet liveries. Godunoff sent for his sister, the Czarina Irene, to inspect the whole, and hear the organs and virginals (spinnets) ("admired especially the organes and vergenalls all gilt, &c., never seeing nor heeringe the like before, woundered and delighted at the loud and musicall sound thereof. Thousands of people resorted and steyed about the pallace to heer the same; my man that plaied upon them much made of, and admitted into such presence often wher myself could not cum"). The great pleasure derived from the articles brought by Horsey from England, was the principal reason why the company obtained some very desirable privileges, and why further advantages accrued to the English residents in Russia.

The house of Nikita Romanovitch Jurgeff Romanoff, the grandfather of Michael Fedorovitch, was close to that of the English, for only the church of St. Maximus Ispovendik intervened. When, on one occasion, Ivan Vassilovitch suddenly ordered that he should be deprived of all his goods and chattels, he sent immediately afterwards to the English for cotton stuffs, in order to have the most necessary articles of clothing made for himself and his children, as well as for Theodore (afterwards Philaret) Nikitisch. For the last-named person, who afterwards, together with his son Michael Fedorovitch, governed as the Patriarch Philaret, Horsey composed a Latin grammar, as well as he could, in the Russian character. The young Theodore Nikitisch found great pleasure in the study of Latin, with the assistance of this grammar, although it certainly must have been very imperfect.

Until the time of the foundation of the city of Archangel, Rose Island was the principal depôt for the Russian trade with England by the North Sea. In 1583, when Theodore Andregevitsch Pissemsky, the ambassador, returned with Sir Jerome Bowes, Queen Elizabeth's envoy, from his mission to England relative to Lady Mary Hastings, whom Ivan Vassilovitch, now a seventh time a widower, wished to marry, at Dr. Robert Jacob's recommendation, the former was quartered at the convent of St. Nicholas, but the latter at the English house in Rose Island.

Pissemsky was a nobleman from Schatzki. His secretary, whom we only know as Ne-udatsch, I found in England, in the translation of the letter delivered by Pissemsky, called Ne-udatsch Gavorloff. Pissemsky's interpreter was Reginald Beckmann; but the person who, in 1583, communicated to Queen Elizabeth the secret desire manifested anew by the Czar, Ivan Vassilovitch, to come to England and marry

Mary Hastings, was Ægydius Crow. The Queen wrote to the Czar on the 8th of June, 1583, that he would be exceedingly welcome; but, as is well-known, Ivan Vassilovitch died on the 18th of March, 1584, just before Bowes returned to England.

Although Ivan Vassilovitch, on the 4th of March, 1583, ordered a city to be built near the old and venerable convent dedicated to the Archangel Michael, according to the plan laid before him by Peter Afanassjevitsch Naschtschokin, then Vaivode of the Dwina, and this command was promptly obeyed. The English subsequently received permission to continue their shipping business at their establishment at Rose Island.

In the before-mentioned charter, obtained by Jerome Horsey in 1586–1587, is the following passage:— "We allow them (the English) to continue to retain the house and warehouses which they have hitherto occupied at the anchorage at the Pudoshem mouth; and they shall not be obliged to remove these buildings to the site of the newly-founded city" (Novo Cholmogorü, afterwards Archangel), "but they shall be permitted, as they have hitherto done, to unload English articles of import, and embark Russian produce for exportation at their old house at Rose Island. The Cholmogorü Custom House shall merely receive lists of such goods, but shall not have the right to examine them." When Horsey, after obtaining these privileges and other advantages for the English Company, again returned to England, Prince Vassily Andreievitsch Svenigorodsky, the Vaivode, escorted him by water with much pomp from the city of Novo-

Cholmogorü, then recently built, to the English factory on Rose Island. "The Duke mett me at the castell gate with three hunderd gonners shott of their calivers and all the ordinance he had in the castell for honnor of my waelcom, all the Dutch and French ships" (even in 1587 several had followed Sauvage, the first Frenchman who, the year before, had arrived at the Dwina) "in that roade shott of also their ordinance by the Duks apointment before I came. He feasted me, the next daie brought me to my barge, had apointed fifty men to rowe and hundred gonners in small boats to garde me to Rose Iland, did me all the honnor he could in his golden coate, told me he was comanded by the king's letter so to doe, toke leave and preied me to signifie his service to Boris Fedorovitsch. Came within four hours to Rose Iland, being but thirty miells, wher all the English masters, agent, and merchants mett me. The gonners landed before me, stode in rancke, and shott of all their calivers, which the ships heeringe shott of also some of their ordinance. The gonners and bargmen made drinccke at the seller dore, and despatched that night back again to the castell. The next day friers of St. Nicholas brought me a present, fraesh salmons, rye loaves, cupps and painted plaetters. The third daye after my arivall (on Rose Island), ther was sent a gentlemann, Sabloch Savera, a captain, from the Duke; delivered me a copy of his comission of the Emperor's and Boris Fedorovitsch, their grace and goodness towards me, presented for my provicion 70 ewe shepe, 20 (16) live oxen and bullocks, 600 henns, 40

(25) flaeches of bakon, 2 milch keyne, 2 goats, 10 fresh sallmons, 10 geese, 2 swans, 2 cranes, 3 young beares, a wild boare, 40 gallons of aquavita, 100 (65) gallons of mead, 200 (60) gallons of beer, 1,000 (600) loaves of white bread, 60 (80) bushells of meall, 2,000 eggs, garlick and onyons store. There was four great lighters, and many watermen, &c., there, that came with this provicion, which wear all orderly dismist. I took some time to make merrie with the master and merchants, havinge some pastymes that followed me, plaiers, danzinge bares and pieps, and dromes and trompetts, feasted them, and divided my provicion in liberal proportion." Horsey embarked with his companions at Rose Island on the 26th of August, and on the 30th of September landed at Tynemouth, in Northumberland, whence he travelled post, by the York road to London, reaching it in four days. Queen Elizabeth had the Russian copy of the charter explained to her at Richmond by Horsey, and said, "I could quicklie learn it." She requested Lord Essex (Robert Devereux) to study the Russian language ("the famoust and most copious language in the world"). The presents from Moscow she afterwards took to Greenwich for inspection, and derived great pleasure from them.

Rose Island remained for a long time the emporium for Russia's foreign trade, and with the Nenccksa shore, where Chancellor landed, well deserves a token of remembrance in commemoration of succeeding events. Our poet of the Dwina should celebrate these places in song, for certainly Somonossoff must, when a boy, have frequently passed Rose Island with his father, in his fishing excursions, from Cholmogorü to the White Sea.

Rose Island is not only to be considered the cradle of our foreign trade, but that of the Russian navy. The navigation to the mouth of the Dwina, commenced by the English, is known to have induced the youthful Czar, Peter, to travel there in 1693. Here he first saw and sailed on the seas, visited the foreign shipping, dispatched the first Russian vessel with goods for other countries, and built his first ship (the "St. Peter"), which he launched himself, and on board of which the Russian flag was hoisted for the first time. To this place he sent the "Peter and Paul," the first ship of the line built by him at Saardam, in 1697, and here was the first foreign ship (a Swede) captured by the Russians in 1701. In the following year Peter had two yachts, which had been built by him at the same place, dragged overland to Lake Onega, partly through forests. With the assistance of these craft, the founder of St. Petersburg took possession of the Neva.

CHAPTER X.

VOYAGE OF TRADESCANT—MEMOIR OF TRADESCANT—HIS COLLECTION OF VARIETIES—DISCOVERY OF A MS. BY TRADESCANT, A NARRATIVE OF HIS VOYAGE TO ARCHANGEL.

IN earlier times, trade usually paved the road for natural philosophy. The commercial route, opened by Chancellor round the North Cape, thus led to the visit of an English botanist and zoologist to the Dwina in 1618. This was John Tradescant.

Who and what was John Tradescant? How, and with whom, did he come to Russia? What did he do there?

John Tradescant, the elder, was the man to whom is certainly due the no small merit of having founded the first museum for objects of natural history and art in England; he also possessed one of the first, and in his time the best, botanical garden. Both establishments were close to each other in South Lambeth, at that time not far from London. This place is now within the boundless metropolis, on the east side of the South Lambeth Road (improperly called the south side); and the buildings stand just opposite to Spring Lane.

The house containing the museum, which was called Tradescant's Ark, where the Tradescants, father and son, as well as Esther, the widow of the latter, and afterwards Ashmole, resided, has been so often changed in its internal arrangements and outward appearance; and, moreover, so many additions have been made to it, that at the present day it can no longer be discerned which were the apartments originally devoted to the museum, and which were inhabited. The whole now consists of two divisions—the older, called Stamford House, is occupied by John Alexander Fulton, who has pepper ground close by according to a patent method; and the other and newest division, Turret House, is inhabited by John Miles Thorne, proprietor of a brewery at Nine Elms.

The objects in the museum, as well as in the garden, have been made known to the world by Tradescant's son, by whom both establishments were considerably increased, in a catalogue published in 1656, the title of which is "Musæum Tradescantium, or, A Collection of Rarities preserved at South Lambeth, near London, by John Tradescant."

To this catalogue a portrait of the father, as well as one of the son, both painted by Hollar, are added. We find that, in the museum, amongst other things, there was a stuffed Dodo from the Mauritius. This is the only complete specimen of this bird existing in a European cabinet, its race having been extinct for about two hundred years. I have already mentioned that Francis Willoughby bore testimony that he had seen it in the Tradescant Museum. Perhaps it is the same which, in the year 1538, was exhibited alive in London. Now, all that remains of it (at Oxford) is its head, which was cut off in 1755, and one of its feet. Of the first I have laid before the academy a plaster cast, and of the latter several photographic sketches of the bones and sinews. In the British Museum another foot is preserved, which is, perhaps, that seen by Clusius before 1605, in the collection of Professor Pauff, at Leider, when brought from the Mauritius. I have, likewise, laid a plaster cast of this last before the academy, and preserve one of the Dodo's head, now in the Royal Museum of Natural History at Copenhagen, originally in the Paludam collection. At Oxford there is a large oil painting of a Dodo, by John Savery, with the date of 1651, which I have copied, on account of the colouring. Rowland Savery, the uncle of the Savory just named, has represented the Dodo in the painting of Orpheus charming the wild animals, executed by him in 1638. The large painting of the Dodo in the British Museum was taken from the Sloane collection, but the artist is unknown. With the materials collected by me, a Dodo has been modelled here (in Russia) by Herr Jenssen, a pupil of Thorwaldsen, from which we are enabled to place coloured casts in our collections.

Tradescant the elder died in 1638, and his son, who was born in 1608, departed this life in 1662. The only son of the latter (the Christian name of all three was John) was carried off by death before his father, viz., in 1652; and, consequently, the second Tradescant, who had no heirs, on the 16th December, 1659, bequeathed the whole collection at South Lambeth to Elias Ashmole.

Ashmole, who was born in 1617, had already made himself known by three works—two of which, published in 1650 and 1652, treated of Alchemy—and the third, in 1658, of the philosopher's stone, the title of which was, "The Way to Bliss." It may be worthy of notice, that the work with which Ashmole first made his appearance before the public, in 1650, "Fasciculus Chemicus," was composed in Latin in 1629, in Russia, and, indeed, at Moscow, by Dr. Arthur Dee, physician in ordinary to the Czar, Michael Fedorovitsch.

The complete title of this small work is, "Fasciculus chemicus abstrusæ hermeticæ scientiæ, ingressum, progressum, coronidem, verbis apertissimis, explicans, ex selectissimis et celeberrimis authoribus, tali serie collectus, et depositus, ut non modo huius artis tyrombus, sed candidatis, summo emolumento, instar speculi Philosophiæ habeatur, a nemine hac methodo distributus, opera et studio Arthuri Dee, Archiatri Magni Imperatoris totius Russiæ." The preface to the reader is dated, "Ex Musæo nostro, Moscuæ, Kalend. Martii, 1629." This little book was afterwards published at Basle, in 1629, and then, in 1631, at Paris, translated into English by Elias Ashmole, and laid before the public with the latter's name anagrammatized into James Hasolle. Dr. Arthur Dee, who was born in 1579, was the son of the well-known Dr. John Dee, of Mortlake, and in 1621 accompanied the Ambassador, Isaac Ivanovitch Pogosheff, to Moscow, where, until 1626, and again, after a visit to England, from 1627 to 1634, he was physician in ordinary to the

Czar, Michael Fedorovitch. His own house was near the Ilgin Gate, and the usufruct of an estate was likewise granted to him. His father was esteemed a good mathematician, but, moreover, considered an enthusiastic astrologer and alchemist. He probably arrived at Moscow in 1586, about the time when Horsey was endeavouring to fulfil his commissions for the Czarina, Irene Fedorovna, at Oxford, Cambridge, and London. Owing to the recommendations of the English at Moscow, an advantageous proposal was made to him by the Czar, whilst he, together with Kelly, happened to be carrying on his trade in Bohemia, as he had already done in Poland. His son was strongly infected with the father's enthusiasm; in youthful Russia, however, there was fortunately but little sympathy for such folly. A certain Franz Murrer, then at Moscow, must have been familiar with astrology; this I discovered from a MS. of Arthur Dee's, at Oxford, which refers to him, " Murrerus was an astrologer of some account at Moscow."

The second work published by Ashmole in 1652, was his " Theatrum Chemicum Britannicum," a collection of old medico-philosophical writings.

This work had also become known to two Livonian amateurs of chemistry. At Oxford, I discovered in the second volume of Ashmole's own copy, a memorandum in Latin pasted in, which a Livonian knight, Nicholas von Vilcen, wrote whilst in Ashmole's house; viz.—" Generose et nobilissime Domine, adfuerunt hic duo nobiles Germania, artis chymicæ amatores, qui viderunt et legerunt librum Dominationis

Vestræ Theatrum chimicum Britannicum, quædam cum Dominatione Vestra communicaturi, si grave non est et hora commoda designabitur. Commorantur in S. Steefens alle (St. Stephen's alley), at the 3 glasses of Mumm. Nicholas von Vilcen, Eques Livonus, 18 Oct., 1670."

Subsequent to 1650, Ashmole as well as his wife repeatedly visited Tradescant, the younger, at South Lambeth. The former was then married to his second wife, and he was her fourth husband; they were united in 1649. She resided at the Tradescants' from the 20th of November, 1652, until the 17th of January, 1653. On the 14th of December, 1652, they observed the comet. We see that Ashmole succeeded in making himself important in the eyes of Tradescant the younger, probably by boasting of his astrological and alchemical knowledge. He was likewise of great use to Tradescant, at the commencement of his acquaintance with him, in making out the catalogue of the museum and garden, which he did in common with Dr. Thomas Wharton (born in 1614), for whom he then busied himself in finding out a good wife by astrological calculations. As Tradescant had now no hopes of children by his second spouse, Esther, he in his will, as already mentioned, appointed Ashmole, who was in no wise related to him, his heir.

Esther Tradescant who, in 1662, when a widow, erected a joint monument (still existing) to the memory of the three John Tradescants, in the churchyard of St. Mary's, Lambeth, close to the palace of the Archbishop of Canterbury, protested for many years against the will made by her husband in favour of Ashmole; and at last (in 1674) lost her suit, and was obliged to deliver up the museum to the latter. In 1676, she signed a declaration, probably not of her own free will, that she was wrong in proceeding against him, and in 1678, drowned herself in a pond in the same garden in which her father-in-law and husband had done so much for the cultivation of plants and trees.

Ashmole, whose before-named second and rich wife (who, by the way, endeavoured to get rid of him in 1657, and for this purpose filled no less than eight hundred folios of paper with strong complaints against him) died in 1668, soon afterwards married a daughter of Sir William Dugdale, who sometimes resided at Oxford and sometimes in London, in order to make use of the libraries of those cities for the publication of his works ("Monasticon," "Baronage," &c.). Ashmole, in 1672, published the "History of the Order of the Garter," and made collections of antiquities, coins, seals, &c., of which he lost a part by a fire in 1679. Then he also lost that library which, in the great fire of 1666, he had brought in safety to Esther Tradescant's. In a letter dated the 1st of September, 1680, written by Sir Thomas Herbert at York, to Ashmole, with whom he had become acquainted in his travels, I find that the latter had then returned to Tradescant's house, in South Lambeth. Herbert wrote as follows:—

"I find by your letter that you do not frequent the Court as you have formerly, having retyred yourself to your house in South Lambeth, a place I well know, having been several times at M. Tredescant (to whom I gave severall things I collected in my travels), and was much delighted with his gardens, so as you have sequestered yourself to a place of much pleasure als well as privacy."

The University of Oxford presented Ashmole in 1669 with the diploma of a Doctor of Medicine, and was offered by him the Tradescant collection as a present, on condition that they should erect a building expressly for it. Sir Christopher Wren, well known as the builder of St. Paul's Cathedral in London, was requested to draw out a plan, and the foundation stone was laid in 1679; on the 16th of August, 1682, Ashmole travelled to Oxford in order to inspect the new house, and in 1683 the collection sent from Lambeth (in February and March) was installed there by Dr. Robert Plott, who had been appointed its first superintendent. Dr. Plott had already published (in 1677) his "Natural History of the County of Oxford," and from 1682 was one of the secretaries of the Royal Society. After his appointment to this post, he was also a Professor of chemistry, and in 1686 published his "Natural History of Staffordshire."

This building is situated near the University Theatre, which was likewise built by Sir Christopher Wren in 1664-69, at Dr. Sheldon's expense, and in which the highest mark of honour which the University had the power to offer, was shown by the presentation of a Doctor's diploma to the Emperor Alexander in 1814, to the now reigning Emperor Nicholas in 1817, and to the Grand Prince Cesarovitch Alexander in 1839. The former edifice is now called the Ashmolean instead of the Tradescant Museum, which would be a much more appropriate denomination; and hence it is, that the true founder's name is almost altogether forgotten. It would now scarcely ever be uttered, had not Henry Bernard Rupp, in his "Flora Jenensis," published in 1718, given the name of Tradescantia to a particular class of plants, after the Pelagium Ephemerum Virginianum Joannis Tradescanti; so called by John Parkinson in 1629.

Tradescant the elder was gardener to the Earl of Salisbury, Robert Cecil (son of William), who died in 1612; afterwards to Edward Lord Wotton, at Canterbury, and then to George Villiers, Duke of Buckingham, the first of whom died in 1628, and the latter was murdered in the same year.

Edward Wotton, Baron of Merley, was employed as a diplomatist in France, Portugal, and Scotland, and afterwards filled important offices at Canterbury, where he had a palace formed of part of the ancient convent of St. Augustine. From Lord Wotton's garden at Canterbury, Tradescant the elder sent plants to Parkinson. Dr. Ducarel mentions, in his letter to Dr. William Watson, published in 1773 ("on the early culture of botany in England, and some information with reference to John Tradescant"), that Parkinson, (page 141 of his "Paradisus Terrestris") had erroneously written Canterbury, by which he must have meant South Lambeth. We see that Ducarel knew nothing of Tradescant's activity at Canterbury. Near the portraits of the Tradescant family in Ashmole's

Museum, the latter of whom appears to have inherited them and Tradescant's collection at the same time, is also the portrait of Lord Wotton. Doubtless, it belonged to Tradescant the elder, for Lord Wotton died ten years before him. The Tradescants were also gardeners to King Charles the First, and to his consort Queen Henrietta Maria. According to the epitaph on the tombstone, father and son were "Gardiners to the Rose and Lilly Queen."

Tradescant's contemporaries, John Parkinson, the London apothecary and royal herbalist, who, in 1629, published his "Paradisus Terrestris," and, in 1640, his "Theatrum Botanicum;" and Thomas Johnson, likewise an apothecary in London, who, in 1633, published John Gerard, the surgeon's, general history of plants, "The Herbal," with many additions of his own,—both repeatedly gave him the character of an extremely diligent and indefatigable collector, and this in expressions which testified the highest respect for him. Parkinson calls him, in his "Paradisus Terrestris," page 152, a "Painful industrious searcher, and lover of all nature's varieties;" and again, he says at page 346,— "that worthy, curious, and diligent searcher and preserver of all nature's rarities and varieties, my very good friend, John Tradescante;" and at page 575,— "my very good friend, Master Tradescante, has wonderfully laboured to obtain all the rarest fruits hee can heare off in any place of Christendome, Turky, yea, or the whole world." Johnson says of him in his edition of "Gerard's Herbal," page 184,—" Studious in the knowledge of plants;" and calls him at page 260, "the great treasurer of natural rarities." Tradescant is also mentioned in many other places, in the " Paradisus," the " Theatrum," and the " Herbal."

Shortly before Tradescant's death in 1638, the University of Oxford intended to appoint him superintendent of their " Physic garden," which had been established by Henry Danvers, Earl of Danby, in 1632.

At Oxford, soon after the establishment of Tradescant's collection in the Museum, it was called " an inestimable treasure of natural objects "—" thesaurus inæstimabilis rerum naturalium." That the Dodo also accompanied it from South Lambeth to Oxford, we gather from a work published in 1700, by Hyde, Professor at Oxford, who was likewise librarian in the Bodleian Library. Its name is " Veterum Persarum et Parthorum, et Medorum Religionis Historia." Hyde knew the Dodo by the description given of it by Herbert in his travels, and says, " ejus exuviæ farctæ in auditorio anatomico Oxoniensi servantur." This definite information is particularly important, because Isaac Walton, in the 1676 edition of his " Complete Angler," where he speaks of the fishes and animals to be found in the Tradescant Museum, then belonging to Ashmole, says nothing of the Dodo. Ashmole, who died in 1692, bequeathed to it his collection of books, manuscripts, coins, and other things; and it had likewise received presents of books and manuscripts from his father-in-law, Sir William Dugdale, and afterwards from Anthony Wood, the well-known historiographer of Oxford, and John Aubrey, the antiquarian. In 1697, the statutes of the Museum were published, when

Edward Shwyd was custos. I have found it stated that Peter the Great, in 1698, about three weeks before his departure from London, honoured the University of Oxford with a visit. If this be correct, the inquisitive monarch undoubtedly cast a glance over the Tradescant Ashmolean Museum.

Such knowledge as we have hitherto acquired of Tradescant the elder, is to be met with principally in the herbals published by his aforesaid contemporaries. I found a passage in Parkinson's "Paradisus Terrestris" (1629), where the author, speaking of the hellebore, then called " elleborus albus vulgaris," says, at page 346:—" This plant grows in several places in Germany, and likewise in certain spots in Russia in such abundance, that, according to the account of that worthy and diligent searcher after and preserver of all natural curiosities, my much valued friend, John Tradescant, whom I have already mentioned several times, a respectable sized ship, as he says, might be loaded with the roots of the plants which he had there seen in one island." The same is stated, but in other words, in Parkinson's "Theatrum," page 218.

As I have now been unable to discover, either in Moscow or anywhere else, in my researches after old accounts of Russia, anything of Tradescant's visit to that country, this passage has remained fixed in my memory, because I could not imagine in what part of Russia this island covered with hellebore was situated.

In looking through the manuscripts in the Ashmolean Museum at Oxford, I examined all those which related more or less to Russia. Amongst these is one in the catalogue that has just made its appearance, and in the compilation of which Mr. William Henry Black, of the Record Office, a gentleman well skilled in similar tasks, was employed. It is numbered 824, xvi., and thus labelled and described:—" A voiag of ambussad (to Russia), undertaken by the Right Honorable Sir Dudlie Diggs, in the year 1618, p. 175—186 [b]." " This curious narrative of the voyage round the North Cape to Archangel, begins with a list of the chief persons employed in the embassy, and contains observations on the weather, and on the commercial, agricultural, and domestic state of Russia at that time. It is written in a rude hand, and by a person unskilled in composition. The last half page contains some chronological notes, perhaps written by the same hand." This is the account of Mr. Black, the compiler of the catalogue.

I now employed myself in deciphering the MS.; followed the author on the Dwina and its islands, amongst which was also Rose Island; and when I came to the passage, "helebros albus enoug to load a ship," it was as if a sudden flash of light discovered to me that, in the *brochure* on which I had laid my hands, I saw a MS. of Tradescant. A further and more minute examination satisfied me that my conjecture was correct.

I must here observe that in England absolutely nothing was known of Tradescant's handwriting, for his autograph has, in no instance, been preserved. I conclude that Ashmole destroyed the Tradescant papers; but that, fortunately, like other people, he did not recognise the journal of his voyage to Archangel.

The full title of the MS. which I have ascertained to be written by Tradescant, is, "A viage of Ambassod, undertaken by the Right Honorable Dudlie Diggs in the year 1618, being atended on with 6 Genttillmen which beare the name of the King's Genttillmen, whose name be heere notted on, M. Nowell, brother to the Lord Nowell, M. Thomas Finche, M. Woodward, M. Cooke, M. Fante, and M, Henry Wyeld, with every on of them their man, other folloers on Brigges Interpreter M. Jams, an Oxford man, his chaplain, on M. Leake, his secretary, withe 3 Scots, on Captain Gilbert and his son, with on Car, also M. Mathew De Quester's son, of Filpot-lane, in London, therest his own retennunt, sume 13 whearof—*Note on Jonne an Coplie Wustershermen*—M. Swanli, of Limhouse, master of the good ship called the 'Dianna,' of Newcastell, M. Nelson, part owner, of Newcastell."

From documents preserved in the archives at Moscow, I have become acquainted with the Christian names of all the persons who arrived at Archangel with Sir Dudley Digges. Nowell's Christian name was Arthur; Woodward's, Thomas; Cooke's, Adam, Fante's, Joseph. The secretary was Thomas Leak, the chaplain Richard James, the interpreter George Brigges. Then follow in our list Jessy De Quester, Adam Jones, Thomas Wakefield, John Adams, Thomas Crisp, Leonard Hugh, and John Coplie. This latter must be Tradescant. Hence we see that, by his "Note on Jonne an Coplie Wustershermen," must be meant only one person, and that himself. The others need not here be mentioned.

What the words "Note one" (out of the thirteen) "John an" (and?) "Coplie people (?) from Worcestershire," can mean, is not yet very clear to me; at all events, "Jonne" must refer to John Tradescant himself. Perhaps this supposition may yet lead to the discovery that Tradescant was not, as was supposed, a native of Holland, but of Worcestershire. The name of Tradescant might be an adopted one. I will here merely observe, that it has also been written Tradeskin, which might be translated Trade-skin, consequently hide or skin merchant. In 1680, Sir Thomas Herbert wrote it Tredescon.

In Flatman's Poems appears, at page 14, the following distich:—

"Thus John Tradeskin starves our wondering eyes,
By boxing up his new-found rarities."

Sir Dudley Digges, to whom it is probable that Tradescant attached himself in order to learn something of Russian plants and animals, was sent by James the First, in 1618, to the Czar, Michael Fedorovich, who in the preceding year had dispatched Stephen Ivanovich Volünsky, Mayor of Räshk, together with the Secretary, Mark Posdegeff, to the king, principally for the purpose of negotiating a loan; for, on Michael's accession to his throne, he had found the Russian finances in a very reduced condition. The ambassador, Volünsky, who was now returning to Russia started in another vessel at the same time as Sir Dudley Digges. The ship, commanded by Captain Swanlie, of Limehouse, near London, on board of which were

Digges and Tradescant, was called the "Diana," and was from Newcastle. Mr. Nelson, one of her owners, was likewise on board.

I have copied some passages out of the Journal kept by Tradescant on the voyage, from which it appears that on the 3rd of June, 1618, they sailed from Gravesend. On the 16th they anchored in the port of Tynemouth, in Northumberland; and on the following day Tradescant, with some one else (probably Nelson, part-owner of the vessel), proceeded to Newcastle to purchase fresh provisions, through which incident we are made acquainted with the price of salmon at that period. Tradescant thus describes it:—"Tuesday (the 16th June), to Tinmouth haven, to releve our sick men with fresh vittells from Newcastell. Wednesday (the 17th day), boat hoysed to set the people on shore, and myself and another to go to Newchastell for make provisione of beef and muttone, with many other necessaryes, wheare I bought 11 salmons for 6s. the cuple, and some for 4s. the cuple, whiche at London would have been worth 2l. 10s. the cuple." (What a contrast to the price at the present day! The great difference in the relative prices arises, in the first place, from the mode of packing the salmon in ice, introduced by Dempster and Richardson on the Tay, and then from its being brought round in coasting craft.) "Also we went to suppe at the best ordinary in the toune with many dishes; wen being payed for cam but to 8d. the peece, which in London, I think, 2s. the peece would have hardli mached it. On Thursday (the 18th) we returned to the ship with sume 17l. worth of provision.

Sir George Selbe sent to my Lord Imbassator (Sir Dudley Digges) for a present 2 salmons and an hogshead of beare; the Mayre of Newcastell the day before sent him one salmon, using his genttellmen with much courtesie being ashore at Shields, 6 myles short of Newcastell, his Lordship keeping abord all the while." Sir Dudley remained on board the vessel: he was very seasick. Early on the morning of St. Peter and St. Paul's Day (the 29th), Sir Dudley Digges sent M. Volünsky some meat and porter out of courtesy, because he knew that on that day the Russians' fast was at an end. " On Saynt Peetter's day (29 June), on the morning, my Lord (Digges) sent the Russian Ambassator (Volünsky) fresh vyttuals on quarter of mutton, half a fittill porter, &c. 3 live pullets ther lent being but then ended; also at new Castell my Lord sent him two small salmons and 9 gallons of Caynary Sack; the curtiseys hathe passed as yet without requittall."

On the evening of the same day a bird came on board the vessel, which was then in the sixty-sixth degree of latitude, and about sixty leagues from land. The bird was taken alive, and handed over to Tradescant; but he was not acquainted with its name. When the bird died he preserved the skin. " Also on Monday night (29) the cam a strang bird abord our shipe whiche was taken alive and put to my custody, but dyed within two dayes after being 60 leagues from the shore, whose like I yet never sawe, whos case I have reserved. This was in 66 degrees."

On the night of the 1st to the 2nd of July, Tradescant saw a small part of the sun still above the horizon when it had reached its lowest point. "1 of July in 67 (degrees) or a little short (?) whear the sunne did showe sume small part of her boddy all the night." Tradescant had already, on the 23rd of June, alluded to the clearness of the night when they were in the 60th degree of latitude, and when there was sufficient light to see to write by. On the 4th a pinnace left the vessel destined for Greenland. "On Friday the 3 of July a man of Mr. Delcrass cam abord of us to take counsel about sending away the pennas for Greenland, the year being so far spent, as they thought, the Russe being landed the time of the year would be too far spent whear it was decreed that she should goe on of her intended voyage. This man's name was M. Spyke who was made welcom according to the manner of the sea. My Lord (Digges) sent back with him two bottells of his wine on of Sack and on of Clarret even present fit for such people, yet two great as the time required by reason of our long voyage. Satterday the 4 of July the pennas parted with us. That night at 12 we saw the sun shine about an hour higghe just northe." During the four following days there was a fog; on the 5th (Sunday) they saw many whales. On the 6th they saw the North Cape, and on the following day they spoke a Danish man-of-war near Wardöhuys. "Monday morning (6 July) we had sight of the North Cape, which is all covered with snow."

Further on he says: "The air is cold, the land high, all Ilands, with many bayes. Tuesday morning

(7) on of the King of Denmark men of war demanded of us to com on board to show our pase, but we ansered that our boat was stowed, we could not; besid, we had an Inglish Ambassador on board, which he presentlie desisted from his demand. Our consort also tould him in like sort that he had a Russ Ambassator a board. Also in his company we found the Companye's other shepe who had bin from her port from Hamborow 3 weeks with other two in her company, also two Hollanders, who he caused their boats to com abord. We at that time had been out of England 5 weeks lacking a day. The man of war laye to waft or watter the fishermen that fishe upon that coast of Wardhouse whear the King hathe a castell withe great comand of Lapland, whear many Danes live with the Laps, which, if I might have the whole kingdom to be bound to live there, I had rather be a portter in London, for the snow is never of the ground wholly. The King's man of war gave us a peece or gun, which we ansered with another, and our Vise admiral gave him 3, and so for that time partted being now short of Wardhouse 3 leags; being Inglish and strangers 7 sayls bound for Aarchangel." On the 11th some Lapland fishermen from the coast near the island of Ssossnovetz brought them fresh salted salmon, some of which Sir Dudley bought.

Tradescant describes the Laplanders as well as their boat. As he compares this with a Dutch "schuyt," we must suppose that he had been in Holland. The island of Ssossnovetz, on the Lapland coast (in 66° 29′ N. lat.), was named Cross Island by Stephen Burrough in 1557, from a cross which he discovered there. At the mouth of the Ssossnoka, behind this island, there is even now a Lapland fishing station. Tradescant writes:—" 11 July we had a small boat of that country of the Cros Iland that brought his bote laden withe salmon 3 dayes salted. My Lord bought on for 4s. our money 4 very great on. Now after wee were so far as Crose Iland the snowe began to abate and the natur of the coaste to change from russet to a greener coller, the inland being full of shruby trees, and further of we monythe perseve great woods, but all this way no kind of grayne. Now to speak of the boate and the men. On of them was a man aboute 50 yeares withe on eye, hard favord, the yonger man was about 25 years, well favord and well limbed, and both clad in lether, withe the skins of sheepe with the fire side inwarde, bothe having crusifixes about the necks very artificyally mad. Ther boat was small, very neatly mad, lik to the manner of Hollands scuts."

On the 12th, Tradescant saw a large white fish (?), which they told him was a bitter enemy to, and destroyer of, the salmon. "On Sunday, being the 12 of Juley, the wind being coatrary, being some 6 leags short of Foxnose, we had sight of a great whight fish twse (twice?), so great as a porpos, being all over as white as snowe, whiche they say is a great destroyer of the salmons."

Fox Nose is a promontory, so named by Stephen

Burrough in 1557, on the eastern shore of the White Sea, near the small river Kamennoi, three leagues north of Keretz, which latter must be the promontory called by him Dog's Nose, and this is eight leagues north-north-west of Kuiskoi Noss, according to Burrough Coscaynos. Of Dog's Nose he says :—" It showeth like a gurneed's head, and is the better knowen because it is fuller's earth, and the like I have not seen in all that country." Salt works were established there. The fish seen by Tradescant must have been a white dolphin (Delphinus Leucas). This dolphin of the North is at times confounded with the fish Beluga (Acipenser Huso) of the Volga and the Caspian Sea, because with us (in Russia) it bears the same name (beluga). During my stay in Scotland, in 1815, a Beluga, similar to those of the Icy Sea, was observed by the fishermen for several months in the Frith of Forth, and was no small annoyance to them. At length the salmon fishers not far from Stirling succeeded in killing it. It was placed by Professor Jameson in the museum of the Edinburgh University: and Mr Patrick Neill and Dr. Barclay undertook to make a scientific examination of it.

On the 13th many small birds flew on board the vessel, when distant not more than three leagues from the shore. Tradescant captured three, and preserved their skins. He observes that they resembled the English linnet. "On Monday, the 13 of July, ther wer many small birds cam abord the shepe, being sume 3 leags from the shore. I have thre of ther skins whiche were caut by myself and the rest of the company. They did muche resemble the maner of our Englishe linnets, but far lesser." Probably Linaria minor.

On the 13th, the vessel passed over the Bar of the Dwina. It must have been the Beresov mouth. According to Tradescant, the depth of water was twelve feet and a half. In 1557 Stephen Burrough had found thirteen feet. "On Tuesday, the 14 of Jully, we came to the bar, where we spent on daye because it was calme. On the Wednesdaye we went over the bar having only on foote watter mor than the shep drew" On the 6th of August, when the vessel sailed out of the Pudoshem mouth, Tradescant states that she was in ten feet and a half water. The English Company's agent at Archangel sent them fresh provisions immediately after they had crossed the Bar. "At our first entterance over the bar intto the river we reseved from the agent on good bullock, 2 sheep, 10 hens, 2 fesants, 6 pattriges, non like the Inglish." On the 16th, first Valünsky, and then Digges, were welcomed to the port with military honours. The officer who received them, unknown to our author by name, was Peter Perfirjeff, the chief of the Strelitzes at Archangel. "On Thursday, the 16 day (of July) we came unto the harbor, but before we came halfe the way the souldyers cam to sallut ther owne ambassador (Wolünsky), but not us; but in the halfe way passage in the river the Grand Prestave salluted my Lord (Digges) withe main boats full of souldyers, who himself was entterteyned in the cabbin withe a banket of sweet meats, the agent and the rest of the Inglish marchants having had the like enterteynement just before his coming, whear at his departur we gave 3 peeces of ordnance, and he us his small shot, whiche was but poorlie performed, ther peeces being hardli so good as our calliver, neyther had the soulgers any expertnce like to thees in thees parts."

On the same evening some Samoiedes came off to the vessel in a boat, and are thus described by Tradescant:— " That night (16 July) came abord of our ship a boat of Sammoyets, a miserable people, of small growth. In my judgment is that people whom the fixtion is fayned of that should have no heads, for they have short necks, and commonly wear ther clothes over head and shoulders. They use boues and arrowes, the men and women be hardlie known on from the other, because the all wear clothes like mene, and be all clad in skins of beasts packed **very** curouslie together, stockings and all. They kill moste of the Loth deer that the brought. The be extreme beggers, not to be denied." On the same day our author gives us a proof that he was a good observer, for the remarkable appearance of a double flood, the Manicha, did not pass unnoticed by him. He writes : " This night we weighed the anchor on account of the two floods: the first barely lasted two hours, followed by a remarkably strong ebb ; and two hours later a long flood like ours succeeded." "Farther, that night (16 July) we wayed anccor by resen of the two fluds; the first is but 2 houres, and then a swift ebe; and then presentlie after two hower along flud like ours." As we are aware, the Russian Academy has lately caused the Manicha at the mouth of the Dwina, and at some other places situated near it on the coast of the White Sea, to be observed by means of an instrument invented expressly for the purpose by our colleague Senz, which has received the name of the Hypsalograph.

Tradescant's impatience to acquire a knowledge of the plants of the Dwina district lying before him was so great, that he requested to be conveyed to the nearest shore in the ship's boat. Immediately after he landed he fell in with a berry which he describes as resembling the strawberry, but with leaves in some measure like the aveus (*Geum Urbanum*), of which he says that it was used as a remedy against the scurvy. As it was of an amber colour, it must have been the yellow cranberry, *Rubus Chamæmorus*, by us (the Russians) called Moroschka. He dried some berries in order to save the seeds, and afterwards sent part of them to Paris to Robin the florist; probably Vespasian, whose father John had established the first good garden in the French metropolis, whence during the last ten years of the sixteenth century, he carried on a mutual exchange of seeds with Gerard of London. This appears from Gerard's "Herbal" (published in 1597), and is likewise repeated in Johnson's edition. Parkinson also makes mention of Robin in the "Paradisus" and in the "Theatrum." In the latter book, he says that Tradescant had received from Vespasian Robin some roots of Doronicum Americanum (*Rudbeckia laciniata*), and shared them with him. Jean Robin cultivated in his garden, about the year 1600, more than a thousand different plants. The species Robinia is so called after him. He received from Henry the Fourth the title of "herboriste (also simpliciste) du Roy," and it was he who delivered to Pierre Vallet, who bore the title of " Brodeur ordinaire du Roy," flowers from which to sketch the embroidery patterns for King Henry the Fourth's court ladies. A work is extant, called " Le Jardin du Roy très chrestien Henry IV. Roy de France et de Navarre dedié à la Royne par Pierre Vallet, brodeur ordinaire du Roy, 1608." We know, to a certainty, that Vespasian Robin sent American plants from Paris to London for Tradescant.

It was not only our (the Russian) plants which interested Tradescant. " I would have given five shillings for one of their skins," says he, as some birds flew before him, of which one he describes must have been a black cock. Tradescant's description is somewhat strange:—" great to the bignes of a fesant, the wing whit, the bodie green, the tayll blewe or dove collar." Tradescant even alludes to finding a piece of the skin of a snake.

On the evening of the 16th of July, the vessel lay close to the shore, before the English factory at Archangel; and on the following day Tradescant landed with the whole of the party. Sir Dudley was received by the Intendant Perfijeff. Three houses were selected for their residence, of which two belonged to the Dutch, and the third to an Englishman named Wilkinson. " They be all built of wholl trees layd on the top of the other very strong, withe fayr roomes packed betwen the hollowes withe wood moss. Having but four bedsteads, content to lay our bodi on the ground."

CHAPTER XI.

TRADESCANT'S DESCRIPTION OF LIFE IN RUSSIA — FORESTS — FLOWERS — DRESS — ORIGIN OF THE ENGLISH WHALE FISHERY — HIS VOYAGE HOME.

ON the 20th of July, 1618, Tradescant obtained an imperial boat in order to explore the islands in the Delta of the Dwina, northwest of Archangel, and to examine the plants growing on them. "On Monday (20th of July)," he states, "I had one of the Emperor's boats to cari me from iland to iland to see what things grewe upon them, whear I found single Rosses, wondros sweet, withe many other things whiche I meane to bringe with me. We had a comander with us, who was glad to be partaker of coorte cake, as we thear could get, whiche was sower creame and oatmeall pastill very poorli mad, which to them was a great bankit."

On this excursion it was that he found on one island so much hellebore (*Helleborus albus*), the present Veratrum album, or V. Lobelianum. I have already mentioned that what Tradescant says of it has enabled me to recognise him as the author of the MS. He states by the way that this plant was called "Cameritza" by the Russians. Hence we might infer that in the present name "Tschemeritza," as often happens, the C or

K is changed into Tsch; as Komar or Kamar now signifies a gnat, it follows that the Russian name for hellebore is gnat-plant. Russia therefore must have named this plant, not like Germany, from its producing the effect of sneezing, but from the peculiar quality it possesses, mentioned in old botanical works, of killing gnats. Pliny says, "Muscæ necantur albo (sc. Elleboro) trito et cum lacte sparso." In Brunsfel's "Contrafayt Book of Plants," published in 1532, at page lxv., there is the following receipt : " If thou wilt kill all the gnats in August, take hellebore, macerate it in milk, and set the same milk for the gnats to drink." As in the spring the large Russian rivers inundate so much land when the snows melt, and this is favourable to the development of the gnats, which, as is well known, issue from the water, it is important for those who live on and visit the Delta of the Dwina, where also great abundance of these tormentors of men are generated, to have a means of destroying them at hand. Hence, then, the name of Komaritza —now changed into Tschemeritza; I must observe, nevertheless, that at present the hellebore is not put to this use.

Speaking of the "Tscheremucha" tree (Prunus Padus), Tradescant acquaints us that the English at Archangel called the berries wild cherries. The Russian name must be the root of the word Cerasus or Cherry. He took with him several of the branches which had taken root in the ground, in the hope that some of them might thrive in England; consequently he contemplated the application of this supple kind of wood to hoop-making. He mentions that the English coopers at Archangel frequently made use of hoops of this material for caviare casks, because they were tough and durable to an extraordinary degree. The Flemings, Dutch, Hamburgers, and Russians must likewise have used much of this wood at that time for hoops; and it was also conveyed to England for the purpose of binding casks for the Greenland fisheries. "They have littill trees that they make hoops of, which the Inglishe say they be wilde cheryes, but I cannot believe it. It is of that kind, but is like a chery in leafe, and beareth a bery less than our Scarbis" (he means Sorbus), "bery somewhat blackishe, but was not ripe at my being theare; the wood is wondrous pliant, and if a twig chance to tuche the ground it will take roote, as I have seen in many places. I took up of them in July, an brought them over a plant or two, which I hope will growe; for all the unfit season of the yeare they be very willing to grow. Now for the abundance of hoopes that there is mad, 1 may imagine, for our coopers, for the great caske of caveare, and the Fleming, Hollanders, and Hamburgers, and Russes, spend such abundance, yet our people bring them away for the hooping of the cask in Greenland; and by the report of the coopers, they be the best hoops in the world, for they say, in a whole day they break not on."

Tradescant names several other trees and plants seen by him. His four sorts of "Nadelhölzer" (Needlewood, *i. e.* trees with needle-like foliage, firs, pines, &c.) must have been Pinus sylvestris, Picea (abies) obovata or vulgaris, Larix sibirica, and abies sibirica

(Ledeb). He speaks of large birch trees, Betula alba, tapped in May and June for the purpose of using the sap in the preparation of an agreeable beverage. "In the contrie, as 5 parts is woods and unprofitable grounds, I have seen 4 sorts of fir trees an barch trees of great bignes, whiche in the spring tyme they make incistion for the juice to drinke, which they saye is a fine coole kind of drink, which lasteth the most part of May and the beginning of June."

Tradescant further says, with reference to other trees not seen by him: "By report they have most sorts of trees that we have in Ingland, up in the contrie, both oake, elm and ashe, aple, peare and cheryes; but the frut les, and not so pleasant. This have bin tould me, and amongst the rest of a plant that growethe upon the Volga, whiche they call God's tree, whose leaves be much lik to fennell; but the report is, is pasing sweet and of great vertue." This is the Artemisia abrotatum, which plant is called in Russian Boshige derewo, literally God's tree; whence Tradescant was probably led to take it for a tree. Of berries he also names, red, black, and white currants, Ribes rubrum, nigrum et album (he says, that they were larger than any he had seen in England), three or four sorts of vaccinium, one red; red bilberries (Brussnika), V. Vitis idæa, perhaps also whortleberries (Klukiva) Oxycoccos palustris, two blue; common bilberries (Tschernika) V. Myrtellus, and perhaps great bilberries (Golubika) V. siliquosum. "I have seene shrubs of divers kinds, as Ribes, or as we call them currants, white, red, and black, far greatter than ever I have seen in this cuntrie; 3 or 4 sorts of whorts, red ons, and two sorts of blewe ons. The currants, and all other things wear so much biger than ours, as I could gather by the vyger of the somer, which is so quick, that when a thing is in blosom it never fellethe could till it is a perfect frute." He moreover found Angelica (Archangelica?) Lysimachia (vulgaris), Pentafolia major (Potentilla?), Geranium flore cœruleo, as well as pratense, Saxifrage (Pimpinella?), Sorrel (Rumex), Ros solis (Drosera), &c. "Also I have been tould that thear growethe in the land both tulipes and narsisus. By a Brabander I was tould it, thoug by his name I should rather think him a Hollander. His name is Jonson, and hathe a house at Archangel. He may be eyther, for he always druke" (is drunk) "once in the day."

I think that there is an error, either in the MS. or of the press, in Parkinson's " Paradisus Terrestris" of 1629, where, in speaking of a species of strawberry, he says, that Tradescant brought it with him from Brussels; probably Brussels is here put for Russia. The passage is as follows:—" There is another strawberry very like unto this, (the Virginia strawberry, which carrieth the greatest leafe of any other except the Bohemian,) that John Tradescante brought with him from Brussels (Russia?) long ago (1618); and in seven yeares could never see one berry ripe on all sides, but still the better part rotten, although it would every yeare flower abundantly, and bear very large leaves." I must, moreover, observe that Tradescant, with reference to the strawberry, wrote as follows:—" I also saw strawberyes to be sould, but could never get of the plants;

but the beryes wear 3 times at my Lords (Digges's) table; but they were in nothing differing from ours, but only les, which mad me that I did not so much seek after them." It is probable, notwithstanding, that he took some seeds with him.

Tradescant makes some observations, although but cursorily, on the cultivation of the different kinds of grain; on bread, flesh, beer, arable land, ploughs, mode of carriage, on the streets made of wooden logs in the city of Archangel; the skilful use of plain carpenter's work; the building of dwelling-houses, farms, &c. He thus heads his observations: "Things by me observed." Then follows: "Imprimis for the sowing of rye the sewe in Jully, ther wheat in June, these two grazers seeme 13 months before they be reaped by reason of the snow falling in August or September, and so liethe till the May after.

"The harvest is in August and the beginning of September; their barley, oats, and pease they sowe in May the last, and commonly reap the first of August, or the last of July.

"I have bin showed oats whyte, very good, whiche wer sowne, and mowne, and keapet, thrashed in 6 weeks.

"For ther howses they be made all of long peeces of fire, being half cut away on the insyde. They be glased withe glas called slude; their ruffes be flat almost and cut bordes of a handfull thick layd longwayes doune the ruffe; they leave the rinds of birche trees under the borde, which be as broad a yearing calfe or broader, and 3 yards long, whiche they laye the edges on above another, and doo defend the wet, and rayne, and snowe.

"Now for ther warmthe they have stooves wherein they heate ther meat, whiche is so well don that it givethe great content to all strangers.

"For beds I have seene none of the huses but think for the most part they sleep upon bed-steads, and most of ther beding is beare skins, and other skins. The English and Leefelanders, I have seen ther beds lik to thees borded beds in England, of a mean sort.

"For ther meat and bread, it is reasonable god; they have bothe wheat and rie bread, and is full as good os most places of Ingland dooe afford, only they never bake it well, and have many foolish fatyons for ther form of ther loafe, sum littil ons so littill as on may well eat a loaf a two mouthe full, other great onse but much shaped like a horse shooe, but that they be round, and a horse shoe is open in the on end; also they have a broune kind of rye bread, whiche is both fine and good. I have seen at the Inglishe house, and also in the Duche houses, Leeflanders so good bread as I have yet never seen the like in this contrie.

"For ther drinks they be meads made of hony and watter, and also beere; but ther Ruse beer is wonderfull base of an ill taste, but ther best meade is excellent drinke, mad of the hony which is the best honny of the world. I have drunke such beere brewed by a Russe in the Inglishe house, bothe for strength and for good tast as I have never betterd it in England.

"For the mutton and beefe it was bothe small and lean, ther shape much like to the Norfolk sheepe; ther beefes like runts of 4 marks price; ther hens and cokes small, and no capons. Ther pidggs they spend wonderfull small; the hogs short, well trused swine, ther bacon tasts much after oyle, because of the muche fishe ther hogs eate.

"Ther land, so muche as I have seene, is for the earable fine gentill land of light mould, like Norfolke land, without stons; ther maner of plowes like oure, but not so neat, muche like to Essex ploughes, withe wheels, but the wheels very evill made.

"The carts be littill ons, long narrow ons, muche like them of Stafordshir; the wheels be lowe mad of two peeces of slit for timber, being thik weare the exselltre goeth thorow, and so deminishe les till they com to the rime, and follow the cattell withe muche labor. For ther horses they be well shaped, short kryt, well joynted; only ther Tarter horses be longe, much like to the Barbery horses, but of the best use of any in the knowne world, for, as I have heard Captaine Gilbert report, that hathe long lived theare" (I shall show, farther on, who this Gilbert was), " he had on which he hathe rod a whole day together, and at night hathe give him a littill provender, and the next day hathe don the like, and so for many dayes, and yet he confessethe that he hathe not known seldom one of tire.

" For ther streets they be paved withe goodli timber trees, cleft in the middell, for they have not the use of sawing in the land, espetiali in that part whear I was, neyther the use of planing withe the plane, but onlie withe a shave, or as some parts of this kingdom calleth it, a draing knife, and withe muche speed, but that I think is by reson of the softnes of ther woods. The yards of ther howses be all paved withe timber, and divided betwin neybor and neybor with palliadowes of yong timber of 12 or 13 foot highe, the timber being so big, as from post to post they put through a long piece . . . . throw a mortis.

"Also the contrie howses be built like to those of the townes, and pallasadeed whiche be don all in on forme, having the yard rounded withe cow-houses, and places for shepe and horse, being all open to the yardsyde, muche lik cloysters heer in Ingland, ther ploughes and carts amongst ther cattell to mak partission, an over liethe the hay, for the most part they be quadrand, and on corner is the dwelling howse, and on syde the barn whiche is comonly the pont. Farther it is to be observed, that all thees cuntry howses stand on little hills, whiche hathe bin raysed by art at the first, and also without the pallisade, or fence of inclosure, ther stands the bodyes of timber trees some 7 or 8 feet high, and from the inclosure, some 16 foot, and on from an other 7 or 8 foot, whiche they say is to defend the isse whiche at the first thawing, if it be with rayne, makethe a very great flud."

Tradescant was shown oats which, six weeks after they had been sown, were thrashed out. The bread he found to be as good as in most places in England; still he somewhat objected to the baking, and to the external shape. Besides white, and the usual rye bread, he also mentions a finer description of the latter.

The cattle he found small, the sheep similar to those in Norfolk. Beef and mutton lean, cocks and hens small, and no capons. The young pigs, he says, are killed when very small; the hams tasted oily, because the swine (at Archangel) were fed so much upon fish.

The Russian beer was generally bad, but that brewed by a Russian at the English factory at Archangel, was as good as any he had ever drunk in England.

The arable land near Archangel he compares to that in Norfolk; the ploughs he found to resemble those in Essex, but the wheels were badly put together. The carts were small, narrow, and oblong, like those in Staffordshire, the horses tolerably good.

That the Russian carpenters were enabled to work with such simple tools, Tradescant might well explain, at least, as far as regards quickness, by the softness of the wood.

The arrangement of the farms he compares with that of the monasteries in England, for the cells are built in a circle round the court.

With somewhat more copiousness Tradescant gives an account of five varieties of craft which he saw on the Dwina.

In the first place he describes the barges (Lodgen). They have, he says, the appearance of one lighter turned upside down on another: the entrance was from the side; the deck lined inside with the bark of trees (Lubki), and the seams caulked with tarred moss. The masts and sails he found to resemble those of the Gravesend barges. He mentions the streamers usually placed on the mast, together with hawks' or horses' bells, as well as on the long and thick rudder. In shallow places they are propelled along slowly with poles. On the Lapland coast and elsewhere they usually sail only with the wind astern. Tradescant was present when thirty labourers were engaged in launching a lighter into the water with levers, and in so doing, as he says, made as much noise as if all the inhabitants of the city had fallen together by the ears. He thought he might boldly assert that, with five other Englishmen, he could have accomplished more than these thirty Russian labourers taken together.

The boats, carrying from eight to nine persons, in which mostly the smaller cattle and poultry were brought to Archangel to market, he finds smaller than the wherries on the Thames, and points out the difference between them, observable in the rudder.

Craft, with keels made out of a single tree, as much as seven feet in diameter and thirty in length, the sides of which were raised with planks fastened together with ropes from the Tscheremucha (Prunus Padus), and then covered with birch-bark or sealskins, were employed, as he says, in numbers in the seal and other fisheries.

Tradescant admires the strength of the beams employed in building the barks. He thought that they might be useful to the East India Company if they were decked. He further describes the river craft with awnings, for persons of station.

Lastly, in Tradescant's journal of his residence at

Archangel, there is something geological. It relates to the Scandinavian blocks of stone (blocs erratiques) seen by him, which are found in Russia as far north-east as the Petchora and the Ural, and south as far as the Voronesk and Tscheringov Government. Tradescant writes: "In the Dwina district lie a quantity of stones, of which some are half a waggon load, and still more heavy. I requested some one who understood Russian to inquire how these stones came there, as there are none of any other description in the vicinity, and the ground towards the Dwina is marshy." The interpreter (probably George Brigges) received for answer: "Ther lyethe by the river syde many great stones, some of halfe a cart load, and near whiche I demanded one to ask how they cam thear, the land being witheout, being moorish toward the watters syd, and they tould our interpreter that they were brought ought (out) of the land by the isse."

This latter explanation is, in a certain degree, interesting; but the people were of opinion that the Dwina ice brings these blocks of stone from the interior of the country; for that they were transported there from Scandinavia our inhabitants of the Dwina district did not then imagine, although several of them, as even now happens, may have gone a long distance on icebergs in the Icy Sea.

On the 5th of August Tradescant quitted Archangel in the Diana, and at the same time Nelson, part owner of this vessel, returned. For the point of departure, the Pudoshem mouth must have been chosen, for the vessel anchored on the first evening at Rose Island, which is situated between that and the shallow Korelian mouth, which Tradescant visited, in order to botanize there.

"The 5th of August we set sayle for Ingland from the point, a myll from the toune. That night we cam to an ancor under Rose Iland wheare I (and) divers (other) went on shore whear ther was a littill souldyers hous poorly garded withe sum 10 men, whear we bought gras for our live sheepe, whear I gathered of all such things as I could find thear growing, which wear 4 sorts of berries, which I brought awaye with me of every sortt. This Iland is lowe land all over but whear the house stands, and that place is a long bank of drie white sand, the land being eyther woods or meddow, but seldom eyther mowne or fed."

Where Tradescant gives a general account of the plants discovered by him on the Dwina delta, he does not describe the roses which grew wild, at the time that he mentions his visit to Rose Island; but he must doubtless have seen most of them there. When he says that from four to five English acres were bedecked with them, he certainly refers to this island. He compares the roses seen by him with the cinnamon rose. Of the many rose-bushes which he took with him, he says, that he hopes that, at all events, some of them would grow and thrive in England, wherein he was not disappointed. "I have seen roses, only single, in a great abundance, in my estimation four or five acres together; they be single, and much like oure sinoment rose; and who have the sense of smelling, say they be marvelus sweete. I hope they will bothe growe and beare heere, for amongst many that I brought home withe the roses upon them, yet some on may grow."

From the catalogue of the plants in the Tradescant garden, we see that the Rosa Moscovita was to be found there even as late as 1656. That rose was in this case brought originally from the islands of the delta of the Dwina, and perhaps from Rose Island itself. Parkinson describes, in his "Theatrum Botanicum" of 1640, a rose brought from Muscovy ("Sylvestris Russica, the wild bryer of Muscovie"). This must have been an offshoot of that introduced by Tradescant.

I must here remind my readers, that until the year 1630 there were none but wild roses in Russia. It was only at that period that Peter Marselius for the first time brought cultivated roses from the ducal garden at Gottorp to Moscow, which then throve very well. The Russian wild roses were formerly called by us, gul, after the Persian. Hence appears, in old Muscovite receipts for rosewater, the name of "gulafuaga woda," from gulaf, the Persian word for this water. The petals of the wild roses were used for pharmaceutical purposes even long after the introduction of the garden rose. Even in 1764, as much as thirty pounds of the conserve was sent to the apothecaries' hall at St. Petersburg.

Apropos of roses, we learn from Tradescant's

journal, that he was deficient in the sense of smelling, for he says: "those who have it assured me that the roses on the island were marvelous swete."

In another place there is a direct confirmation of this, where he speaks of boiling blubber for train oil. This, he says, spreads a stench which nearly poisons passers-by; "but as I was wanting in the sense of smell, I could not bear testimony to this." Here, then, was a compensation for the pleasure of which he was deprived at Rose Island.

This passage in Tradescant's journal has already been quoted. There we learn, that he saw how distended sealskins were cleansed as much as possible from the oil on their fleshy side, turned outwards for the purpose of covering bottle-cases, which, for the most part, were sold to the Dutch, numbers of whom came to Archangel. These foreigners varnished them over at home, provided them with the necessary iron lining, and then brought them again to Archangel for sale.

On Rose Island, Tradescant likewise found a plant with berries, which was unknown to him, and which he describes as fully. It must have been the Swedish privet (Cornus Secica), which is by no means rare there. He took some branches with him on which were berries, but the ship's boys destroyed them before he was aware of it; nevertheless, to his comfort, he found some on the ground. To water his plants, too, some salt water, instead of fresh, was brought to him at sea, without anything being said to him on the subject, because several casks of fresh water had been thrown overboard when the vessel grounded on the bar at the time of her sailing.

"A sort of plant, bearing his fruit like hedge-mercury (Mercurialis perennis), which made a fine showe, having leaves on the tope of every stake, having in every loupe a berry about the bignes of a hawe, all the three berryes growing close together, of a finner bright red than a hawe, which I took up many roots, yet am afraid that none held, because on our being on ground we staved most of our fresh watter, and so wear faint to watter withe salt watter, but was mad believe it was freshe, whiche that plant having but a long whit thin root, littill biger than a small couch gras; and the boys in the ship, before I pe(r)seved it, eat of the berries, except som of them cum up amongst the earthe by chance. I found this plant to growe in Rose Island."

On Rose Island he also found pinks (Feldnelkia Dianthus), as beautiful as those in England, with deeply-cut petals. "Thear (in Rose Island) I found pinks growing natturall of the best sort we have heere in Ingland, withe the eges of the leaves deeplie cut or jaged very finely."

On the 6th August the Diana went over the bar, where Tradescant, as already mentioned, sets down eleven feet of water. The vessel there touched the ground, but fortunately got off. On the 8th he was at the Island of Ssossnovetz, and on the same evening fell in with the English man-of-war, which had brought Volünsky to Russia. From the 8th to the 10th the wind was contrary, and then to the 13th there was a thick fog, so that the Diana, in four or five days, only made ten leagues. Near Cape Svatoi Noss the vessel appears to have been drawn into the whirlpool described by me, and was in great danger of being wrecked on a rock (probably Kamen Woronucha). On the 14th there were several whales in the neighbourhood of the ship, and Nelson called Tradescant on deck, in order to point out to him how one of them was tormented by a " thresher." On the 16th the Diana passed the North Cape, but it was only on the 22nd of September that Tradescant landed at St. Catherine's Docks, in London.

" The 6 of August we weyed ancor " (from Rose Island) " the wind being fayer, and went, for the bar is but 11 foot watter and our ship drew 10 and a halfe, the tide being then neape whear we cam on, and sat 6 or 8 howers to oure great grefe, a floud presently rising, whiche if it had continewed the shipe must needs have perished ; but, thanks be to God, the next tyde we cam of without any harme. The next day we wear becalmed. The 8 day we mad Cros Iland, the wind being fayre, but small and much raine, in so muche that all the decks wear leake, which for my own part I felt, for it rayned donne thourow all my clothes and beds to the spoyll of them all. The 8 day at night we met withe on of the state men-of-war that the Russian Ambassador cam home in of Cape Grace " (eight leagues and a half north-east of the Island of Ssossnovetz). " From the 8 to the 10 conttrary winds. From the 10 to the 13 extreme foge, so that in 4 or 5 dayes we went but 10 leags a head.

Of Cape Gallant" (Svatoi Noss) " we wear afrayed of being brought upon a rock" (probably Kamen Woronucha), " but, thanks be to God, it proved beter. The 14 daye being Fridaye we saw mani whales, whear the owner of ship" (Nelson) " sawe on chased with a thresher and called me to see it, but they rose no more. The next day (15) being Satterday we had a great storme, the wind being at east. On Sunday (16) towards night the storme seased and the wind changed west; that night we mad the North Cape. On Sunday being the 13 of September I with on were walking on the wash of the shipe, I descreyed lande, which was present aproved by the whole company, which land was to the southward of Boffum Ness, part of cuntrie of Scotland; our master imagined it to be the Frithe, but could no more tell than any other. This is in on iuste monthe we had bine without sight of land, for the Sunday monthe befor wee had sight of the North Cape of the land called Assumtion. On Friday 18 August" (it should be September), " 12 of the clock, we made Flambrow Head. Saturday 19" (again August instead of September) "night we recovered Yarmouth Road, where we anchored and dined in the towne. On Sunday (20) after dinner we wayed anchor, and that night, the wind being fayre, we recovered Al(d)boroug; the next morning being Monday we wayed, and that daye came to Gravesend. On Tuesday the 22 of August" (he must mean September) " we landed at Saynt Katharine neer London, whear, God be thanked, we ended our viage, having no one man sick, God be thanked."

From the passage in Tradescant's Journal, which we have quoted above, we find that as early as 1618 the name of "Thrasher" was in use for the dolphin, well known as the tormenter of the whale, and even called "Balænarum tyrannus," viz., "Delphinus (Phocæna) orca," in Russian Kossatka, although, at that period, barely twenty years had elapsed since the English had practically engaged in the whale-fishery at Iceland, and also not far from the North Cape. I cannot, however, refrain from mentioning that the first plan formed by the English, in 1575, for carrying on the whale-fishery, had immediate reference to those waters where Nelson pointed out to Tradescant a whale pursued by the delphinus orca. In order to take lessons in the practical part of this branch of industry, which was then unknown in England, some Biscayans experienced in the art were engaged. With regard to the necessary experiments, William Burrough, amongst others, was taken into council.

The plan was to send a vessel of two hundred tons equipped for the whale-fishery, with five pinnaces and fifty-five men, to Wardhuus, in April; the fishery was to take place not far from the Lapland coast. The aforesaid Biscayans were to teach the method of harpooning, boiling the blubber, &c., and a skilful cooper was then to put together the staves taken with them from England.

William Burrough, as we have previously mentioned, was the principal agent of the London Company in Russia, in 1574 and 1575. In the voyage with his brother Stephen, in 1556, he had observed a whale close to his vessel, when in the vicinity of Nova Zembla. In the subsequent voyages to Rose Island, the English doubtless met with whales frequently; and this may have given rise to the establishment of the English whale-fishery, which has since become so important a branch of industry.

Just one hundred and nineteen years after Tradescant's visit to Russia, viz. in 1737, the thrasher, as well as the swordfish, were instanced by Dr. John Brickell, by hearsay, in his natural history of North Carolina, as deadly enemies to the whale.

Dr. Brickell writes: "These fish (the whales) are never found dead, or floating to the shoar with their tongues in their heads, for it is the opinion of many in these parts, that the thrashers and sword-fish (which are mortal enemies to the whales, wherever they meet them) eat the tongue out of their head, as soon as they have killed him; but whether this be done by the fish above mentioned, or by others of the same voracious nature, I will not take upon me to determine."

Twelve years earlier (in 1725), Paul Dudley communicated to the Royal Society, that the orcas were called killers by the whalers, and that they pursued the young whales as bull-dogs do a bull, to bite and thrash them. The whales bellow like hunted bulls, and as their tongues hang out of their mouths the orcas eat them.

Paul Dudley's words are: "Our whale men have given this fish (that preys upon the whales) the name of killers. They go in company by dozens, and set upon a young whale, and will bite him like so many bull-dogs; some will lay hold of his tail, to keep him from threshing, while others lay hold of his head, and bite and thresh him, till the poor creature, being thus heated, lolls out his tongue; and then some of the killers catch hold of his lips, and if possible, of his tongue; and after they have killed him they chiefly feed upon the tongue and head, but when he begins to putrefy they leave him." This killer is, without doubt, the orca that Dr. Franguis describes in these words: "Quando orca insequitur balænam, ipsa balæna horribilem edit mugitum, non aliter quam cum taurus mordetur a cane." These killers have sometimes bit out of a dead whale a piece of blubber of about two feet square.

One of the manifold appellations bestowed on the dolphin in question, and indeed a very old one, is " grampus," probably abbreviated from " grand porpois." As this fish is much met with in the neighbourhood of the North Cape, it is likewise called a North Caper. The Russian appellation of Kossatka was bestowed upon it, from the oblique and somewhat crooked wake, almost peculiar to the fish, and usually left by it in the water. Kossa, as we know, means a scythe, and likewise a twisted tail; and the word kosso, curved, is the root of both. The kossatka are even now frequently seen about the spot, where, according to a calculation made at the time, Nelson must have observed them on his voyage with Trades-cant, viz. near the Peninsula of Rübatschy and the Varanger Fiord. An eye-witness told me that the kossatkas very often drive whales into shallow water, and, indeed, ashore, in the Gulf of Motover, which is formed by the south shore of the Peninsula of Rübatschy and the opposite coast; and not only there, but in the northern bight, now called the Harbour of Nova Zembla, and in both the bays situated to the south of the same, on the main-land. In confirmation of this, the shore at those places is actually covered with the skeletons of whales. The easternmost of these southern bays was, probably on that account, called Ketova (from kit, a whale), but is now on our charts set down as Titovskaja. The westernmost bay, which is now set down in them as Kutovoja (which has been derived from kut, an angle or end), may probably have been originally called Kitovaja, especially as the rivulet flowing into it is likewise called on the charts Titovka (sometimes Kitovka). There were consequently two whale bays; that to the west stretching in a south-west direction, and the other and easternmost one to the south. Tilesius saw a shoal of kossatkas form themselves into a sort of battle-array, and drive seals before them, whilst the latter sought to escape by repeated leaps into the air. A sketch of this scene he presented to Pallas.

It is remarkable that Dr. W. Scoresby, who was so experienced in all that relates to whales, mentions nothing of this dolphin. He doubts indeed (in 1820) the existence of the thrasher, for he says, "The sword-fish and the thrasher (if such an animal there be) may possibly be among the enemies of the whale, but I have never witnessed their combats."

As Tradescant doubtless learnt the name of the thrasher from Nelson, part-owner of the vessel, it must be supposed that the latter had already visited the north on former occasions. A river and a light in Hudson's Bay were named after one Nelson, who with Thomas Button was dispatched to the north-west by Sir Dudley Digges, and other members of the Russia Company, and who wintered in this bay in 1612-13.

From imperfect accounts which we possess of Button's expedition we learn that Nelson, who accompanied him as captain of one of his vessels, died in that bay. Button was likewise dispatched, as Hudson had been in the previous year, by Sir Dudley Digges and some other members of the Russia Company, to search for the north-west passage. At the entrance into Hudson's Bay he stopped at an island named by Hudson after Sir Dudley Digges, in order to put together a pinnace which had been brought thither with him in pieces.

It is to be lamented that Tradescant did not remain longer in Russia, for, with his spirit of observation and his indefatigable zeal in the collection of objects of natural history, he would certainly have taken note in his journal, of much which would have been highly interesting to us now.

He took with him to England several articles of dress, as appears from his Catalogue. At page 49, we find the "Duke of Muscovy's vest, wrought with gold upon the breast and armes." The English often called the Czar Duke, but likewise Prince. In 1618, there was no other Prince at Archangel than the Vaivode Audreas Vassilovich Chilkoff: his assistant was Bogdan Borissovich Vojeikoff. Probably this vest, wrought with gold, came out of the wardrobe of Prince Chilkoff. At page 47, a Russian vest is also mentioned. At page 50, Russian stockings, without heels, and Russian shoes, shod with iron. At page 48, boots from Russia; 46, a knife from Moscovy. At page 4, is the Northern Diver or Gorara (in Russian, Gagara), or Colymbus, from Muscovy. Hence I believe it was that I discovered the dissevered head in the so-called Ashmolean Museum. At page 162, is the Rosa Moscovita (Moscovia Rose) before mentioned, from Rose Island.

Parkinson tells us in 1640, in his "Theatrum Botanicum," that Tradescant brought a "Geranium Moscoviticum purpureum" from Russia to England; which has not been described, although it existed for a long time in English gardens.

"G. Muscovit. purpur. groweth in Muscovy, brought to us by Mr. John Tradescant, hath not beene published, although we have had it longtime in our gardens."

In the catalogue of the plants in South Lambeth Garden, which we have often mentioned, there is however no "Geranium purpureum," but at page 116, we find G. Batracoides flore cœruleo; and Tradescant writes in his journal, that he found the "Geranium flore serulle," on the islands of the delta of the Dwina.

Two years after his visit to Russia, he undertook a voyage into the Mediterranean sea, with the expedition destined at that period to act against Algiers. He brought with him from Fermentera Island, "Trifolium stellatum," which Johnson, in his edition of Gerard's "Herbal," describes as "Trifolium stellatum hirsutum;" and he informed Parkinson that he had seen fields full of Gladiolus in the Barbary States. According to Parkinson ("Theatrum Botanicum"), Tradescant received "Trifolium fragiferum Lusitanicum tormentosum," from Guillaume Boel of Lisbon.

Seven years later, in 1627, Tradescant accompanied the ill-fated expedition undertaken by the unfortunate Duke of Buckingham (George Villiers), under whom he was gardener, to La Rochelle and the Isle de Rhé the year before his murder. He brought from the latter island "Leucojum marinum maximum Parkinsoni." Tradescant, the younger, made a voyage to Virginia before 1640. He brought with him from thence, "Aquilegia Virginiana" (Park. Th. Bot., page 1367; "Musæum Tradescantianum," page 84. A. Canadensis, L.); "Spargianum maius, sive ramosum Virginianum (Park. Th. Bot., page 1206; Mus Trad. page 169); "Gelseminum sive Jasminum luteum oderatum Virginianum scandens sempervirens" (Park. Th. Bot., page 1465; "Gelsenium nitidum," Mich.); "Cupressus Americana" (Park. Th. Bot., page 1477; "C. Virginiana," Trad., Mus. Trad., page 106; "Taxodium distichum," Rich.). Probably also, "Arbor siliquosa locus nostratibus dicta" (Park. Th. Bot., page 1550; "Locusta Virginiana arbor," Mus. Trad., page 135). William Watson mistakes in saying ("Phil. Trans." vol. xlvi.) that Tradescant, the father, was the first who introduced the cypress.

I have already mentioned that the three Tradescants, father, son, and grandson, were buried close to the palace of the Archbishop of Canterbury, in the churchyard of St. Mary's, Lambeth.

In the so-called Ashmolean Museum, there are several portraits in oil of the Tradescants, the father and son; of the young grandson and his stepmother Esther there are also portraits. Of the elder Tradescant, a portrait was likewise taken immediately after his decease, and a plaster cast of the head preserved. Besides the portrait of the father and son previously alluded to, taken by Wenceslaus, the Bohemian, for the catalogue of the Museum, it has been twice engraved by John Thomas Smith. That of Esther Tradescant is engraved by Caulfield singly, and together with her stepson (not her son). The Tradescants' house at Lambeth was originally engraved by the J. T. Smith just named, for his "Antiquities of London and its Environs" (1791–1800). Under the portrait of Tradescant the father, there is this inscription:—"Johannes Tradescantus Pater, rerum selectarum insignem supellectilem in Reconditorio Lambethiano prope Londinum, etiamnum visendam primus instituit ac locupletavit." Under that of the son:—"Johannes Tradescantus Filius, genii ingeniique paterni verus heres, relictum sibi rerum undique congestarum thesaurum ipse plurimum adauxit et in Museo Lambethiano amicis visendum exhibet." It is possible that the worthless notes which cover the blank paper of the last page of the MS. on which I have written the name of the elder Tradescant, originated with the younger one who was connected with Ashmole. The scrawl commences :— " Simpathetical and antipathetical working of herbes, plants, stones, minerals, with other utemost virtues, sometimes taught by the devil " . . . . and farther on :—" Theare was never any callende mad publik before the captivitie of babilon, by which they were divided the yeere into twelve parts," &c.

Even as early as the middle of the preceding century, the English gardeners named some plants after Tradescant. First ; the " Phalanguim Ephemerum Virginianum," already mentioned, which was then set down by Rupp, in Germany, as the parent of the Tradescantia genus. Secondly; the " Narcissus pseudonarcissus," which was named by Parkinson in honor of Tradescant, and from the number of its petals, as well as its yellow colour :—" Pseudonarcissus aureus maximus flore pleno, sive roseus Tradescanti;" and last and thirdly, the aster which Tradescant received from George Gibbes, a physician at Bath, who brought it with him from Virginia, and which is also set down by Linnæus as " aster Tradescanti," so that in botany, not only a species of plants, but likewise a tribe is named after Tradescant. In 1749, William Watson visited the Tradescant garden with Dr. Mitchell. They found there still growing "Borrago latifolia sempervirens (anchusa sempervirens);" "polygonatum vulgare latifolium (convallaria polygonatum);" " Aristolochia clematitis rector, Dracontium dodonæi (Arum dracunculus);" a "Rhamnus catharticus" twenty feet high, and nearly one foot thick, and two large arbutus trees, which plants we find inserted in Tradescant's catalogue. Dr. Andrew Coltie Ducarel, the antiquary and historian, during the latter part of his life, which terminated in 1785, inhabited a portion of Tradescant's house, at the same time that John Small occupied the other part, which had been added by Ashmole, and which Small purchased in 1760. In 1773, Ducarel wrote a letter about Tradescant to the before-named Dr. Watson, wherein he attempts to remove some erroneous ideas with respect to him; and this was published in the "Philosophical Transactions," vol. lxiii. He supposes, for instance, that Tradescant the elder was not a gardener at Canterbury, and was not alive in 1656, and that Ashmole purchased the collection from his son.

The fame which, by means of Parkinson and Johnson, accrued to the founder of the garden at South Lambeth, doubtless hastened the laying out of other botanical gardens. The Oxford physic gardens I have already mentioned. Soon afterwards the apothecaries' garden at Chelsea, which still exists, was formed; it was superintended first by Watts and Drody, and more recently by James Petiver and Philip Miller. Private gardeners likewise displayed zeal for progressive improvement in the science. Rose, King Charles the Second's gardener, visited Tradescant's garden in 1669, when the widow Esther's suit with Ashmole was still pending; and two years before the transfer of the Tradescant collection to

Oxford, viz. in 1681, four gardeners formed an association for bringing the cultivation of fruit-trees to perfection. Their names were Roger Locker, Queen Catherine's gardener, who was likewise superintendent of many other gardens; George London, gardener to the Bishop of London (Henry Compton), at Fulham; Moses Cooke, gardener to the Earl of Essex (Arthur Capel), at Cassiobury and Hadham; and John Field, gardener to the Duke of Bedford (William Russel), at Woburn Abbey. Of these gardeners, George London and Moses Cooke are likewise known as authors. The former translated, with Henry Wise, two small French works, which he published under the title of "The Retired Gardener." Moses Cooke wrote, "The Manner of Raising Forest Trees."

Sir Hans Sloane was, in 1712, proprietor of a piece of ground which he afterwards ceded to the Apothecaries' Guild. Not far from this garden, at Chelsea, he spent the latter part of his life, and there he died. Sloane's collections of specimens of botany and natural history served as the foundation for the British Museum in London. His monument stands on the left shore of the Thames, near Chelsea church, whilst the founder of the Oxford Museum rests on the right shore of the river at Lambeth. Of the now somewhat indistinct bas-reliefs on the monument of the three Tradescants, there are sketches amongst Pepys' papers, at Magdalen College, Cambridge, which Dr. Ducarel has had engraved ("Philos. Tran." vol. lxiii.). The epitaph placed on the monument at its erection in 1662, which was repaired by subscription in 1773, runs as follows:—

> " Know, stranger, ere thou pass, beneath this stone
> Lie John Tradescant, grandsire, father, son:
> The last dy'd in his spring; the other two
> Liv'd till they had travelled art and nature thro',
> As by their choice collections may appear,
> Of what is rare in land, in seas, in air;
> Whilst they (as Homer's Iliad in a nut)
> A world of wonders in one closet shut.
> These famous antiquarians that had been,
> Both gardiners to the Rose and Lilly Queen,
> Transplanted now themselves, sleep here; and when
> Angels shall with their trumpets awaken men,
> And fire shall purge the world, these hence shall rise,
> And change their garden for a paradise."

May the discovery of Tradescant the elder's MS. described in these pages, serve to refresh our remembrance of this enthusiastic friend of Flora, and the first founder of a museum of natural history in England; and teach us to value as it deserves, his hitherto insufficiently-acknowledged merit.

CHAPTER XII.

GEOGRAPHICAL DISCOVERIES PROMOTED BY MEMBERS OF THE RUSSIA COMPANY—SIR FRANCIS CHERRY AND OTHERS.

In order to give our readers a better account of Sir Dudley Digges and some other persons, in whose company Tradescant visited Russia, it may be necessary next to consider what Sir Dudley and the Russia Company, founded at Sebastian Cabot's instigation, have contributed towards the great geographical discoveries in the north.

A review of the history of the expeditions undertaken in the last half of the sixteenth and the first twenty years of the seventeeth century, to the north, north-east, and north-west, shows that they were either fitted out by the Russia Company itself, or that at least some of its members gave them a helping hand.

It has been shown that this was the company which, in 1556, dispatched Stephen Burrough, and in 1580, Arthur Pet and Jackmann, for the purpose of seeking a north-east passage. An active member of the same company, William Sanderson, was the chief investigator of the expedition commanded by John Davis, in which Davis' Straits were discovered to the north-west, and Hope Sanderson was reached.

All the Russian historians repeat a mistake at first made in the extract from the "Dwina Annual Record," which was unfortunately lost, viz. that Dutch vessels sailed to the Dwina as early as 1555, which was but the second year after Chancellor's first arrival there. This was not the case, for we have seen that the first Dutch vessel dispatched to the Lapland coast at Philip Vinterbonig's instigation, arrived there in 1565; but that it was in 1577 that the first reached the Dwina, and which belonged to Gilles Hoofman. Nine years later, in 1586, the first French vessel appeared there, from Dieppe, commanded by Jean Sauvage.

The frequently-repeated visits of the Dutch to the Dwina led to the three expeditions undertaken by them in 1594, 1595, and 1596, with the object of searching for a north-east passage. With reference to the last voyage, I have had an opportunity of making some observations on the return to Kola. Here I am reminded that, in sailing northwards from the North Cape, an island was discovered in 74° 30′, which the Dutch named Bear's Land, or Bear's Island, because they had a long contest there with one of these animals, and that this island being, so to say, discovered anew by the English in 1604, was, in the ensuing year named, by a member of the Russia Company, Cherry Island.

If, on a globe, or on a chart of the Arctic Regions, we look at the appellations bestowed on different places towards the north, east, and west, after passing Cherry Island, the following observations occur:

On Spitzbergen, which is situated due north of it, we see a mountain named after the "Muscovie Company;" and on this island we likewise find the names of some active members of the same company. One of these, whose name occurs three times in the northern part of the island, Sir Thomas Smith, was, as we shall hereafter mention, in Moscow, in 1604–5, as the first Ambassador sent there by King James the First, and was for some time at the head of the Russia Company. Another member, Benjamin Deicrowe, was the London agent of the same, and is incidentally mentioned by Tradescant in the "Journal" of his voyage, where he speaks of the whale-fishery. In the British Museum I have seen a MS. of his.

Round half the globe, to the right, we read mostly the names of our countrymen (Russians), as monuments to the fame of the Russian spirit of enterprise; and to the honour of our country's navy, Russian navigators have accomplished, eastwards of Nova Zembla and Matvejeva Zembla, what was impracticable for English and Dutch voyagers, on account of the ice. To the left, however, in the farthest part of North America, stands, far beyond Hope Sanderson, in Baffin's Bay, the name of Sir Dudley Digges; and still higher, even on the most northern point of America which has been explored, we again discern Sir Thomas Smith's name. Between both, we see that of another active member of the Russia Company, John Wolstenholme, in a bay, in the neighbourhood of which, at Serillack, is situated, according to Ross, the northernmost settlement of Esquimaux, whence Baron Wrangel proposes that an expedition be undertaken in sledges drawn by dogs on the ice to the North Pole. The names of the three members of the Russia Company whom we have just mentioned, we find at the entrance into Hudson's Bay.

The existence of the names we have quoted in the high north, is owing to the expedition undertaken by the great geographical discoverers, Hudson, Button (with Nelson), and Bileth (with Baffin), whose names will only perish with the world itself; and who were sent forth by Sir Dudley Digges, Sir Thomas Smith, John Wolstenholme, and some other members of the Russia Company, in order to follow out Sebastian Cabot's earlier discovery. Thus through the Russia Company was it that two empires now entirely surround the world in the north, and that the possessions of England and Russia join just opposite to Cherry Island.

This great and important result requires a review of the persons who brought it about.

Francis Cherry, whose name now figures on the map of the world, at the northernmost point of the continent of Europe, devoted himself in Russia, and particularly at Moscow, to a practical life. In the time of Ivan Vassilovitch he was employed by the English factory on the Varvarka at Kitai Gorod. He acquired so good a knowledge of the Russian, that he was employed at Court as interpreter ("Mister Francis Cherry was the Emperour, Ivan

Basilivich, his interpreter"). In our public documents he is named "Frangike Tsarei." He is also mentioned as "Frangike Ivanoff," whence it appears that his father's Christian name was John.

About the period when, through Jermach, the extensive Transural region, "with the golden soil," came into the possession of Russia; when Anthony Marsh, the company's agent at Moscow, sent a Russian Commissioner, with a Samoiede, over the Yugorian chain for sable skins; when some Promuschlenniks from Pustosersk proposed to this Marsh to sail past Matvei's Land to the Oby; and when the Stroganoffs, through Oliver Brunel, thought of exploring Siberia from the Icy Sea,—Cherry travelled to Permia ("he has travailed in person into Permia, farre to the east in Russia"). He appears to have advanced farther than the Strogonoffs' possessions, viz. to the east side of the Ural, for he ate sturgeon from the Oby ("Francis Cherry saith that he hath eaten of the sturgeon that come out of the river Obi"). Some of the natives, who had been great travellers, told him that in the east there was a warm (not frozen) sea ("the Russes that are great travellers say, that beyond Ob to the southeast there is a warme sea, which they expresse in the Russe tongue—Za Obu reca moria teupla"). We know that in 1567 two Cossacks traversed the whole of Siberia, and advanced as far as Pekin.

When Jerome Horsey was about to embark for England in 1587, Francis Cherry delivered him at Rose Island a piece of goldstuff and beautiful sable furs, as a present from Boriss Federovitch Godunoff, in order that he might have a dress made from them in remembrance of him. Soon afterwards Cherry came to England with a letter from the Czar, Theodore Ivanovitch, to Elizabeth. In 1591 he again brought letters to the Queen from the Czar Theodore, and Boriss Godunoff, and from the latter likewise to Lord Burghley. In 1596 we find Cherry elected a member of the Russia Company.

On the 2nd of July, 1598, he returned to Moscow with letters from Elizabeth to the Czar, Theodore Ivanovitch, and to Boriss Godunoff, it not being known at the time of his departure from London that the former had died on the 7th of January. On the 11th of July he had the honour of delivering his letters to the new Czar, Boriss Godunoff, and on the 20th he reported to England that the rumour which had been spread of Elizabeth's having supplied the Sultan with cannon and warlike stores, originated with a Pole. In December, Cherry was sent back to London by way of Novogorod and Pskov, and there gave the first information of a projected marriage between the Czar's daughter, Kseni Borissovna, and Prince John the younger of Denmark, and stated that the Lubeckers sought to extend their trade to Moscow. It was also Cherry who, in 1599, negotiated the engagement of Dr. Timothy Willie, who was to succeed Dr. Mark Ridley at Moscow, where he had arrived in 1594, and whence Elizabeth ordered him back in 1598. In 1601, he was employed in London as assistant in the translation of some Russian letters from Godunoff, brought to Elizabeth by Richard Lea.

In 1603, the well-known Cherry sent a vessel, named the Grace, to Kola, where Josias Logan, who had been appointed factor or agent for the management of the business, was to be left. From Kola the vessel sailed to the north, according to the instructions given by Cherry, in order, if possible, to reach the 80th degree of latitude, and make geographical discoveries. William Gordon from Hull was appointed factor for this part of the voyage. On the 16th of August the vessel made the above-mentioned island, which lies in 74° 30′. Gordon and Bennet seem to have been ignorant, notwithstanding the accounts of the Dutch voyages in 1596, which were then in existence, that the island had been previously visited.

Cherry desired to have this island examined more closely, particularly as Gordon and Bennet had discovered traces of its being frequented by walruses. Consequently, in the following year, 1604, in which he likewise escorted Sir Thomas Smith, who was on his way to Moscow, as far as Gravesend, he dispatched another vessel, named the Good Speed, under the command of the same Captain Bennet, and with Thomas Weldon as factor. Bennet was first to sail to the Kola, and the Petschenza Bights, on the Lapland coast, where a commodious bay is still called the foreign station ("nemetzkoe stanowischtsche"), and then to endeavour to reach that island a second time. On it were now found a great many walruses, and as they did not yet understand how to kill them with lances, they fired at them; but when all the powder and lead they had taken with them were exhausted, the idea struck them of shooting these unwieldy but powerful animals in one eye with a blowpipe, and then attacking them on the blind side—(our promüschlenniks are accustomed, where the nature of the ground allows of it, to throw shovelsful of sand on the heads and into the eyes of the walruses before they fall upon them with lances). On the return of the vessel with a large quantity of walrus-teeth and hides, the island was named in London after Sir Francis Cherry.

To these first two expeditions in 1603 and 1604, now succeeded many others; which gradually acquired importance in a commercial as well as in a geographical point of view.

Bennet and Weldon were again sent to Cherry Island in 1605, and as in this voyage they had the misfortune to be plundered, by Dunkirkers, of almost all their firearms, they were compelled again to adopt the method, still pursued, of killing the walruses with lances. From their blubber oil was boiled on the island in cauldrons, taken with them, and eleven tons of it were brought to London as a new product of industry.

In 1606, besides the former vessels with the persons already mentioned, a pinnace was sent equipped by another member of the Russia Company; the commander was Jonas Poole, who had made the previous voyages in the vessel of which Bennet was captain. They now understood this new description of sport so well, that in the course of six hours about eight hundred walruses were slain.

In the following year (1607) another ship, the "Paul," commanded by Thomas Weldon, sailed for Cherry Island, dispatched by a London brewer of the name of Duppa. The trip was repeated in 1608, but the master was instructed by the company to touch at "Tipany," in Lapland. We can scarcely suppose that by Tipany, the harbour ("Korabelnaja guba") between Cape Tipunov and Cape Korabelnoi (in the map Cape Sergejev), at the east end of Rübatschü, is meant. Waida Bay, at the north end of this peninsula, was then often called Wedagoba, or also Kegor from Cape Kekur, which was near it. On this occasion a thousand walruses were killed in seven hours, and a pair of young ones were captured, of which the male was brought to London, and even to the palace, to be shewn to King James. Another vessel, the "Dragon," not belonging to the company, had arrived at Cherry Island; she was also dispatched by Duppa, and commanded by Richard Stevens.

In 1609 two vessels sailed for account of the company, one, the "Lioness," with Jonas Poole and Thomas Weldon, went straight to Cherry Island, and on the 8th of May took formal possession of it for the Russia Company. In the other, the "Paul," was Thomas Edge, an apprentice to the same company, as factor, and who was first to go to "Tipany," in Lapland, for the purpose of loading fish. Edge arrived later at Cherry Island, and took Josias Logan with him. The "Lioness" then went to Archangel, and the factors returned to London in the "Paul," now commanded by Poole. They brought with them two young bears, which for a long time were exhibited to the public in Paris Garden (in Southwark, not far from the Thames, between Blackfriars and Southwark Bridges).

In 1610, the Russia Company once more dispatched two vessels, the "Lioness," with Thomas Edge, to Cherry Island, and the "Amitié," with Jonas Poole, to make discoveries in the north. Poole, whose lieutenant was Nicholas Woodcock, arrived in May at Spitzbergen, which had been seen by the Dutch in 1596, and in 1607 by Hudson, but which the English now maintained had been discovered by Sir Hugh Willoughby in 1553. Poole named the high mountain, the peak of which was first discerned by him, Muscovie Companies Mount. Walruses were killed there likewise, and twelve tons of their oil brought to London. The horn of a narwhale, then usually called a sea-unicorn, which was considered a great curiosity, formed part of their spoil.

Henry Hudson, who in 1607 had made a voyage to the north, in 1608 and 1609 others to the northwest, and in the latter year one also to the west, and had discovered the river named after him, was again dispatched westward by Sir Dudley Digges, John Wolstenholme, and some other members of the Russia Company. His ship appears to have been the "Discovery," the same in which Button with

Nelson, and then Bileth with Baffin, afterwards made their voyages. In our most recent Arctic chart (published in 1845), it is stated by mistake that Bileth was under Baffin's orders. When Hudson, in the joyful hope that he had at last discovered the long-wished-for passage, entered the straits which will ever be called after him, he bestowed names on the capes and islands in the following order:—God's Great Mercie, Hold with Hope, Magna Britannia, Henry (after the Prince of Wales, successor to the throne), James (after the King), Ann (after the Queen), Charles (after the second son of the King, and afterwards King himself), Salisbury (after Robert Cecil, son of William), and lastly, at the entrance into the bay, likewise named after him, Digges and Wolstenholme.

It happened that the cape to which Sir Dudley Digges' name was assigned, did not form a part of the main land, but of an island. Digges' Island became frequented; and when the sailors were returning with the vessel in the following spring, after the wicked deed perpetrated on Hudson, the principal supercargo, Henry Green, and some others, were murdered on it by the savages. Abacuck Pricket, who was in Sir Dudley Digges' service, gave such an account, on his return, of the strong westerly current near Digges' Island, by which the vessel which had touched on a rock there was floated off, that Sir Dudley determined on sending another vessel there in the following year (1612).

In 1611, Sir Thomas Smith, Governor of the

Russia Company, dispatched two vessels, the "Mary Margaret" and the "Elizabeth," to Spitzbergen, which had been visited by Poole in the preceding year; the first of these was commanded in chief by Edge, whilst Bennet was the sailing-master, and Poole was captain of the other. The latter was to endeavour to reach the North Pole from Spitzbergen (New Land, Greenland), but only advanced as far as the eightieth degree. With Edge were six skilful whalers from St. Jean de Luz. The ice in the bays was an obstacle to the fishery, nevertheless they caught one whale, and from its blubber oil was boiled, for the first time in Spitzbergen, in the bay which, in 1610, had been named Crosse Road by Poole, and which was probably situated in the north part of the island. Oil was likewise obtained at Foule Sound, from the walruses which were killed there. Both vessels were lost, and the whole of the crews returned in a vessel which arrived at Spitzbergen from Hull for the whale fishery, viz., the "Hopewell," commanded by Captain Thomas Marmaduke. Some of the oil which was on board the other vessels, was likewise brought in her to England.

Sir Thomas Smith, at the same time that he sent the two above-named vessels in 1611, dispatched Josias Logan, whom Cherry had placed as factor at Kola, with William Pursglove, an assistant, and Marmaduke Wilson, an apprentice, to Pustosersk, not far from the Petschora river, in order, if possible, there to establish a direct trade with England; for at Moscow, at that time, no attention was paid to commercial affairs. On board the "Amitié," a vessel commanded by James Vaden, and which brought the above-named persons to the Petschora, the pilot was William Gordon, the same who with Bennet was sent by Cherry to the north in 1603, and first arrived at Cherry Island; moreover, the interpreter was Richard Finch, who had learnt Russian at the factory at Moscow, and who, as we shall see, was in 1605 dispatched by the pseudo-Demetrius after Sir Thomas Smith, who was on his road from Moscow to Archangel.

On the bar across the Petschora mouth, formed by Petschorsky and Medgansky-Savorot, the vessel touched the ground, but was got off and passed over without any damage. The cape, now called by us Russky Savorot, which bounds the Petschora mouth to the west, is always named by Finch Petschorsky Savorot. It is thus set down in the chart of our north coast, which we shall hereafter mention more particularly, and which Isaac Massa has preserved for us, and this is probably a better appellation than the other. Finch correctly indicates the position of the islands of Dolgoi and Ostroff, which are inside this Savorot in the Ssuchoe Loch, and remarks that they must not be confounded with the other Dolgoi islands, situated to the south of Matvejeff Ostroff. The Mangasei coasters sailed to Matvejeff Island from the mouth of the Petschora in thirty hours with a fair wind, and from thence to the Yugorian inlet in nine hours. Linschoten, in 1594, copied the inscription found on a large wooden cross, discovered on Matvejeff Island, which was then named by the

Dutch, Mauritius Island. This cross stood on the west side of a narrow spit turned to the north. Forster confounded the islands of Matvejeff and Dolgoi with each other. Logan calls the Medünskoi Savorot of the present chart, Medenskoi, and Finch, Mendanetzkoi.

The "Amitié" lay at anchor in the bay, when, on the 11th of July, Logan, Pursglove, and Gordon were rowed in the shallop by six men through Ssuchoje More to the Petschora river, in order to ascend it as far as Pustosersk, which they reached on the 16th. On the way they called at several fishermen's huts, the owners of which fled, because they took the strangers at first sight for Poles; indeed, in one instance they fired on the sailors remaining in the boat. The people's terrors were usually dispelled by *aqua vitæ*.

In 1611, Pustosersk, notwithstanding a destructive fire which had taken place shortly before, still contained about one hundred houses and three churches. It had no Vaivode; for the last, as Logan related, set fire to the castle in the winter of 1610-11, by which a hundred houses perished in the flames; and he then took his departure. Logan said: "In times past these places have been good for trading; but now, by reason of a bad Governour, in these troublesome times, upon a spleene he has fired the towne, and burned above an hundred houses, and so by that means they have fallen into poverty, and trading has decayed by reason of his great exactions." Now, on the arrival of the English, the tax-gatherers were the highest public functionaries in the place. It was only after eight days' deliberation that they gave Logan and his two companions permission to take up a temporary residence at Pustosersk. " In the meantime wee made much of them, and feasted them with our aqua vitæ, biscuit, and figs, that we might the better obtayne their love." It was a fortunate circumstance that just at the commencement Logan was recognised by a native of Cholmogorü who was present, at whose uncle's he had resided for a twelvemonth at Kola, and where he had been previously seen by him. They did not fail, moreover, to display copies of the different charters granted by the Czar up to that time. Logan afterwards dwelt, strangely enough, at the house of a Pole, Jurgevitch (Uriavich), who had been some time before a prisoner at Tobolsk and at Beresov, but had returned to Moscow. At the time of his conversion to the Greek Church he received the name of Trifon. On the 25th, Gordon and Pursglove returned to the "Amitié" with some wares they had purchased—the former to sail further on, but the latter with the intention of going back to Pustosersk with Wilson, and bringing with him from the vessel sundry commodities for trading.

From Logan and Pursglove, as well as from Gordon, who accompanied them from the vessel to the city, we learn much of that region, especially with reference to its branches of industry and trade. Josias Logan was an acquaintance of Hakluyt's, then a canon in Westminster Abbey. Hence it was that Logan and Gordon (on the 17th of June) bestowed

Hakluyt's name on a river on Koljujeff Island, in the same way that similar testimonials of respect had been given him elsewhere by the Russia Company's agents. Thus his name appears on the north side of Spitzbergen, and likewise in Baffin's Bay, quite close to that of Sir Thomas Smith. Logan wrote to Hakluyt on the 24th of July, viz. on the evening prior to Gordon's return to the vessel which was awaiting him in Petschora Bay, that in the winter two (he afterwards says three) thousand Samoiedes arrived at Pustosersk with goods, amongst which might be some that the English had not even dreamt of ("which may be such as we dreamed not on yet"). He heard of the Jenisei river, which flows near China, and as he by chance saw a piece of an elephant's tooth, which had been purchased from a Samoiede (and which was probably procured from a fossil), he believed himself to be on the right road to China ("you may perceive what hope there is of this enterprise"). On the 16th of August he wrote again from Pustosersk to Hakluyt, mentioning the abundance of salmon, beluga, walrus, and seal-oil; white foxes and feathers. He points out the route by water through the Jugorsky to the Oby, and mentions the Jenisei, the Tungousi, &c. Logan considered this information so interesting, that he requested Hakluyt to furnish the Earl of Salisbury (Robert Cecil), Lord High Treasurer, with a copy of the letter. This information was repeated in 1611 to Hakluyt, the celebrated historian of voyages. As he died in 1616, when he had made no use of Logan's letters, they afterwards came into the possession of

Purchas, who published them. At Pustosersk, the young Andreas Artamonovitch Matvejeff spent three years (from 1677 to 1680) with his exiled father, Artamon Sserjevitch, and his preceptor, Poborsky the Pole, who had voluntarily accompanied him. The father was, as we know, a favourite of the Czar, Alexis Michaelovitch; and in his house the latter became acquainted with Natalia Kirilovna, Peter's mother. In 1691 the son was Vaivode of the Dwina district, and in 1699 Ambassador to Holland. In 1708 he was Ambassador to Louis the Fourteenth of France, and in 1707 to Queen Anne of England, where (in London) he was arrested in the street for a small debt. In 1712 he was Ambassador to Vienna, and in 1715 Count of the Holy Roman Empire. His eldest daughter was grandmother of the imperial chancellor, Count Rumanzoff.

The chief industrial occupation of the Pustoserkers was the fishery of the Beluga Dolphin ("Delphinus leuca"), near Cape Bolvan, to the east of the extensive delta of the Petschora, for the purpose of extracting their oil, and of salmon ("Salmo nobilis"), and salmon-trout ("Salmo omul"), for their own use as well as for salting them down for exportation. Pursglove was himself present, in 1612, at the fishing for belugas at Bolvanovsky Cape. About fifty boats, each with three or four men, had arrived there from Pustosersk, distant two days' sail, on the 23rd and 24th June. He describes the size of the belugas, the mode of harpooning them, and the abundance of oil which they produce. This fishery lasted from the 24th of June until the 20th of July, and then they proceeded to their chase after the ducks, geese, and swans. The walrus-hunt, for the oil, teeth, and hides, was carried on by the Pustoserskers at the same places frequented by the natives of the Mesen, Pinega, and Dwina, viz. at Waigat and on the coast of Nova Zembla, as well the Karian Sea. In Isaac Massa's very interesting map, we find seventy mouths of the Dwina set down at the Petschora delta. This map, published by Hassel Gerard in 1613, and unseen by Muller, was originally drawn up at Moscow, with the names of the places in the Russian language, including all that existed up to the year 1601, for it contained the city of Tasovskoi-Gorod, which was built in this year on the eastern shore of the Tas, which was also called Mangasei.

Logan said that in 1610 the Pustoserskers caught fifteen thousand salmon, and describes them as very fat. Three of them usually weighed a pood. As much as from one to four Russian pence (dengi) were paid for the fish. From eighty to one hundred salmon were exchanged for a pood of salt. The salmon were so plentiful at Cape Bolvanoff, that at the end of the summer the fishermen knew not what to do with them, and many were actually spoilt, especially when salt was dear.

Finch wrote that the Omuli (wandering salmon) were caught particularly near both the Selennüja Islands (great and small), situated opposite to Medjansky Savorot. He describes them as resembling mackerel ("like maccarels"); and Logan says that it was a fish of very good flavour ("a very sweet fish").

The Pustoserkers also carried on a chase after geese, ducks, swans, and white grouse (the English wrote partridges), partly on account of the flesh, which was used fresh, and salted for winter, and partly on account of the feathers, with which they traded, and of which Logan immediately purchased a considerable quantity (five-and-forty sacks full), and shipped them on board the vessel which was returning with Gordon and Finch. White grouse feathers were sold by the Pustoserskers at five altins the pood; duck feathers, including the down, at seven to eight altins. Formerly white grouse feathers had been given away by the Cholmogorü people for two-pence (dengi) a pood and a piece of soap, which at Cholmogorü cost ten pence (dengi).

From Logan and Pursglove's descriptions, it appears that Lamposhna (on an island on the Mesen) was no longer, in 1611, the place it was for some years after Chancellor's arrival in Russia, where a great market was held; but instead of this fair, there was then an important village, where now stands the chief town of Mesen. This place was founded by the Okladnikoffs from Novogorod. It is to be wished that the lower portion of the river Mesen—at all events, as far as a little above Lamposhna—were properly set down on a chart. One place, called Mesen, was formerly situated higher up the river of this name. Hither, twice every winter, viz. before Advent and before the great fasts, "Permacks" and Samoiedes came in great numbers to carry on a trade by barter with the Russians, who assembled there from Cholmogorü, Vologda, and other places. The inhabitants of Pustosersk were wont to bring principally salmon and omuli (omellies) in sledges drawn by reindeer. From Sslobodka they were conveyed farther on by horses. Almost all the Pustoserskers travelled with their own reindeer. Some of them possessed as many as twenty or thirty, which in winter were let out for the conveyance of fish, and in summer were entrusted to the care of the Samoiedes. In November, 1611, about seventy reindeer sledges proceeded with fish from Pustosersk to Sslobodka.

On the 23rd of November, 1611, Pursglove travelled from Pustosersk to Sslobodka with the reindeer caravan, named "Argish," which consisted of two hundred and ten sledges (Narten), to almost all of which two reindeer were yoked. About two hundred loose reindeer likewise went with them.

The road from Pustosersk to Sslobodka, the present city of Mesen, lies over the chain of mountains which we are accustomed to call Timan, and to which the name of Tschaitzin Kamen is also often applied. Pursglove simply calls it "Camen;" and as he had newly arrived in the country, he probably repeated the name just as he had heard it from the Russians in 1611. Loschak, the master of the fishing-boat, speaking to Stephen Burrough in 1556, gave the mountain chain at the Yugarion Inlet the name of "Bolschoi Cumen." One continuation of the Ural we clearly see at Waigat, and we might well expect to discover one of the Timan at the Peninsula of Kanin. Might not, then, Kanin be a corruption of Kamen? Kanin Noss then would properly have been called Kamennoi Noss, and meant the Cape of the Timan chain. If Russians, who, like Pursglove, had travelled by the land route between Sslobodka and Pustosersk, and thus had passed over the Kamen, stretching to the north-west, were now to undertake to go thither by water, they would again find the Kamen at the solstitial point of their voyage. This Kamen the Samoiedes, or other strangers, may have turned into Kanin. For the reading world, the present Kanin Noss received this name on the 8th of July, 1556. On this day Stephen Burrough wrote in his journal, " We plyed neerer the heedland which is called Caninoz." This name he heard from the fishermen whom he brought in his company from the Kola Gulf, and may, like so many others, have noted it down incorrectly. The Dutch, in 1594-1597, had made Candinoes and Candenoes out of Burrough's Caninoz. In Linskoten's map, Camenkh still stands, together with Candenos. On the before-mentioned chart, representing the south coast of the White Sea, Waigat, Nova Zembla, and the Karian Sea, (which Isaac Massa succeeded in procuring at Moscow,) we find Canninoos and Caninoos. In 1611, Gordon wrote that in conversation the Cape was " corruptly" termed Candinos, for that it was really Callinos. Is it not probable that Gordon here intended to write Canninos? The Russian explanation on the large map ("bolsckoi tschertesh") has it,

"Konez gorü Schamagodskago (Ssamojedskago?) Kamini" (end of the Samoiede Kamen). The word Kanin does not here appear. At Pustosersk the distance from "Menschoi Kamen," the Timan, is quoted. Linguists should examine whether Timan may not have gradually been produced from Kamen. We find the word likewise changed into Kimin (Cuminum, Carraway), Timon, and even Tinin.

Ten altins were paid for the hire of a yoke of reindeer from Pustosersk to Sslobodka, which journey, a distance of nearly five hundred versts, was generally performed in sixteen days. At Sslobodka, where Pursglove arrived on the 9th of December, he unexpectedly found an Englishman established, named Thomas Ligon, who was glad to be able to entertain him in his house. This Ligon had been servant to Richard Cockes, one of the persons previously employed by the company in Russia. Cockes, together with five others, was alluded to by Queen Elizabeth in a letter to the Czar Theodore Ivanovitch, dated the 14th of January, 1592, as faithless to the company. Cockes was nevertheless a member of the company in London at a later period, and his name appears in the charter granted to it in December, 1604 by the pseudo-Demetrius. In writing of his meeting with Ligon at Sslobodka, Pursglove says: "Saluting mee in English, he marvelled much to meet me there, and caried me from the rest of my company to his lodging, and gave me there very kind entertaynement. The next morning I departed thence in his sled, having overnight hired a horse to the next towne, which was fifteen versts off, and so travelling day and night, changing horses at every convenient place." From Sslobodka Pursglove travelled in a horse-sledge to Cholmogorü, where he met Fabian Smith, the Anglo-Russian Company's agent. This journey was performed by the loaded sledges in six days, and fourpence (dengi) per pood were paid for carriage. Pursglove went back to Sslobodka in the like manner, for the purpose of returning with the reindeer-caravan to Pustosersk, which this time consisted of two hundred and fifty sledges. He reached that place on the 5th of January, 1612.

Ust Zülven is a place situated more than two hundred versts south of Pustosersk, higher up the Petschora, just opposite to the embouchure (ustje) of the Zülven. Logan embarked in a boat to proceed up the Petschora, with his host, the Pole, Jurjevitch, on the 26th of May, 1612; the passage lasted four days. On the 9th of June he quitted Ust Zülven, and on the 11th returned to Pustosersk.

He had been informed, as Finch had been before him, that he would find at the Petschora many elk-hides, as well as beaver, and other furs. He took with him principally cloth and copper kettles for barter, but did not succeed in trading as much as he had expected. The place he describes as a village, with about forty houses. According to the description of the " Bolschoi Tschertesh," there was then, as now, a church dedicated to the miracle-working St. Nicholas. Formerly it was written Tschilma, as well as Schulma. Logan found the barley growing near

Ust Zülven to be nearly as white as rice; and rye was likewise cultivated there.

On the 24th of June Pursglove was sent by Logan to the mouth of the Petschora, where the fishery of belugas and omuli then began, with orders to purchase all the beluga oil on the spot. On the 5th of August, Logan and Wilson joined him there, with a view to assist at the conclusion of the oil-boiling. The casks were then placed on board a fishing craft (Lodge), and brought by Logan and his two companions to Archangel, whence all three proceeded to Cholmogorü, and arrived there on the 29th of September.

The "Amitié," the vessel which brought them to Petschora the previous year, had set sail immediately after Gordon's return from Pustosersk, on the 1st of August, 1611.

The day before its departure from the Petschora Gulf (on the 31st of July), a fleet of about thirty kotschen, or lodgen (coasting and fishing craft), sailed into it. These came from Ustjug, Cholmogorü, Pinega, and Mesen. Mangasei had been their destination; but, through contrary winds and the late season, they had given up the voyage, and decided on leaving the craft with their cargoes at Pustosersk for the winter, proceeding themselves to their homes in small boats on the Zulma, and then on the Pesa, and other rivers. They were loaded with meal, bacon, butter, oatmeal "tolokno" (pounded and dried oats), and salt, as well as with some yeast, leather, and cloth. For Pustosersk itself only two craft had arrived in 1611 with similar commodities. As they mostly fed on fish, little meal and that of poor quality, was consumed.

I here quote some remarks from Logan's journal, with reference to his stay at Pustosersk, because we really know so very little of the habits of the people at that time in this remote spot. On the 12th of January, 1612, an order reached Pustosersk for a complete fast to be observed during three whole days and nights; even infants were not to be exempted. It began on the following day: "They neither eating nor drinking so much as water, neither admitted they their sucking babes, save those that fainted, to whom they gave a few figs and a little water." On the 23rd, the "Carritchey" (properly Churjutschi) Samoiedes arrived at Pustosersk. Logan invited their chief, with his son, grandson, and nephew, to dinner on the 30th. He related that they were in open war with the Samoiedes of Mangasei, and that consequently on this occasion they had been able to bring but few commodities with them. He mentioned that two years previously they had seen some other vessels near Waigat, but had been afraid to show themselves. "They seemed to be glad of our coming, when they saw our behaviour, and the entertainment they had of us. Nevertheless they are very timerous, and unreasonable covetous, as by more acquaintance I perceived by them." On the 2nd of February most of the Samoiedes proceeded with their goods to Sslobodka (on the Mesen). On the 1st of March the Russians departed, with the goods they had obtained by barter. On the 11th of April the Pustoserskers returned from Sslobodka, bringing rye, rye-meal, and other provisions. On the 21st of June seven "Ssoimas" belonging to Pustosersk, Ust Zülma, Pinega, and Mesen, sailed for Mangasei—Logan and Pursglove wrote Molgomsey, Gordon Mongauzey and Munganzea. According to Müller, the Samoiedes inhabiting the country about the Tas were called Mokassei. This was the origin of the Russian name of Mangasei, bestowed upon this region, as well as upon the city built there in 1601, but in no way was it derived from the European word Magazin.

In London orders had been given to Gordon and Finch, that, if they did not find walruses (mohorses) somewhere in considerable numbers, they were to endeavour either to reach the Oby from the Petschora, or discover Sir Hugh Willoughby's (problematical) Land. After this they were to touch at Cherry Island on their way home. But as the vessel had been obliged to lie at anchor for so considerable a period in the Petschora Gulf, they could neither approach Nova Zembla on account of the ice in the Straits of Waigat, nor was any Willoughby's Land to be discovered; and when they reached Cherry Island, Poole had not long before quitted it in the "Elizabeth" for Spitzbergen, as they learnt from a letter which he had left behind him. They set sail, therefore, in the "Amitié," for the Thames.

CHAPTER XIII.

EXPEDITIONS OF THE RUSSIA COMPANY FROM 1612—THEIR UTILITY IN THE ADVANCEMENT OF SCIENCE.

In 1612 the Russia Company sent two vessels to Spitzbergen, the "Seahorse," under the command of Thomas Edge, and the "Whale," under John Russell. On board of one of these was Gordon, who, as we have just seen, had, with Finch, accompanied Logan to the Petschora, and likewise visited the town of Pustosersk. They fell in with a Dutch and a Spanish ship, both commanded by Englishmen who had been in the company's service. One of them, Allen Sallowes, had made many voyages between the Thames and the Dwina, and the other, Nicholas Woodcock, had served under Jonas Poole. Both these foreign ships were ordered off by Edge.

Edge ordered Sallowes to come on board his ship, but allowed him to depart in freedom. Woodcock, on his return to London, was imprisoned for eighteen months, but in 1614 we find him again at Spitzbergen, as commander of the "Prosperus."

Thomas Marmaduke, from Hull, who, without the Russia Company's permission, often sailed to Spitzbergen, attained the eighty-second degree of north latitude in 1612, with his ship, the "Hopewell." In the preceding year, Woodcock, who, after the loss of Edge's vessel, had returned to Spitzbergen with some others of the wrecked crew who were proceeding to Cherry Island in boats, piloted him into the bay of "Crosse Road," which was well adapted to the whale fishery; and this moreover led, after the loss of the second vessel, to the safety of the crews of both. Marmaduke presumed to erect a cross at Spitzbergen in 1612, as if he were the first that had discovered it. I must here observe, by the way, that an English vessel, the "Diana," commanded by "Thomas Bustion, dwelling at Wapping Wall," arrived at Foule Sound in 1612. The vessel in which Tradescant and Sir Dudley Digges made their voyage to Archangel, was called the "Diana," and belonged to Newcastle.

In the ensuing year, 1613, seven vessels were dispatched to Spitzbergen by the Russia Company. Amongst them was a man-of-war, the "Tigris," of 21 guns, commanded by Captain Benjamin Joseph. In this vessel William Baffin, afterwards so well-known, served in a subordinate capacity; but he has been incorrectly called the chief of this expedition. He had already, in the preceding year, accompanied James Hall on his fourth voyage, and given a description of it. During the summer many vessels of other nations arrived at Spitzbergen. One of these was again conducted there by Thomas Bonner, an Englishman, who had been in the service of the company. Captain Joseph, who had a royal commission, under the Great Seal, sent all these vessels away, taking Bonner, and the Dutch vessel commanded by him, to England.

In 1614, three vessels and two pinnaces dispatched by the Russia Company sailed for Spitzbergen, where they found eighteen Dutch ships, of which four were men-of-war, each of thirty guns. Against such a force it was natural that the company's vessels could do nothing. Robert Fotheby, who commanded the ship "Thmasine," on board of which was also William Baffin, set up in Maudlen Sound, on the 23rd of June, a cross with the escutcheon of King James the First, under which was nailed a sheet of lead, with the Russia Company's cipher, and a sixpence. He took some of the earth with him, and made another voyage to the north, but this had no further result, although he maintained that he had advanced beyond the eightieth degree of latitude.

In the year just mentioned, William Gordon, with whom we are already well acquainted, made a journey from Pustosersk to Yugoria, which is interesting; for, in the first place, it shows us with precision that, contrary to Lehrberg's opinion, Yugoria was, at least partly, to the west of the Northern Ural; and, secondly, because we thence see that the assertion made by Fischer, that in 1607 the Pustoserskers' travels extended only as far as Rogovoi Gorodok, and that the place was desolate, is not well founded, for here we find that Gordon also proceeded as far as Rogovoi Gorodok. Logan likewise wrote, during his residence at Pustosersk in 1611, that, on the 4th of December, the inhabitants of the town departed by land to

Yugoria (not "Ingoria"), for the purpose of trading with the natives of that place and the Samoiedes.

On the 19th of January, 1612, the Pustoserskers, who had travelled as far as "Ingoria," returned. They had been unable to purchase much ("had but a hard voyage"), because the Karatschei Samoiedes had been prevented from proceeding thither by the hostilities then existing with those of Mangasei, viz. with the Mokaseis at Tasowskoi-gorod, whence came the best sable furs which found their way into Russia. On the 8th of September, 1611, Logan had noted down that a Pustoserskan craft (a "soyma") descended the river in order to sail for Yugoria, but did not leave the Petschora, and was obliged to give up the voyage.

As Logan then knew the Russian language, and had resided at Pustosersk since July, the names he gives are doubtless correct.

Gordon writes that on the 20th of November, 1614, about four o'clock, he started from Pustosersk for Yugoria (" to Yongorie "). All the rivers across which his journey lay, are named by him, and he mentions in which direction they flow, and likewise where they disembogue; the distances travelled are likewise given. Each day's journey is set down, and the weather, the state of the road, and incidents of every kind described. The following are the names of the rivers :—The Schapkina (which flows into the Petschora), the Novgorotka (falling, according to Gordon, into the Schapkina, but I have not been able to find this river on any map), the Habeaga (which joins the Petschora), the Hargena (according to Gordon, a tributary of the Kolva, perhaps the Charajaga), the Colvoy (Kolva, falling into the Ussa), and the Ssandavets. This tributary of the Kolva is now called Ssandivei. Gordon, with his company, ascended the Kolva six or seven miles in an east by north direction, and reached its conflux with the Ssandavets. The Kolva there flows from the north-east, the Ssandavets from the south-east. Here they traversed the plain lying between both rivers in an east and somewhat southerly direction, for twelve miles, when they took up their quarters for the night, and on the following day, the 6th of December, the festival of St. Nicholas was kept, which is thus described by Gordon:—" The sixth being Saint Nicholas day, which, with the Russes, is held a principall day, in the morning they caused their Images to bee brought into the chrome, lighting wax candles before them, making their prayers to them, according to their order; after which, I gave them a bottle of aqua vitæ, with which the guides were drunk that they could not guide their deeres, but set me to direct the way by compasse, which I did all the day, although I had but little skill: we went south-east and by east twenty miles. The seventh day being very faire weather, our guides lay all the day with *Pohmeall* and could not goe forward." For those who do not understand Russian it is to be observed that the word Pochmelje, which Gordon here quotes, means the sickly feeling which follows intoxication. The root of the word is chmel, humulus: hops. The common people who naturally had no idea of the formation of alcohol during the chemical process of the fermentation of the beer, appear to have supposed that the hops gave it its intoxicating quality.

Gordon next notices a rivulet, without name, which flows into the Ssandavets, the Hoseada (which falls into the Ashva), and the Azua (Ashva, a tributary of the Ussa). The road then lay over a considerable ridge, named Yangorda (nowhere marked on the map), then over the smaller Rogovaja, and a plain called Koräpunia Tundra, after a Russian of the name of Koräpa (Correapa), who died and was buried there some thirty years before. At last they reached (on the 18th of December), at midnight, the greater Rogovaja, where was situated the Gorodok of the Russians, who here carried on their trade by barter with the Samoiedes. I have nowhere found two rivers of the name of Rogovaja marked on the maps. Gordon says of each of them, that it falls into the Ussa. (It might be an addition to Krestinin's reputation to state that he mentions two rivers Rogowaja.) Gordon remained here until the 6th of January, 1615. On the 30th of December he took an observation with his astrolabe, and found the sun to be two degrees above the horizon. He sets it down as in 65° 8' latitude, but it must have been at least a degree lower. Fischer has set down Rogovoi Gorodok on his map in 65 degrees and about 25 minutes latitude. On the 6th of January, 1615, Gordon commenced his journey homewards, which lay exactly along the same route, and reached Pustosersk on the 19th. The accounts given by Gordon, Logan, and Finch, of the annual journeys from the other side of the Yugorian chain, made by caravans of trading Karatscheja Samoiedes to Rogovoi Gorodok, and by way of Pustosersk to Sslobodka on the Mesen, make it probable that the fifty Samoiedes and two hundred reindeer, which were captured on the Yugorian chain, when the Princes Uschatoi and Kurbsky took the field against the Yugorians about the year 1500, formed such a caravan proceeding to the west. It fell in with a detachment of the Russian troops, because it was not aware of their line of march. The place where our warriors quitted the Petschora, up whose stream they had ascended, may have been Us Ussa. Neither Müller nor Lehrberg knew what to make of this word, which had been incorrectly copied Ustascha. It is much to be regretted that we have not a map of the Ussa and its surrounding country. Here, for a considerable period, was carried on the communication between Europe and Asia.

According to Gordon's calculation, he had travelled to and fro nine hundred and eighteen miles with reindeer. The last hundred and fifty miles were traversed without resting. Travellers were accustomed to leave the " Argisch " with the loaded sledges behind them, and hasten forwards with the finest animals. This Gordon, as well as Pursglove, calls travelling post ("riding post"). Gordon writes with reference to this posting and the " Argisch," as follows :—" Two deere being yoaked to a sled, they will runne with such swiftnesse and so long to continue, as is not to be believed, except to those that have seene the same. For riding post, they will ride without rest or sleepe two hundred miles in four and twentie hours, but with their argish or stuffe thirtie miles in twelve houres; their women usually doe guide their argish, which is ten sleds, and to every sled a bucke, all made fast one after another." When Pursglove, in January, 1612, travelled back from Sslobodka to Pustosersk with the argish ("argeshey"), he traversed, in company with seven other post-sledges, the last hundred and fifty versts in forty hours.

It is greatly to be desired that the course of both the Rogovaja rivers and the site of the ancient Gorodok on the easternmost and largest of them, were correctly fixed by inspection of the spot. It is probable that this place was, a considerable time since, the solstitial point for commercial relations between two continents. It occupied the same position between Europe and Asia as Kiachta now does with regard to Russia's trade with China. So early as 1092, Nestor had heard from the mouth of an inhabitant of Novogorod, named Gury Rogovitsch, what had been related at Gorodok, to his clerk, who had travelled from Pustosersk to Yugoria. It had reference to the chain lying between the place visited by the traveller and a gulf of the sea. Similar journeys may have been by no means uncommon, if not for the Novogoroders themselves, at all events for their tributaries the Pustoserskers; and it is possible that the place in Yugoria, to which Nestor alludes, was the very same where local circumstances contributed to the establishment of the Rogovoi Gorodok, visited by Gordon. The coincidence between the name of the place and that of the native of Novogorod seen by Nestor is remarkable.

The generally circumspect Lehrberg has allowed himself to be so far misled by partial and incorrect statements, as to maintain that Yugoria did not lie in European Russia, but just to the east of the Ural. Gordon, whose journey took place about the time that this description of the map of Russia was drawn up, convinces us that this assertion of our historian is unfounded, for a part of Yugoria was situated in Europe and another in Asia.

That Yugoria extended west from the Ural to the sea, is evident, amongst other things, from the instructions given to Stephen and William Burrough, at Rose Island, at the beginning of August, 1568, for the expedition which was to sail in the summer of 1569, from the Dwina, or rather from the Petschora to the East, for the purpose of making geographical discoveries and observations along the coast on the further side of Waigat. Both brothers had, as we are aware, accompanied Chancellor to Russia, in 1553, and in 1558 made a similar voyage to Waigat and Nova Zembla. They had, on this occasion, brought the Ambassador Randolph from England to Rose Island. James Bassington (Bassendine) was to sail in their track from the Petschora along the sea-coast of Yugoria ("by the sea-coast of Hungorie") to the passage between this and Waigat. The position of this island and of Nova Zembla the Burroughs had laid down on a chart ("which islands you shall find noted in your plat"). On the other side of Waigat, they write, there was a bay extending southward into Yugoria ("a bay that doth bite to the southwards into the land of Hugory"), and into which two rivers, the Kara and the "Naramsy," flow. This Gulf of Kara is probably that to which, in the eleventh century, the Yugorians, in speaking to Rogovitsch's clerk, gave the name of Luka (a bay), Morja (the sea). If Rogovitsch's travelling agent was, like Gordon, on the greater Rogovaja, the geographical part of the communication made by Nestor is intelligible, for between this Rogovaja and the above-named Luka morja is situated the Yugorian chain, which is above five thousand feet in height. So soon as this is examined in a geographical, geological, and especially in a scientific point of view, we shall be enabled to determine more accurately what was the true meaning of the account given by the Yugorians to the traveller alluded to. The whole question probably reduces itself to this: viz. that, at that time, Chürgutschi or Mugassi (arrowless) Samoiedes hunted on the Yugorian mountain chain, and desired to barter their peltries for iron with the Yugorians, who accidentally fell in with them. This latter commodity they required for their arrowheads and other purposes. Nestor's explanation shows his extensive reading.

Gordon's Rogovoi Gorodok was, perhaps, a place formerly inhabited by the Yugorians. Even without being better acquainted with the locality, we may hazard a conjecture that this was one of those Gorodoks or Gorods (towns) which the Novogoroders sought to overcome by force of arms, in 1193. The Yugorians, as we know, brought silver for barter with the Novogoroders, besides sables and other wares. Consequently that metal must have been a production of mining industry in the East at that remote period, of which so many traces have been discovered in Siberia.

Wilson, who at the time of Gordon's journey to Rogovoi Gorodok, was at the village of Ush-Ulma, previously visited by Logan, in 1612, had there spent the whole winter of 1614-15, for trading purposes; and on the 9th of June, 1615, returned to Gordon, at Pustosersk, with the peltries he had collected. Neither Logan nor Gordon says anything of the ores found in the upper part of the Zülma. This mineral treasure had, even so early as the end of the fifteenth century, attracted the attention of the Government, so that in 1491, by order of the Czar Ivan Vassilovitch, two miners, who had been engaged abroad, were sent there, accompanied by the before-named Greek, Manuel Ivanovitch Raleff, as interpreter and escort. In 1839, at the instigation of Michailo Ivanoff Resarzoff, the Vätten merchant, not only was a fresh inspection of the spot ordered, but smelting works were established, which, however, were soon abandoned. Okladnikoff, the before-named native of Mesen, who was appointed to superintend this business, assures me that a favourable result might have been expected; but unfortunately we possess no geological, and, indeed, not even one good geographical description of this district, which is so interesting to industry in a double point of view. We say this, for in the neighbourhood of the spot where the earliest discovery of ores took place in our country, of which we have any account, there was also the important portage ten versts over land and five over lakes, through which the Rotschuga (the Pjesa) is brought into connection with the Tschirten (Zülma), and, consequently, the north of Russia with the Petschora country, Yugoria, and the Ural. Resanzoff might, however, have found the copper ore near the Ssula, about one hundred versts above its mouth, better than that smelted in the neighbourhood of the Zülma. The Ssula falls into the Petschora, somewhat south of the village of Velikovussotschnaja. Near the Rudjanka and Tshirten the ore must be very rich in silver. On the 21st of August, Wilson and Gordon sailed, together with John Copman and Thomas Dogget, from the Gulf of Petchora, for Holland.

At the time of Gordon's description of his residence at this Bay, the Islands of Glubokoi and Lovezkoi, the Sacharjeff Bereg shore, and the Kusnetzkaja bight, ("Casnet's Nose;" Messa has it Coscaja Nusnaja,) were known under the same names. To the shallows (Gulajevskija Koschki) Gordon gives that of "Drie Sea:" in 1611 he also quoted, as Russian names, "Suchoi morie." Massa has on his map "Socchoiamore."

While Gordon was active in the remote Petschora district, the Russia Company, notwithstanding the foreign competition which they encountered, had dispatched two large ships and two pinnaces to Spitzbergen; Captain Joseph commanded one, and Edge the other vessel. The Dutch arrived with three men-of-war and eleven other ships, consequently nothing could then be done against them. From Denmark three men-of-war arrived, for the purpose of levying a duty on the English. These were the first Danish vessels which visited Spitzbergen, and they were shown the way by James Voden, the same who in 1611 piloted Josias Logan, William Gordon, and their companions, to the Petschora, but was now faithless to the Russia Company. Fotherby went on a voyage of discovery to the north in a pinnace, but did not advance further than his predecessors.

In 1616, eight large vessels and two pinnaces, under Edge's command, sailed from England for Spitzbergen, and reaped so rich a harvest, *i. e.* 1300 tons of train oil, that they could not take all with them. Four Dutch vessels were there at the time.

One of the English ships discovered the island named after Edge, where about a thousand walruses were killed, and their teeth taken to London.

In the ensuing year fourteen vessels, placed under Edge's command, started, together with two pinnaces, for Spitzbergen, on which occasion the venture was good, 1900 tons of train oil having been obtained. One ship went on an expedition of discovery to the East, and fell in with the island which was named after Richard Wiche, a member of the Russia Company. A Hull vessel, probably commanded by Marmaduke, also visited the east side of the island. Ten Dutch ships, of which two belonged to the navy, had preceded the English vessels to Spitzbergen. Three were from Zealand. Edge allowed these last to take away the produce of their fishery.

The Russia now joined the East India Company, and in 1618, sixteen vessels, with two pinnaces, all again placed under Edge's orders, were dispatched to Spitzbergen; but from Zealand more than twenty heavily-armed ships had arrived, and on the 19th of July a bloody battle was fought. By Tradescant's journal we have seen, that on the 4th of July a pinnace, equipped by Benjamin Deicrowe, left the vessel which conveyed Sir Dudley Digges, together with Tradescant, to Russia, in order to sail to Spitzbergen (Greenland). After this year, the English whale-fishery at Spitzbergen was abandoned.

The owners of the vessels suffered a considerable loss in 1618. Nine of the ships, with two pinnaces, were indeed dispatched in the ensuing year, by the united companies, but returned altogether unsuccessful in their venture. In 1620, some members of the Russia Company, Edge, Deicrowe, Ralph Freeman (an Alderman, from whom a Strait at Spitzbergen takes its name), and George Strowd, undertook this business on their own account, and equipped seven vessels, but met with no success. In the following year, the seven ships again dispatched to the fishery, fared somewhat better; but in 1622 the proprietors lost one out of nine vessels which they had fitted out; and this led to the abandonment of this branch of industry to the Dutch, from that period.

In the year after the return of Hudson's vessel, it was sent by Sir Thomas Smith, Sir Dudley Digges, and another person, under the command of Thomas Button, to the bay discovered by Hudson in 1610. She passed the winter of 1612–1613, as already mentioned, in the bay named after Nelson, into which the river, likewise so called, flows; and afterwards remained for some time at Digges' Island.

After Captain Gibbon, who had been to Hudson's Bay with Button, had visited it again in 1614, without any result, Robert Bileth, who had made all three previous voyages, was sent thither in 1615, when he discovered some new places.

In 1616 he was dispatched by Smith, Digges, and others, to Davis' Straits, when William Baffin was his pilot; and they succeeded in attaining the high latitude of eighty degrees north. A cape was then named after Sir Dudley Digges, a gulf after John Wolstenholme, an island after Richard Hakluyt, and a bay after Sir Thomas Smith. It is a remarkable circumstance, that the bay navigated for the first time by Bileth on this voyage should not have been named after him, but after Baffin, who was subordinate to him.

I think that I shall be enabled in the sequel to adduce proofs, that a careful examination of the MSS., very few of which were unfortunately left behind by the English who were in Russia, in the sixteenth century, might lead to not unimportant geographical elucidations.

Our geographers give the name of Nova Zembla not to one but to two islands lying north of Yugoria and Waigat; but, according to old English documents, this appellation properly appertains only to the southernmost, for the most northern of the two had originally another name, which it would now be correct to restore to it.

On the 21st of February, 1584, Russian navigators from Pustosersk acquainted Anthony Marsh, the English trading agent at Moscow, that in sailing to the Oby three islands were passed, viz. Waigat, Nova Zembla, and Matvejeva Zembla. The words rendered in English are: "If you would have us travell to seeke out the mouth of Ob by sea, we must go by the isles" (observe the plural number) "of Waygats and Nova Zembla, and by the Land of Matpherve, that is, by Matthew's Land." Christopher Holmes, who at that time (1584) was agent at Vologda, wrote that Marsh had been made acquainted with another north-eastern route from Kanin Noss to the Oby, namely by Nova Zembla and Mätjŭschin Jar, ("he learned another way by Nova Zembla Matthuschan Yar") in addition to that from "Medemsky Savorot" (in the Petschora Gulf), into the Bay of Kar (and consequently through the Yugorian straits, which separate the mainland from Waigat). From Mätjüschin Jar to the island situated opposite to the mouth of the Oby (thus Beloi Ostroff was then already known, viz. in 1584), it is five days' sail. It is, moreover, remarked that Matjuschin Jar is forty versts broad in some places, but in others not more than six. Naturally enough the discoverers did not venture to call this latter country an island; and as the southern shore (Jar) lying opposite to Nova Zembla is now called Matvejeva Zembla, this appellation has gradually been extended to all those portions of the country which were afterwards discovered towards the north, and is now applied to the whole island. The Bays or "Fiords" of the east coast, which indent the land so considerably, appear to have been known in 1584, although too small an estimate is made of the breadth of the country, viz. less than sixty versts of the present day: it was then merely conjectured.

That the judgment I have pronounced on the English documents of 1584 is the correct one, is proved by the before-mentioned map, drawn up at Moscow probably in 1604, but at the latest in 1608, and engraved for Massa in 1612 with a Dutch title. The island of Waigat is set down on it beyond Yugorsky Schar (Yugorian Inlet), which is here changed into "Gorgoscoi Tsar," and written "Weygats." Towards the north, in the broad opening of the Kara passage, is set down in Dutch, "Here you may pass over at high water, elsewhere it is dry." Then comes a large, oblong island, sloping to the north north-west, against which is written, "Nova Zemla." North of this is a channel, at whose western entrance stands "Matsei of Tsar." This should be called "Matvejeff Schar;" and proves to us that the present appellation of Matotschkin Schar is incorrect. To the north of this channel (Matvejeff Schar), we find land as far as the edges of the chart, which is altogether but six inches and a half from top to bottom. This is the land which, in the letter from Pustosersk, dated the 21st of February,

1584, is mentioned as Matvejeva Zembla (Semlja) (Matvei's Land).

From what we have adduced, it appears, 1st, that even in 1584, the straits to which the name of Matotschkin Schar is now assigned, were not only known, but used as a passage; 2ndly, that Matotschkin Schar is a corrupted name, and Mătjūschkin or Matvei's the true appellation. The name of the discoverer of this channel, situated to the north of Nova Zembla, as well as of the land in question, must have been Matvei; whence the diminutive Matjuscha. Consequently the land situated to the north of Matvei's Straits, and which we know to be an island, must have been called Matvci's, or Mătjūschin's Land. The appellation of Matvei's Land might be preferred, because a small island already mentioned, lying to the west of Yugorsky Schar, bears the name of Matvejeff Ostroff; perhaps from the same person; this original appellation is moreover analogous to that of the southern island (Nova Zembla). The small island, cape, mountains, and bay, situated not far from the passage, at the south-west corner of Matvei's Land, (and from which the first three were called Mitjuscheff, but the latter Mitjuschicha,) in all probability received their names from the same discoverer, Matjuscha, for they are all close to each other, and not far from the straits named after him. The same reasoning applies to Cape Matotschkin, which is likewise in the neighbourhood, but in Nova Zembla, and to the small river Matotschka.

Were a proof still necessary that " Matsei of Tsar"

really means Matvejeff Schar, it is to be found on Massa's map itself; for the Matvejeff Island so often mentioned lying north of Dolgoi Ostroff, and to which De Veer, in the journals of Dutch voyages, from 1594 to 1597, gives the name of "Mat Flae, Matflo," and other similar names, is there set down as "Matserf;" and in the annexed explanation of Russian names, it is said, that "Matseof means Mathy's eylant."

On the map which was first published by Massa in 1612, and then in 1613, it is observable, that after it was engraved in accordance with the Russian design, the outline of the west coasts of Nova Zembla and Matvejeff Zembla was added to it, according to Dutch maps drawn up after Barentz' voyages. By these means the position of Kostin Schar was set down very high in Nova Zembla; and the name which was placed even still higher, resembles the real one just as closely as the "Matsei of Tsar" does Matvejeff Schar, for it is Costintsarch. On the map of all Russia, dedicated by Hessel Gerard to the Czar Michael Fedorovitch, soon after his election in 1614, the "Matsei of Tsar" was omitted; probably because it was not known what it could mean; and to the channel the name of Costintsarch was given. It seems to me, that originally the year MDCXIII. was engraved on this map, and that subsequently a fourth I was added, probably because it was not ready in 1613. Gerard embodied the most essential part of Massa's small map; and this might have led people at Moscow to observe that the map of the north coast which had been drawn up there, had found its way to Holland. Massa carefully avoided mentioning the name of the person who procured him the Russian map, for he feared that he would suffer for it. ("Est sola hæc tabella rudis duntaxat illius oræ delinatio maritimæ, eamque magna molestia mihi comparavi; si vero resciscerent illi quorum interest, actum esset de Moschi illius vita, nomen ideo illius non prodimus.") The incorrect insertion of Costintsarch first in Massa's and then in Gerard's map, is also the reason why the Dutch at a later period sought a passage in vain at Kostin Schar. Kostin derives its name just in the same way as the Matsei Channel, from the diminutive of that of its discover, viz. from Kostja, which is formed from Konstantin, just as Mütajuscha is from Matvei.

Kostin Schar had already been visited by Oliver Brunel, a Netherlander, before Barentz' well-known voyage, for this is noted down by DeVeer in his journal, on the 8th of August, 1594. We have hitherto been unable to discover who this Brunel was. Foster and Barrow maintained that he must have been an Englishman. The former supposed De Veer's "Costinsarch" to mean "constant search," and the latter that it meant "coasting search."

I find it likely that this Brunel was that "Belgian" whom Johannes Balach, of Arensburg, furnished with a letter of introduction, on the 20th of February, 1581, to the well-known cosmographer Gerhard Mercator, of Dinsberg; from which it appears that his Christian name was Oliver (Olferius). He had been a prisoner in Russia, and was afterwards employed by the Stroganoffs, who were landed proprietors, first at the Vutschegda, and subsequently at the Kama and the Tschussovaja. Anika Fedoroff Stroganoff established salt works at Solwütschegodsk, as early as 1517, and commenced an important trade to the Oby with the Samoiedes. He repeatedly sent people there over the Yugorian Chain, and Oliver (Brunel) likewise travelled to the Oby over the Ural, in the Stroganoff's service. He moreover made a voyage, probably down the Petschora River, and then through the Yugorian Straits, and by the Karian Sea to the Mutnaja, up this river to the Volok, and down the Selenaja to the Oby. From Siberia, he must also have visited the Gulf of the Ta, where Tasoffskoi gorod (Mangasei) was afterwards built.

" Adiit ipse fluvium Obam tum terra per Samoedarum et Sibericorum regionem, tum mari per littus Pechoræ fluminis ad Orientem."

The "Yaks Olgush," mentioned in the letter to Mercator, quoted by Hakluyt, the meaning of which has hitherto remained a riddle, can relate to nothing else than the Ta Gulf. Perhaps Oliver mentioned it to Balach as " Taesof guba." Now (1580?) the Stroganoffs ("Yaconius et Nuekius," probably means Jakoff Anikieff, for he might still be alive at the time of Oliver's departure from Russia,) sent him to Antwerp, for the purpose of engaging experienced sailors to make voyages to the Oby, in two vessels which a Swede was then building at the Dwina for them (the Stroganoffs).

"Qui et Samojedicam linguam pulchre teneant et fluvium ob exploratum habeant, ut qui quotannis ea loca ventilant."

Oliver himself was to bring from Holland a vessel of small draft of water, into the bay near the convent of St. Nicholas, and then to Rose Island, in order to man her there with Russians, who, through their annual journeys to the Oby, knew the river well, and spoke the Samoiede language. He was then to start from Rose Island at the end of May, and employ one day in the Petschora Gulf in determining the latitude, surveying the coast, and sounding the shallows (he had previously observed a channel with but five feet water), with a view of fixing upon a good entrance channel

"Quoniam Pechoræ Sinus vel euntibus vel redeuntibus commodissimus est tum subsidii tum diversorii locus propter glaciem et tempestates." Dolgoi Island is named; probably that in the Petschora Gulf, not far from the Western Savorot, is meant.

The vessel was then to sail by Waigats to the Karian Sea.

"Sinus qui per meridiem vergens pertingit ad terram Ugoriæ, in quem adfluunt exigui duo amnes, Marinesia atque Carah, ad quos amnes gens alia Samoedorum accolit immanis et efferata." The river, which in the letter to Mercator is called Marmesia, is probably the same which, by Stephen Burrough, according to the testimony of Loschak the coasting captain (1556), is named Naramsay, but in the instructions drawn up by Stephen and William Burrough, in 1568, Naramsy. In Massa's map it is to be found considerably to the north of the Mutnaja (here Moetnaia), and set down as Nearontza. From the description given in the "Bolschoi Tschertesh" (historical sketches of the Volga), it appears that the whole western shore of the Peninsula of the Oby is called Njaromskoi, Njarmskoi, and likewise, although probably less correctly, Narümskoi bereg. In our most recent map, this river is altogether left out, as are also the historical and still more important Mutnaja and Selenaja. In Massa's chart, the Scharapovüja Koschki is set down as Sarapovi coosci. In its neighbourhood the Mutnaja, which has a lake on its south side, debouches into the Karian Sea, and on the other side of the Volok the Selenaja flows into the Gulf of Oby. In the same latitude, between the Mutnaja and the river Paderitza, is an inlet specified as Monguitzar, which, to my knowledge, is not described by any of the later navigators. My idea is, that the channel between the coast and the island to which the name of Lütke has been lately assigned, is here meant.

With reference to the inlet situated opposite Kolgujeff, Linschoten, as is well known, supposed that the word Schar, which he changes into Toxar, relates to the island lying before it, now named Ling; and he merely terms the mouths of the Schar, " ooster " and " wester gat." On Massa's chart, at the eastern mouth, is set down " bolsoitsa " (bolschoi Schar), and at the western, " tsermensei " (Schar menschoi); between both we read also " mesoetsar," which unquestionably is a repetition of the last name, menschoi

Schar. West of Kara, in the Karian Gulf, which, be it remarked, really bears some resemblance to an arrrow-head, no rivers are set down in our latest charts, whilst Massa has several; the names of those given by him as flowing into the Gulf of Karatjeff, and further west, deserve also to be taken into consideration.

Oliver was instructed next to reach the Oby, the mouth of which must, according to the testimony of the Samoiedes, be divided into seven branches: probably the Petschora is here confounded with the Oby. On the Oby he was to endeavour to get to the Tas River Gulf, which had been previously visited by another route.

The Tas River, in the neighbourhood of which, as already mentioned, the Mokasse, or, more properly the Mugassi Samoiedes dwelt, and where the best sable furs were procured, was thus known to the Stroganoffs in 1580. According to the explanation given in the "Bolschoi Tschertesh," the Tas flows into the Icy Sea.

Oliver hoped to advance still further towards the unexplored country in the east, and even to the confines of China; but in the event of his being obstructed by the ice, he contemplated returning to the Petschora, or even to the Dwina, in order to winter, and proceed with the voyage in the ensuing spring. As Vetsen now apprises us that Oliver Brunel had been to the Petschora Gulf with a vessel from Enkhuisen, but which was lost, probably in the "Ssuchoje more" (arm of the sea), now Gulajeffskija koschki, I think it may be taken for granted that he was the person dispatched to Holland by the Stroganoffs in 1580 (?), and moreover, that he was the Olferius recommended by Balach of Arensberg (on Oesel Island), to Gerhard Mercator, in February, 1581.

From what we have adduced, it appears to follow that the Stroganoffs, to whom the route across the Yugorian Chain to the Mugasse Samoiedes had long been known, at the time that they assisted Jermak, contemplated advancing along the Tschussovaja, and over the Ural into Siberia, *i. e.* in the year of the second English expedition to the east, for the purpose of exploring that country, from the coast of the Icy Sea, and, if possible, as far as China. As we are quite aware that at that time a route to the Petschora was known through Mätjūschin Schar and round the peninsula of the Oby, it is probable that Brunel would have made his way through these straits, had his vessel not perished, as already mentioned, in the Petschora Gulf. The decease of the brothers, Jakoff and Gregory Anikieff Stroganoff, and, still more, Jermak's conquest of Siberia, may have been the reason why the exploration of the north coast was considered by the remaining Stroganoffs, Semen Anikieff, and his uncles Maksim Jakoffleff and Nikita Grigorjeff, as a matter of minor importance, and consequently abandoned.

It is likely that Brunel, when a younger man, visited the Lapland coast, in one of the first Enkhuisen vessels, sent there on one of the trading voyages, commenced by Philip Vinterkonig, in 1565, and on that occasion proceeded, without permission, to the coast of the White Sea, in the same way that Cornelius de Meyer himself and Simon von Salinger travelled to Moscow, in disguise. Dutch authors, indeed, state that he came to the Dwina, and therefore either to Rose Island or to Cholmogorü, and was taken by the English for a spy, and sent to Moscow, which led to his being imprisoned for some years at Jaroslaf, whence he was released at last, through the intercession of the Stroganoffs. In Dutch the passage runs thus:—" Op verzoek van de voernaamste kooplieden te Cola, de Ameckers ontslagen." I think, however, that the word Ameckers must mean Anikieffs, and that Cola is substituted for Sol (Vütschegodskaja). Probably Brunel inspired the Stroganoffs with hopes of disposing of their stock of peltries advantageously, in Holland. He appears also to have undertaken an expedition to the latter country in their service, for in 1577 he came from thence with Jan Van de Valle to Moscow, by land. The latter was the agent of Gilles van Eychelenberg, named Hoofman (who had been previously settled at Antwerp, but then at Middleburg), and he, de Valle, was the person who set up a competition in Russia against the English Company. The first Dutch vessel, which, in 1577, came to the Dwina, belonged to Gilles Hofman; it was from Zealand, and sailed, as well as those that succeeded it, not to the Korelian mouth, which was frequented by the English, but to the Pudoshem entrance, where the Dutch then erected their warehouses. In 1584, Michael Moucheron, as agent for his brother, Balthasar, ordered his captain, Adrian Kruyt, to sail up the Pudoshem Straits as far as the convent of St. Michael the Archangel, where the city of Novo-Cholmogorü (Archangel) had just then been built; and hence it was that the Pudoshem branch of the Dwina was for a long time called Moucheron's River by the Dutch. According to the Czar's decree, promulgated in compliance with a petition presented by the Dutch, through the Chancellor Andreas Jahovlevitsch Schtschelkaloff, in 1586, they immediately removed their warehouses from the Pudoshem mouth to Novo-Cholmogorü, whilst the English, who saw this with much displeasure, remained at Rose Island until 1591.

The erroneous name of Mătjūschin Schar was given to this in 1769, and was, indeed, introduced by Pilot (who had the rank of lieutenant) Fedor Rosmüssleff, who spent a long time in this "Schar," with a view to make himself better acquainted with it. In his descriptions, journals, and charts, he incorrectly assigns to this passage the names of Matotschkin and Matotschnik Schar. Rosmüssleff's error must have been corrected, for at present the name is written Mătjūschin, Matvejeff, or Matvei's Schar, in honour of the discoverer, who unfortunately is not better known.

I must here observe, that in 1769 Rosmüssloff set down a small island of the name of Matvejeff, opposite to Besimjannoi Bay, on the west coast of Nova Zembla.

One of the principal reasons why our early knowledge of the passage between Nova Zembla and

Mătjūschĭna Zembla was lost was, that Isaac Massa himself, in his larger map "Russiæ, vulgo Moscovia dictæ, partes septentrionalis et orientalis," which is better known, and found at Blaev and elsewhere, has omitted to insert Nova Zembla as it was delineated in the chart of the west coast, drawn up by the Dutch in 1594–97. As the Dutch had not seen the passage between Nova Zembla and Matvejeva Zembla, it is naturally not set down in their charts, for it is only near Costintsarch that they have placed a narrow inlet, not stretching far inland. The places lying to the east of "Gorgoscoitsar" are introduced by Massa, in accordance with the small map he obtained at Moscow.

He has, however, forgotten to name the selenaja on the Peninsula of the Oby, whilst the "Reebnaia" and the "Tsernaià," as well as the "Pyr," are set down in his maps; he has also omitted the river "Michalova," in the neighbourhood of Yugorsky Schar, and near the Ssokolji ludü and Meescoi Islands (by us called Mässnoi and Mestnoi). The same is the case with the small river "Motsianca," which, according to the small chart, reaches to the Volok from the Tas, and from thence flows into the Turuchanka (here Toergaefhoeck), which joins the Yenissei (according to Massa, Teneseia reca), and where (in 1662) Tasorskoi gorod or Mangasei was subsequently removed. Opposite to the mouth of the Yenissei, in like manner as before that of the Oby, is an island here termed Ostorf. The mouth of the Pjassida (Peisida reca) is likewise shown on the map. Hence it appears probable that this river was known at Moscow in 1605. As the Pjassida is the last river included in this chart to the east, so it ends in the west with Una Bay, where Chancellor's ship the Bonaventure passed the winter in 1553-1554, and where, in 1694, the Czar, Peter, manufactured and placed the cross which has been preserved in the Cathedral Church at Archangel since 1805. As several of the rivers, bays, and capes situated to the west of Yugorsky Schar are omitted in our most recent charts, I will here give a list of all the names to be found on Massa's small chart:—Oscoriagoeba; to the right, the Pertomin convent, and to the left, as it appears, some salt works are set down. Testia (?) Usma Neuvonsa (the river where Chancellor landed in 1553), Ozera (a lake, from which it flows into the sea), and landwards Nenocsa osoil (this place is of importance, from its salt works), Tostieberg (berg probably stands for bereg, shore, consequently it means Tostie shore; to the eastward of it buildings are represented), Sooltsa, Codina, and monastery of Coreelscoi. The nearest mouth of the Dwina is also here called Corelsca, not Nicolskoe; then follow Podesemscoi, Monnanscoi, and Berasova. To the right of the shore of the Dwina stands the Casteel Archangeli, resembling the view in Gerard's map; along the seashore follow Moedescoi, Sechomov, Cocia osoil (the salt works are mentioned), Solotitsa (here is a village set down with a church), Morsovitz (the island), Cosci (represented as two islands), Coeloeia, Gorigorscoi noos,

Mesen (the river). As far as the Koloi and Mesen, the region is termed Somersyde. To the east of the Mesen follow Slabota, Zeitza, Malgaia, Nees, Titsa, Polosona, Kia, Toina, Canninoos, Crinca, Moscuica, Zicopa (?), Promoi, Totsa, Kolgoi (the island), Tetscaiagocba (the bay), Teesca landouve (the land lying nearest to the shore), Goloebintza, Goloebeica (?) Otma, Oitmitsa, Peisa, Peisitsa (?) Voloinga, Nidega, Swetenoos, Garnostail, Beelt. Here now comes the before-mentioned Schar, to which the names of Tsermensei, Mesoetsar, and Bolsoitsar are given. Colcolcova, Pitzaniza, Petseerscoi Savoroot, Coscaia Niesnaja, Dolgoi Ostrof, Socchoiamore, Petchora riviere, Petzora, Semdeceta ostei, Bolvanscaia goeba, Tserneia, Menseiborandey, and Bolsoiborandey. Here, near the Varandei Island of the present day, is an Inlet set down, and the names I have mentioned are placed at its mouths; Petsianca Borlovaicas. Goltsi stands near the rocks, not far from Dolgoi Island, which, although inserted, is not named, probably because an island of the same appellation is to be found so near it in the Petschora Gulf. Zelentsi, Korotaca goba, Corotaeva reca, Moltsiancova (?) Troscovaja (according to the explanation, Cabelian riviere). Then follows Gorgoscoi tsar, and west of Waigat some small islands are set down, and against them Zemostrof. West of the port of Kar is an important island, by name Poronovo. Against this is engraved the Dutch Laaghe Eylandt, as well as Costintsarch. Westward of the Oby we find Siberia, and there, higher up, is likewise set down Toboll as the " Metropolis Sybiriæ." The chart is headed in Dutch, " Map of the North-East of Russia, or the Land of the Samoiedes and Tungouse, as it was known to the Russians and described by Massa." Isaac Massa was likewise sent to Moscow just at the commencement of Michael Fedorovich's reign, in 1614, 1616, 1618, as well as subsequently, in 1624, to fulfil diplomatical missions from the States-General. Rechta incorrectly names him Maas, where he mentions that in 1616 Doctor Job (Hiob) Polidanus accompanied him for the purpose of being chief physician to the Czar. He farther calls him erroneously Mahs, where he speaks first of the son of the apothecary, Arensen, then of "Godseiuus," an apothecary, whose true name was Hassenius; and, lastly, of the physician, Damius, who came to Russia in 1624. Massa contributed essentially to the extension of the trade of the Dutch with Russia, and, as a well-informed man, sought to make himself useful in other departments of industry. He is called by the Russians, Macca, Abraham's son.

It may be here observed, that Dutch navigators, such as Teunis Ys and Willem de Vlamingh, appear to have originally changed the name of Mătjŭschin into Mătotschkin, for they likewise wrote Matthysstroom, as Mātushinzaar. Witsen copied them, where he has set down Matys and Mathys-stroom as Matiskinjar, and Mathys hoeck. To foreigners, the word Mătjŭschka was better known than the name of Mătjūscha.

On the north-east end of Matvei's Land, the flag of the Russian navy remains yet to be hoisted. For two hundred and fifty years that part of the country has been trodden by no human foot. When the Dutch wintered here in 1596-97, the island, for at least twelve years, had been called not Nova Zembla, but Matvejeva Semlja. It is scarcely to be believed, that north of Mătjūschin Schar (inlet) another strait is to be found. Vlamingh, as is well known, sailed round the north-east corner of Matvei's Land in 1664, and one, Cornelius Jelmerts (Kok), who was on board of his vessel, saw land in the south-east quarter. For this reason Dirk Rembrantsz van Nierop first applied the name of Jelmerland to the Peninsula of the Oby, and which other mapmakers have since copied; on several of our Russian maps is still to be seen the word Jalmal. A grandson of Alexis Ossipoff Otkupschtschikoff, a burgher of Mesen, assured me that the latter had sailed round the north-east coast of Mātjŭschin's Land into the Gulf of the Oby, and returned thence to Mesen with reindeer. His son, Pawel, accompanied the Lütke expedition of 1823 as pilot. The father was better known under the name of Pücha. Krestinin, however, bears witness that at Archangel, in 1788, he heard from Otkupschtschikoff, who was then seventy-four years of age; that from his thirteenth year he had been once every summer, and sometimes oftener, to the northern part of Nova Zembla, *i. e.* Matvejeff's Land, but had not thought of making a voyage into the Gulf of the Oby.

Ssava Fofanoff Loschkin, the Olonetzer, appears to have passed two winters, probably those of 1742-1743, and 1743-1744, on the east coast of Matvejeva Semlja. In 1835 Issakoff, a native of Kemi, sailed from the north to the east coast, and appears to have seen two islands to his left. It might, however, soon be shown how much the north-east corner of Matvejeva Semlja, according to Barentz' sketch of 1596-1597, is pushed out too far to the east, in the charts.

The same Pustoserskers to whom we are indebted for a knowledge of the correct name of Matvei's Land, and the straits between it and Nova Zembla, consented, in compliance with Marsh's request, to travel to the Oby by land. For this purpose they received fifty roubles, and a man who could write was appointed to accompany them. They were to proceed up the Petschora and the Ussa in two small craft, each with ten men, and then (on one side availing themselves probably of the river Jeletz, and on the other of the Ssob) travel on to the Oby. On this river they would then pass by five gorodki (towns) which are here named. I mention this because it may lead to a geographical *eclaircissement*. The first halt, according to the English translation of the letter, would be at the *embouchure* of the "Padou," which flowed into the Oby. By that river must be meant the Pad-jaka, in Russian simply Pad, and which, according to the "Bolschoi Tschertesh," was likewise called Sba. It does not appear to have occurred to our hydrographers that this problematical Sba-river can be no other than the Ssob, which is also written Ssoba, and which the "Bolschoi Tschertesh" incorrectly supposes to flow into the Ussa, for its stream really joins the Oby; so uncertain is the "Bolschoi Tschertesh" with reference to a river, which however forms the communication between the Petschora and the Oby by the Ural route.

Marsh, taking advantage of the privileges conferred on the company, sent the before-mentioned Pustoserskers with Bogdan, a commissioner, and a Samoiede boy to the Oby by this route. They probably also visited the environs of the Tas. They bartered goods for a thousand roubles' worth of sables and other furs. These were, however, taken from them, and Marsh the agent was prohibited from sending out similar expeditions.

I think I must make here another remark, that the Pustoserskers reported in 1584, that an English vessel had been wrecked at the mouth of the Oby ("your people have been at the river of Ob's mouth with a ship"), and that the crew were murdered by the Samoiedes, because they imagined that they came to plunder or subjugate them. What vessel can this have been? One of Jackman's? Hakluyt indeed says that he wintered in a Norwegian harbour in 1580–1581, and sailed in February in company with a vessel whose destination was Iceland. Of this information, however, there is no documentary evidence. That in 1581, an English vessel really did reach the Oby is confirmed by Horsey, who acquaints us that the "Sibirian Emperor" who was brought to Moscow, told him that two years previously he had seized a vessel with people like himself, who had intended to pass by the Oby to China. "I heerd him tell he had som Englishmen in his countrie, at leastways such men of countenance as I was, taken with a ship, ordinance, powder, and other riches, but two years befor, that would have passed the River Ob to seek Catay by the North Sea."

Horsey can have meant no one else but the Czarovich Mametkul, who was dispatched to Moscow in 1583–1584 by Jermak. Now as Jackman was lost in 1581, we must suppose that, after wintering in a Scandinavian harbour, he made another attempt to advance in an easterly direction. He was furnished with provisions for two whole years, and the instructions given to the expedition were, that if it became necessary to pass the winter in harbour, it should be in one as near the Oby as possible; but she was to sail up that river in the ensuing summer, and endeavour to reach the city of Siberia. "If you so happen to winter, we would have you the next summer to discover into the river Ob, so farre as conveniently you may; and if you shall finde the same river (which is reported to be wide or broad) to be also navigable, and pleasant for you, to travell farre into, happely you may come to the citie Siberia, or to some other towne or place, habited upon or neare the border of it, and thereby have liking to winter out the second winter: use you therein your discretions." The vessel arrived at the Oby just as Jermak was engaged in hostilities with Siberia, and it is likely that she was believed to be in alliance with him. Thus did Jackman and the crew of his vessel (in all nine persons) perish in consequence of the conquest of Siberia. The Pustoserskers were well acquainted in 1584 with the fish taken in the Oby. They showed Marsh the following: Sturgeon, large and small, (Acipenser sturio et ruthenus); Tschir (Salmo nasutus); Nelma (Salmo nelma); Pidle (perhaps Pelet, Salmo pelet); Muksun (Salmo muksun); Sigi (Salmo lavaretus). There is no Salmon (Salmo solar) in the Oby. They reported that it was an easy thing to sail to the mouth of this river: "and assure thy selfe that from Vaygats to the mouth of Ob, by sea, is but a small matter to sayle." These words prove that our Promüschlenniks at that time often made the voyage round the peninsula of the Oby.

Siberia was then conquered, and soon afterwards, in 1585, Manssuroff's cannon completed, higher up the Oby, the subjection of that part of the country which he made tributary to Russia, and where, in 1586, Tjumen, and in 1587, Tobol, were built. These towns consequently became the chief points of communication between Russia and the conquered country, thus depriving the early northern routes over the mountains of their importance. The Stroganoffs, a short time before they invited Jermak to join them, had done their best, by means of Oliver Brunel of Enkhuysen, to attract the Dutch to Russia for the sake of trade; and this led, not as is supposed to the introduction of the art of ship-building into Russia, but to their three well-known maritime enterprises of 1594, 1595, and 1596.

I cannot allow it to pass unnoticed, that Storch has erroneously deduced from Balach's letter to Mercator, that the Czar Ivan Vassilovitch had the first vessels built on the White Sea in 1581, by Dutch carpenters; and that many authors, some of them even Dutch, have repeated this error. Hakluyt says, however, that the Stroganoffs had two ships built on the Dwina by a Swede (in Balach's letter it is Sueno, (Sueco?) artifice).

At the time when the English sought to establish a direct trade with the Samoiedes at the Oby and the Tas, in 1584, the Dutch had already obtained a firm footing at Moscow, through the exertions of De Valle, and likewise sailed with their vessels to the Dwina, and as far as the convent, where by that time the present city of Archangel was built.

When Sir Jerome Bowes was appointed envoy to Moscow in 1581, he was commissioned to complain that Van de Valle the Dutchman was permitted to trade freely there. "That the Duche man, John de Wale, who endeavoreth to overthrowe the trade of her Maiesties subjects, is not onely suffered to continnewe his traffike in those places directly against their privileges, but also remaineth free from all taxations." At the coronation of the Czar Fedor Ivanovich, on the 10th of June, 1584, it was proposed that Jan Van de Valle, as a subject of the King of Spain, should take precedence of Horsey the Englishman; but the latter succeeded in obtaining it. He said "he would have his legges cut off by the knees, before he would yield to such an indignitie offered to his sovereigne, the Queene's Maiesty of England, to bring the Emperor a present in course after the King of Spaine's subject, or any other whatsoever." Richard Relph, one of the many faithless clerks of the English Company, who had been established at Kasan, wrote as follows from Rose Island in July, 1584, to two of his friends at that place, (Kasan), who were similarly disposed, viz. Nicholas Spenser and George Henenge:—" Our English Compagnie has but small friendship at Mosco at this present, and John Dowall he is aflote. This Emperor (Fedor Ivanovich) has made proclamation that his land shall be open to all strangers, and hath sent his letters into France and other places with the said effect." I have, however, seen in England, and copied, a charter neatly written on parchment, granted by Fedor Ivanovich in May, 1584, and consequently just before his coronation. This document is unfortunately much injured by fire.

Moucheron, whose vessel was the first that arrived at Archangel, was the same who, ten years later (in 1594), dispatched his captain, Cornelius Corneliszoon Nay, who had already made frequent voyages to the Dwina on his account, to search for the long-desired north-east passage. This Nay, as is well-known, reached the Karian Sea in the same year, proceeding as far as the west coast of the peninsula of the Oby, where the names of both his vessels, the "Mercurius" and "Swaen" (Swan), were bestowed upon two rivers, of which one was probably the Mutuaja, which for a long time before had been frequented by our Promüschlenniks.

The whole of what is now Siberia, from the Ural to Kamschatka, had already been discovered and conquered in an extraordinary manner. The Russians had already advanced beyond the islands in the Kamschatkadale Sea, and visited the coast of America, when Catherine the Second, in May, 1764, gave orders for the islands' complete exploration. Almost at the same time the Empress issued an ukase for the equipment of an expedition to the north, and which with the pretext of a revival of the whale fishery at Spitzbergen, was to ascertain whether a vessel could not reach the north pole from Archangel or Behring's Straits in a north-west direction, and so proceed to India.

Captain Krenitzin was instructed to take possession and give an account of the islands lying between Kamtschatka and America; but this could not be carried into effect until 1768 and 1769. Captain (of the first class) Vassily Jakovlevich Tschïtschagoff was appointed to the chief command of the polar expedition.

The official report drawn up by Captain Krenitzin on his return to Kamtschatka, where he was drowned, was communicated, probably through the medium of the Princess Daschkoff, to Dr. William Robertson, the royal historiographer of Scotland and Principal of the University of Edinburgh; by him delivered to William Coxe of Cambridge, who was at St. Petersburg, in 1778, and published by the latter in 1780. Princess Daschkoff had consulted Robertson in writing in 1776 with reference to placing her son at the Edinburgh University, and subsequently when she resided at Holyrood House in that city, during the studies of the young prince, from 1778 to 1779, became more closely acquainted with him. She then likewise became acquainted with other Scotchmen celebrated in the annals of literature, of whom we will only mention Dr. Joseph Black, Dr. Hugh Blair, Dr. Adam Ferguson, and Adam Smith.

Müller has described both Tschitschagoff's voyages in 1765 and 1766 very correctly from the original documents, and delivered his work to Pallas shortly before his death. The assertion, however, that Lomonossoff was consulted when the plan for these northern voyages was drawn up, is not to be found in it.

When on the 13th (24th) of May, the Empress, Catherine the Second, signed the Ukase relative to this so-called whaling expedition, she commissioned Count Ivan Grigorjevich Tschernischeff to signify her commands to the Admiralty College, that in the event of its appearing desirable, Lomonossoff should be consulted on the subject. The latter consequently gave in the sketch of a plan which he afterwards completed. Tschitschagoff received his formal instructions from the college in question.

Orders were given that several Promüschlenniks from Mesen and other places on the north coast, should be sent for from Archangel, in order that their experience might be rendered available for the voyage. Amongst these was the before named Alexis Ossipoff Otkupschtschikoff.

The probability of Lomonossoff's having given the first impulse to these expeditions of ours to the north, may be inferred from the fact, that, in a memoir drawn up by him in Russian on the 10th (21st) of September, 1763, which he dedicated to His Imperial Highness the High Admiral, Paul Petrovich, he not only recapitulates the earlier voyages to the Icy Sea, and speaks of the possibility of reaching the East Indies by the Siberian Ocean, but even proposes that the north-east corner of Nova Zembla, or rather Matvei's Land, should be made the point of departure for so important a sea-voyage. Lomonossoff unfortunately allowed himself to be carried away by a vague idea which had neither experience nor probability in its favour. His Imperial Highness the young Cesarovich, by an Ukase issued by the Empress, his mother, on the 21st of December, 1762 (1st of January, 1763), at Moscow, was appointed High Admiral and President of the Admiralty College, where he was present for the first time on the 18th (29th) of August, 1763.

The above-named work of Lomonossoff is one of the last productions of our academicians. In its historical part, in which the well-known northern expeditions, the voyages of the Normans to our coast, and the ancient trade of the natives of Novogorod with the regions of the Petschora and the Oby, are the topics, the "Dunki" (the name formerly given to sable furs) are likewise mentioned. Lomonossoff also speaks of these Dunki in his old history of Russia. In a document dated nearly five centuries and a half ago, I have discovered the most extraordinary names given to different descriptions of peltries exported from Riga.

At Spitzbergen, whence, properly speaking, Tschitschagoff's northern expedition was to take its departure, ten wooden houses were to be erected, with ovens and a magazine. In fact, five habitations, together with a storehouse and a bathing-room, which had been conveyed there together from Archangel, were erected at Bell Sound in 1764, and sixteen persons located there. This small Russian settlement was situated in 77° 32′, consequently in a somewhat higher latitude than Wolstenholme Sound, and in one somewhat lower than Sir Thomas Smith's Sound in Baffin's Bay.

The Admiralty College recommended that five masters or pilots, with three assistants, and three apprentices, should be instructed in the Academy of Sciences during the winter of 1764-1765, under the superintendence of Lomonossoff, in the mode of making astronomical observations. They were then dispatched to Archangel, and thence, for the most part in reindeer-sledges, to Kola. Rumovsky had then been for four years chief astronomer at the academy, and for a year director of the observatory. He had observed the first transit of Venus at Selenginsk, in 1761, and travelled to Kola in 1769 to witness the second. The above-named pilots were dispatched from St. Petersburg on the 4th (15th) of March, 1765. By them a quadrant belonging to the academy, and which Popoff had made use of at Irkutsk, in observing the first transit of Venus, was sent to Tschitschagoff, together with a chronometer received from England, and a memoir on the declination of the magnetic needle at St. Petersburg. In this memoir, which the college had obtained from the academy, it is stated by Taubert that, according to the latest observations, the variation amounts to four degrees and a half west, but it is known to be far greater. One month after the departure of the pilots, on the 3rd (14th) of April, Lomonossoff died.

The three vessels built for this expedition at the Dwina, in 1764, by Lamb Yames, an Englishman, had wintered in Catherine Harbour, viz. the "Tschitschagoff," the "Panoff," and the "Babageff." They sailed thence on the 9th (20th) of May, 1765, but, owing to the ice, only reached the latitude of 80° 26', a height which, in the earlier period of the navigation of the Northern Seas, had been attained by the vessels of the Russia Company from England, under Edge's command. Edge, in his map of Spitzbergen, has set down "Deicrowe's desier" and Point Purchas as the northernmost points observed. To the northernmost promontory in the island the latter name appears to have been assigned; but it has been since called by the Dutch "Verlegen Hook," which appellation the Russians adopted literally. James Bisbrown, from Liverpool, appears to have reached 83° 40′ in the summer of 1765, and then to have seen open sea before him towards the north. The unexpected and speedy return of our three vessels to Archangel, without carrying out the proposed object, aroused the displeasure of Count Tschernischeff, as the letter written by him to Tschitschagoff testifies.

Orders were given that they should be immediately sent back to Catherine Harbour at Kola, and make a fresh attempt thence in the ensuing year (1767). F. U. T. Aepinus, member of our Academy of Physic, drew up a memoir for the Admiralty College. He was one of the academicians who made speeches when the Empress Catherine the Second, on the 2nd of July, 1763, honoured a public assembly of the Academy of Sciences with her presence. He was tutor to the Czar Cesarovich, and at the academy he was one of the first who laboured in the departments of electricity and magnetism. This voyage commenced on the 19th (30th) of May. On this occasion, however, they again only attained the latitude of 80° 30′, and from the small colony at Bell Sound, then but two years old, took away seven persons, who were all that remained alive out of the sixteen first landed, returning with them to Archangel. Jonathan Wheatley, an Englishman, sailed nevertheless, in the same summer, in a northwest direction from Hakluyt's Headland as far as 81° 30′ without encountering any ice. Thomas Robinson even reached the latitude of 82° 30′. The well-known North Pole expedition of Captain Phipps (uncle of the Marquis of Normanby), which started in 1774, had no better result than Tschitschagoff's.

The idea that a passage, available in a commercial point of view, might be found along the coast of Siberia, in an easterly direction, is now, and indeed with reason, abandoned. Russia might, however, in my opinion, obtain from the White Sea and the Northern Ocean an article of very essential advantage to her industry and, indeed, to agriculture; for Nature here affords us a material wherewith to impart a considerable degree of fertility to the large tracts of arable land which border the rivers flowing into these seas. It is well-known that from the walruses, beluga-dolphins, and different varieties of seals, only the hides and oil are taken, besides the tusks from the former animal, whilst the entire carcasses are lost. On the strand at the mouths of the Mesen and Petschora, as well as on the shores of the White Sea, lie thousands of these hideless animals, which, although turned to no account for industrial purposes, naturally acquire a value by chemical decomposition; and were this scientifically promoted, it might assist in providing nourishment for thousands of men and domestic animals. At suitable places along the sea-shore, means should be adopted for the preparation of a concentrated manure from this azotic produce of the seas. The compost should then be brought up the rivers in barges to those districts which admit of cultivation, but are not at present productive through a deficiency of manure, whence meal, salt, and other necessaries, might be conveyed to the coast. Russia has in the Northern Ocean and the White Sea an inexhaustible abundance of such matter, fit for promoting the growth of vegetables. At one time, plans were formed for the preparation of manure at the oil boilings at the mouths of the Dwina, the Mesen, and the Petschora, from the oleaginous animals caught in their neighbourhood, and it has been calculated whether whole walruses might not likewise be brought there from remote places, as the craft ("Lodjen") employed in the walrus fishery, on the coast of Nova Zembla, could carry five thousand, but seldom bring more than a thousand pounds of oil and hides : it might often be profitable to extract the former substance at the above-mentioned places, and then a shorter time would be spent on remote coasts. The capture and conveyance of the animals might, perhaps, in many instances, be altogether a separate business from the subsequent operations.

It seems as if a beneficent Providence affords us the means of fertilizing that ground in the northern districts which is least productive, whilst, in the interior of the empire, where the supply of a similar substance for the preparation of manure is not met with, it has given us a black soil, which does not stand in need of it. Neither Great Britain nor Ireland, nor, indeed, any other European country situated near the sea, is as highly-favoured as ours in this respect; for the seas we have named contain not only, as well as theirs, animal nourishment prepared for men, but likewise afford a material for the production of large quantities of potatoes, corn, and other vegetable food for domestic animals. This is a treasure which must be dug up: a gold mine, which is not brought suddenly to an exhausted *caput mortuum*, but produces a fresh harvest from year to year.

The herring, salmon, and other fisheries in the White Sea and in the Northern Ocean, ought to be carried on much more extensively than at present, and with better appliances for the preservation of the produce than are at present in use. Herrings might then at once become an important article of export, instead of large sums leaving the country, as they now do, for purchasing them. As it is to be hoped that on the Lapland coast, also, the Russian fishery will soon be carried on with more activity, it is certainly to be lamented that our boundary-line on the maps should no longer extend as far as it did a short time since in the direction of the Varanger Fiord, for on that portion which has been curtailed a much more profitable fishery might be carried on. In reference to the herring-fishery, the example given in the north of Scotland deserves to be adduced. Formerly the Dutch caught and salted the herrings as they annually descended from the north, and then they were purchased by Great Britain. Thirty years ago I was on the spot, and saw what the Government and private individuals did towards securing this branch of industry to the natives of the coasts of

Caithness and Sutherlandshire, and I lately found it permanently established to a great extent at Wick, Helmsdale, and other places on the north coast. At Wick alone about eight thousand men are employed during the fishing season. During my first residence in Sutherlandshire, I was an eye-witness to the unwillingness displayed by the small tenants, who had lived for several generations in the interior of this district, to quit their miserable smoky huts in order to be settled on the coast, in accordance with measures adopted by the mother of the present Duke of Sutherland. I now found them living in pleasant villages, and deriving a comfortable subsistence from the sea by fishing, whereas formerly they led such indolent lives on the heaths of the mountains and valleys, that those of the Samoiedes, on the mossy plains along the Northern Ocean, might, in comparison, be called more active and useful. On the heaths, which were previously turned to no account, now wander countless sheep, whose instinct teaches them to search out the tender blades of grass sprouting up between the heath, and when they have attained a suitable age, they are, for the most part, conveyed to London in steamers.

The commercial house of Eribanoff, Fontaines, and Lührs, at Archangel, is shortly (in connection with Alexander Ivanoff Dengen, the burgher of Vologda) to make an experiment, with the instrumentality of Captain Michael Plakiten, from the Kena, in the collection of the guano on Kolgujeff Island. If here and elsewhere on the north coast a certain quantity of a substance resembling the Peruvian and African guano should be discovered, it must be, in a great measure, deprived of its soluble and fertilising portion by the frequently-repeated thawing of its covering of snow, and, on this account, no extraordinary result can well be expected from this speculation, at all events, for any length of time.

CHAPTER XIV.

COMPANIONS OF TRADESCANT IN HIS VOYAGE TO ARCHANGEL—
SIR JOHN MERRICK — SIR THOMAS SMITH — SIR DUDLEY
DIGGES—DR. RICHARD JAMES — CAPTAIN DAVID GILBERT—
CAPTAIN ROBERT CARR—JESSY DE QUESTER.

LET us now turn to the persons with whom Tradescant came to Archangel, in order to ascertain their motives for visiting Russia.

As the object of Sir Dudley Digges's mission to Russia was of the same nature as that of his predecessors, I must make some mention of these members of the Russia Company, and amongst them of one who had been previously established in our country for a long time at the factory at Moscow.

John Merrick had already, when a younger man, served at the factory at Moscow. I take him to be the son of that William Merrick, one of the original members of the company founded by Cabot, in 1554. From a letter written at Rose Island in 1584, it appears that John Merrick had at that time been appointed agent at Jaroslavl. (Robert Peacock had then arrived at Moscow, in William Turnbull's place, the latter having been removed by William Burrough.) In May, 1592, Queen Elizabeth wrote to Godunoff that John Merrick was named agent at

Moscow. In 1596 he was already a member of the Russia Company in London, but remained as agent at Moscow. In March of the same, and in January of the following year (1597), the Queen exculpated herself to Godunoff from the calumnious accusations which the Pope and the Emperor had transmitted to the Czar, as to her having rendered assistance to the Sultan, to the prejudice of the Christian world. Elizabeth had received notice of these intrigues from Merrick.

On the 14th of March, 1598, Merrick reported to London the death of the Czar Fedor Ivanovitch, which took place on the 7th of January—until that time he had been unable to obtain permission to dispatch a courier. He made known at the same time the election of Boriss Fedorovitch Godunoff, and added that he was particularly well-disposed towards him and the English. In July of the same year Francis Cherry was despatched by Elizabeth to Moscow, in order to contradict the reports circulated with reference to her diplomatic proceedings with the Sultan.

In the summer of 1600 the noble Gregory Ivanovitch Mikulin, accompanied by Ivan Sinovjeff, as secretary, were sent to Elizabeth by Godunoff, with a view to cement the friendly intercourse then existing. Merrick proceeded to England at the same time. He took with him two young foreigners who understood the Russian language, a Frenchman, of the name of Jean Parquet, and William Colliers, an Englishman.

Mikulin landed at Gravesend on the 18th of September, amidst the firing of cannon. Sir William Russell, knight, whose son Francis was the founder of the ducal line of Bedford, was sent by the Queen to escort him up the Thames to London, where he was received by the Earl of Pembroke (Henry Herbert), accompanied by many other persons of rank. The Queen sent two state carriages, one of which conveyed Mikulin, opposite to whom sat Lord Pembroke, whilst on his right was Sir William Russell, and on his left John Merrick. In the other carriage was Sinovjeff. The audience took place at Richmond, on the 14th of October. I found the original letter delivered by Mikulin to the Queen in the Tradescant Ashmolean Museum, at Oxford. It is dated the 13th of May, 1600, and embraces no details, for the ambassador was to fulfil his mission verbally.

On the 6th of January, 1601, Mikulin and Sinovjeff dined with the Queen. On the 16th of May, she wrote to Godunoff by Mikulin, who returned to Moscow in July.

The journal of Mikulin's mission to London, kept by Sinovjeff, is not uninteresting. We here have in the Russian language some notes on London in 1600 and 1601, mentioning the Tower, the city, and the only bridge over the Thames by which the city was connected with Southwark, with the houses and booths thereon. The honours paid to Mikulin and Sinovjeff were great. Guns were fired off at the Tower as they passed by it. Lord Bothwell, ambassador from the King of Scotland (who two years later became also King of England), visited them twice, the first time under a feigned name. The Journal contains all kinds of details, even that at the Queen's table Mikulin declined washing his hands in the silver vessel presented to him by her orders for that purpose, which much amused her.

In February, 1601, Mikulin assisted in fighting for the Queen of England, when the conspiracy—of which the mad Earl of Essex (Robert Devereux) was the instigator, and in consequence of which he was executed on the 25th of the same month—broke out in London. With Mikulin an apothecary came to Moscow, but he immediately returned to England. This ambassador, as well as Sir Richard Lea, who was at Moscow somewhat later, begged James Trencham, the apothecary who had returned to England with Bowes in 1584, to revisit Russia; and he brought a letter from Elizabeth to Godunoff, of the 11th of March, 1602, not, as Richter says, in 1601. We possess a list of the multifarious drugs and chemical preparations imported by him. Sir Thomas Smith found Mikulin at Jaroslavl in 1605. Mikulin actually appears to have taken the pseudo-Demetrius for Ivan's son; and several Strelitzes, who were of another opinion, were cut down by their comrades at a feast given by him. Mikulin had done some service in the field before Narva in 1590, with a hundred Circassians.

Whilst Mikulin and Merrick were on their way from Russia to England in 1600, Elizabeth had dispatched Sir Richard Lea as ambassador to Boriss

Fedorovitch, and he returned to her in the summer of 1601. To John Merrick, who had remained behind in London, and Francis Cherry, who was then settled there, the translation of Godunoff's confidential letter delivered to Queen Elizabeth by Lea, was entrusted. In the same year, too, Merrick was sent to Boriss Fedorovitch with an answer from the Queen. He was also commissioned to oppose a marriage which was on the tapis between the Czarina Ksenia Borissovna and a member of the Austrian house, an attempt to impede which was also to have been made by Lea. Through the latter the Queen had proposed a daughter of Ferdinand Stanley, Earl of Derby ("being of our blood royall and of greater possessions than any subject within our realm"), as bride for the Czarovitch Fedor Borissovitch, but she subsequently learned that the latter was but thirteen years old, and consequently four years younger than Lady Stanley. Lord Derby had no son, but three daughters: the eldest, Anne, married Grey Brugges, Baron Chandos; Francis, the second, John Egerton, Earl of Bridgewater; and Elizabeth, the third, Henry Hastings, second Earl of Huntingdon. Elizabeth provided Merrick with a memorial (a "minute") for Boriss Fedorovitch, wherein, amongst other things, she says: "We have thought it our part by this lettre to lett you knowe howe the case standeth, and to assure you that, if we had any of our blood (nay, of our own bodie) answerable to your expectacon, that we would thincke ourself both honored and strengthned by such a match, not only in regard of yourself from whom the Prince is descended, but in respect of the great towardlinesse which we doe understand to bee in him. Seeing therefore that it hath pleased Allmightie God (who holdeth the hartes of all kinges in his hand) soe to dispose our mynde as it could never geve way to those affections which might have been the meanes to raise an issue of our owne person (a matter whereof we have noe cause for our owne mynd to be sorye . . .), wee think it also our part to hold you no longer in expectacon but to return you this our speedy answere, which we wish would present you the grief we have because the earnest desires in both of us of such a union could not take place." As Godunoff now left it to Elizabeth to propose another, Merrick was to lay before him a list of the whole of her relations ("a draft of the pedigree"), so that he might not only select a bride for the Czarovitch, but a bridegroom for the Czarina. Merrick reached Moscow on the 10th of February, 1602, and took up his quarters, according to his desire, at the English house on the Varvarka.

On the following morning the Chancellor, Afanassy Ivanovitch Vlasseff, politely invited him to his house, and the day after visited him personally at his place of residence, in order to request him to hold himself in readiness in the evening to accompany him to the Czar. The Chancellor himself conveyed Merrick in his sledge to Boriss Federovitch, who was in the Kremlin. ("His Majestie then sitting in private, and not in state, having his ffeete placed on a footstoole covered with sables;

he gave me his princely hand to kiss.") When the Czar learnt that his last letter to the Queen had been entrusted to Merrick (and Cherry) to be translated, and that, because the contents were thus known to him, he had been selected for the present mission, he conversed with him so much the more freely. He praised Christopher Rietlinger, the physician who accompanied Lea, and who was an Hungarian. Lea requested the Czar to confer on this physician the title of Doctor. Godunoff published some very bitter remarks, condemning the proceedings of the Pope with reference to the Queen. Merrick was commissioned to translate into Russian, with the Chancellor Vlasseff's assistance, Elizabeth's letters, and the list of her entire pedigree and relations.

As he was engaged in this occupation on the 23rd of February, Vlasseff produced a paper from his writing-desk, and asked Merrick how it was that the Queen did not mention the families of the Earls of Hertford and Huntingdon. On the 3rd of March, the persons sent by Godunoff to Denmark returned; and on the 13th, those dispatched to Moscow by King Christian the Fourth arrived: the latter delivered the portrait of Prince John, and it was decided that he should receive the hand of Ksenia Borissovna. On the 22nd of June Merrick had his audience of leave-taking. Boriss Fedorovitch recommended four young Russians to him, whom he took to England to place in an educational establishment. Merrick reported that Godunoff had told him "that he did the rather make choice of this our country for the especiale love he beareth her Maiestie, and the good opinion he hath of our Naçon; and that I should make them known to her Maiestie, and desire her, in his name, that she would be pleased to give leave that they may be trayned up in learninge, and not be drawn to forsake their religion."

On the 24th of July Merrick travelled from Moscow to Archangel, and thence sailed on the 30th of the same month. On the 5th of September he delivered Godunoff's letter to the Queen at Oatlands, not far from London. The original of the letter sent by Godunoff to Elizabeth in June, 1602, through Merrick, was discovered by me in the Tradescant (Ashmolean) Museum at Oxford. Boriss Federovitch therein states that he had given an audience to Merrick, her envoy, in order to receive her letter, and that the verbal communication entrusted to the bearer had been delivered to him.

Elizabeth's reply to the Czar was couched in very friendly terms. She proposed a young Englishwoman, whose name she did not mention, as a bride for the Czarovitch Fedor. The father of the latter thereupon asked who and of what rank this lady was, but received no reply, the death of the Queen having occurred in the interim. Elizabeth had departed this life on the 24th of March, completing her glorious reign of five-and-forty years, which exercised so highly important an influence on Russian trade and industry.

In the ensuing year (1604) her successor on the throne, James the First (until then James the Sixth of Scotland), dispatched to Boriss Federovitch Godunoff the already frequently mentioned Sir Thomas Smith, who, for several years in succession, had been Governor of the Russia Company. He was presented to the King at Greenwich, by Lord Salisbury, before his departure. The ship John and Francis brought him to Archangel.

Smith had his first audience four days before the intelligence of the advance of the pretender, Demetrius, reached Moscow, viz. on the 11th of October. He obtained from Godunoff all that he desired for the company's benefit.

During his residence at Moscow, John Merrick continued to be the principal agent of the company, and William Russel (previously Dutch agent) was Merrick's assistant. At Smith's audience, the chief person present was Peter Fedorovitch Bassmanoff. Smith calls him "a very gallant nobleman." Merrick and Edward Cherrie, probably a brother of Francis, were invited to dinner.

Shortly after Smith again quitted Moscow, Boriss died, viz. on the 13th of April. As Smith decided on waiting at Vologda for the favourable season for navigation, he was enabled to return thence the papers he had received from the deceased Czar to the latter's son and successor, Fedor Borissovitch, who, on his part, then confirmed them; but, before Smith quitted Russia, he, too (Fedor), had departed this life. Demetrius, the pretender, sent after him Gavvilo Ssamoilovitch Ssalmanoff, who, in 1600 and 1601, had been Vaivode of the city of Verchotvije, then recently built, and as interpreter, the Richard Finch, who, as we have seen, accompanied Logan and Gordon, in 1611, to the Petschora. These persons overtook Smith at Archangel n the 31st of July, and delivered him a letter, in which the usurper requested Sir Thomas to express to King James his wish to be on friendly terms with him, and to mention, that immediately after his coronation an embassy should be sent to him; at the same time he requested to have Godunoff's letter returned to him. Smith reached London only in September, still, in the same year (1605), he published an account of his travels ("Voyage and Entertainment in Rushia, with the tragicall ends of two Emperors and one Empresse within one month").

Samuel Southeby, who had been at Moscow as chaplain with Sir Thomas Smith, likewise thought of laying his observations before the public, but did not fulfil his intention.

Merrick likewise continued in Russia as English agent during the disturbed period which commenced in 1605. On the 8th of June of the same year, Demetrius, the pretender, invited him from Zula, when Merrick was on the road to Archangel to pay him a visit; in consequence of which, he visited the usurper at his camp at Kolomenskoje, near Moscow.

Here he received, on the 18th of June, a free pass for travelling through the country, and to England, as well as permission for the English to carry on their trade free of duty. Tunofei Matvejevitch Lasareff, the Vaivode at Archangel, and the Secretary Roman Makarieff Voronoff, received orders to permit Merrick and the other English, to pursue their traffic without hindrance. In December of the same year, Merrick obtained from the pseudo-Demetrius, at Moscow, a formal charter, which he sent to England by Oliver Lysset during the winter.

In this document, Sir Thomas Smith's name stands at the head of the members of the company. I have already mentioned, that Richard Cockes, whose clerk (Thomas Ligon) discovered Pursglove in 1611-1612, at the village of Okladinoff, on the Mesen, is also named. John Merrick and Edward Cherry are likewise set down as members. Amongst other things, the permission formerly granted, and still existing, for vessels to load and unload at Rose Island, was renewed.

Vassily Ivanovitch Schuisky granted a fresh charter to the English, at Merrick's request, on the 4th of June, 1606, and sent him to England with it, as well as with an account to King James, of the events which had lately taken place in Russia. He promised that a Russian embassy should speedily follow.

During Merrick's absence, Mark Brewster remained at the head of the factory at Moscow. In the summer of 1609, George Brighouse, one of the clerks, arrived at Moscow from Cholmogorü, travelling post by way of Vladimir, and took up his quarters for a short time with Brewster. On his return, at the beginning of September, he gave an account which was transmitted to England. It referred to occurrences at and near Moscow, the battle near the Chodünka, Butschinsky's protracted arrest (Brewster daily sent him food from the English factory), &c. One piece of intelligence which has come to us by these means, relative to one of the three wives of Ivan Ivanovitch, is worth noticing. Brighouse dined with her in her cell at Vladimir, both on his journey to, and his return from Moscow, and was received by her in a very friendly manner. He says:—"The Princesse, wife to Evan Evanovitch, that was eldest sonne to the old Emperor, she whom you gave the good entertainment to, made very much of him; he dined in her presence; after dinner, sent him a great present of many dishes and drinkes for your sake, and often remembered you and your great kindnesse to her and hers, still remembering T. La, and kept him so a longe time in her owne cell." I consider, therefore, that the last of the three consorts whom the Czarovitch had in the course of two years is here meant. Karamsin could not tell what became of her. According to Passevin, she was the cause, owing to her light behaviour, of the tragic end of her consort in the Alexandrian suburb, on the 19th of November, 1582. Her name whilst a maiden and wife, was Helena Ivanovna; her brother was the celebrated General Fedor Ivanovitch Scheremeteff; her father, Ivan Vassilovitch, died in a convent in 1578; when she became a nun, she assumed the name of Leonida. Two letters written by her under this name, and with her seal attached, are extant; one of the 20th of August, 1583, and the other of the 21st of July, 1587; both dated from the Novodevitch convent, at Moscow. The first is preserved in the Trotzkisch convent, and the other is in the possession of M. von Bütschkoff, Librarian to the Imperial Public Library at St. Petersburg. The contents of the latter letter show that this Czarina was a joint-proprietor with her brother, of the village of Borissoglebsk, in the then Kostroma district on the road from Nerechta to Nishny Novogorod. Brighouse's account is the only one which we have, since 1587, of this lady, who is interesting in an historical point of view. According to the same, she must have been still resident in 1609, in the Uspenkisch convent at Vladimir, which is now nearly seven centuries and a half old.

Mark Brewster continued to preside over the factory until the eventful summer of 1611, residing still at the Varvarka. After that dreadful day (the 8th of September), on which Kitaigorod was sacrificed by our people, in order to compel the Poles to retreat, Brewster received permission, through the favour shown him by Prince Fedor Ivanovitch Motislavsky, to dwell in a cellar of the palace at the Kremlin. Merrick, who had remained at Cholmogorü and Archangel, quitted the latter place for England in the autumn.

Captain Jacob Margeret, who, three days after the

destruction of Kitaigorod, left the Kremlin, and with Michailo Glebovitch Ssaltükoff removed to Poland, wrote from Hamburg on the 29th of January, 1612, to Merrick in London, that a fire had broken out, kindled by the red-hot balls of the Russians, and that the English house behind the great Caravanserai had been consumed, so that but three buildings remained standing and uninjured in the town. He mentioned Chodkevitch's arrival at the Kremlin, and his expedition against Rjäsan. In the prognosis which Margeret gives of Russia on this occasion he makes a considerable mistake, for he says :—" If the Russes have no forraine helpe, as there is no appearance, no question it will come to pass, as I writ last to Your Worship, that they will be forced to yield." Margeret, as is well known, ventured to return to Archangel as early as 1612, to offer his assistance to Russia; but Prince Demetrius Michailovitch Posharsky sent him back in the disgrace he merited.

Michael Fedorovitch, soon after his accession to the throne, dispatched Stephen Michaelovitch Uschakoff, and Ssemar Saborovsky, not only to the Emperor Matthias, but to Holland and England, in order to announce his election to the sovereignty of Russia, and pave the way for friendly intercourse. In Holland and England, moreover, they were to apply for assistance in concluding a peace with Sweden, and to negotiate a loan. Purchas witnessed the landing of our envoys at Gravesend—their honourable reception in London, the part they took in the amusements (" the running at tilt at White Hall"), and the audience granted to them by the King, on the 24th of March, 1614. Russia, on which so much misfortune had fallen between 1605 and 1613, required money in order to be enabled to defend itself against the hostilities which still continued on the side of Poland.

In 1615, Merrick, the ci-devant clerk and trade-agent at the Varvarka, now knighted by James the First, and appointed to the Privy Chamberlainship, arrived at Archangel as ambassador from that King, with a suite of no less than four-and-forty persons, and a nobleman named Michael Jelisarovitch Vikentjeff was sent from Moscow to meet and receive him. Sir John Merrick announced that King James was ready to advance Russia a sum of money, which was a communication naturally much longed for. He was further commissioned, to act as mediator of a peace between Russia and Sweden; and subsequently, he and the Russian Commissioners proceeded, in November of the above-named year (1615), to the province of Staraja-Russa, where the negotiations were to take place, and where a Dutch embassy also arrived.

Merrick was at first lodged with his suite in a desolate country house, near the village of Romanoff, where the Swedish General Jacob de la Gardie then was. The Dutch embassy, which arrived on the 20th of November with Reynbout van Broderode at its head, were at first quartered in the neighbouring village of Milagona, but subsequently provided for in the village of Glebovo. The Russian Commissioners had quarters allotted to them in the village of Diderina, to which (on the 17th of December) De la Gardie, and Merrick, with their suites, afterwards removed. Here the treaty was to be celebrated in tents erected for that purpose on the snow; but the cold, which was exceedingly great, afterwards compelled them to assemble at Merrick's. In his lodge an armistice for three months was at length concluded on the 4th of March, 1616. This was the whole result of the long negotiations which were carried on with unspeakable inconvenience, owing to the desolate nature of the country, and the intense cold. We are indebted to Anthonis Goeteeris, who accompanied the Dutch Commissioner as treasurer, for an account of the manner in which the negotiations were carried on, as well as for illustrations of all the townships named. At Diderina, even the tents behind which was the house inhabited by Merrick, were depicted, as well as the procession to them.

Goeteeris has handed down to us two views of Ivangorod as it was at that time. In March, Gustavus Adolphus sent a letter to Merrick at Moscow, whither he had returned, by Christopher Woldek, who travelled thither by way of Ostaschkoff. It was also through Merrick's mediation that the King raised the siege of Narva at the commencement of October; and now really began the negotiations for a peace. On the 20th of November, Merrick made a provisional arrangement with the Swedish Commissioners. In the "Chronological Record," which appeared in 1845, it is not correctly stated that a Dutch Ambassador was present at the celebration of the Stolbov peace. The first negotiation between Merrick and the other Commissioners ended in an armistice. The substantial treaty of peace was first agreed to at a subsequent meeting at Stolbova between Tichvia and Ladoga, by the above-named Russian Commissioners, without the assistance of the Dutch, on the 27th of February, 1617. In virtue of this treaty, Russia received back Novogorod Staraja-Russa, Porchov, Ladoga, Gdov, and some other provinces; but transferred to Sweden the whole tract of country from Ivangorod (Narva) as far as Nöteburg (Oreschek Schlüsselburg); including, consequently, the ground on which St. Petersburg now stands.

The treaty of Stolbov, to the completion of which Merrick's mediation had very essentially contributed, was signed by him as witness. He returned to London immediately afterwards.

In August of the same year, 1617, Stephen Ivanovitch, Volünsky, Mayor (Namestrick) of Räshk, and Mark Posdejeff, Michael Fedorovitch's secretary, were sent to England, as already stated, partly with a view to cement the existing friendly relations between both realms, and partly to urge the fulfilment of the promise made of the loan of a sum of money (a hundred thousand roubles). I discovered the letter from the Czar Michael Fedorovitch, delivered to King James the First, by Volünsky, amongst the Cottonian papers in the British Museum. It is inserted in the Catalogue under the head of Nero, B. XI. 92, as " a paper Russian."

The English Government was ready to make a loan,

but wished to impose sundry conditions, viz. that the navigation on the Volga, and across the Caspian sea, should be free to the English; that a contract should be entered into for the supply of hemp, flax, and cordage, and that the Dutch should not enjoy commercial privileges equal to those of the English; lastly, good security was required for the repayment. I found these conditions in the British Museum in London (Lansdowne No. 160, 71, Fol. 246).

It was considered advisable that an embassy should be dispatched to Moscow, with special reference to this loan; and Sir Dudley Digges, the active member of the Russia Company, so often named, and in whose suite Tradescant came to Archangel, was appointed its chief.

Sir Dudley Digges was the son of Thomas, and the latter of Leonard Digges. Both were known as authors of mathematical, geometrical, and other scientific works. The first written by Leonard, " A general Prognostication," appeared in the year of the Willoughby expedition (1553). The title of the second book, published two years subsequently, was: " A Prognostication everlasting of right good effect, fructfully augmented, contayninge playne, briefe, pleasant, chosen rules to judge the wether for ever, by the sunne, moone, starres, &c." The "Tectonicum" appeared in 1556 ("a book named Tectonicum, briefly shewing the exact measuring and spedie reckoning of all manner of lands, squares, timber, stones, steeples, &c."). The "Pantometria" ("a geometrical, practical treatise, divided into three bookes, Longimetria, Planimetria and Stereometria") was published by Thomas, with corrections and additions in 1591. Of the latter's works I will here only name: " Scalæ mathematicæ Stratioticos ("an arithmetical military treatise"), and "a brief discourse what orders were best for repulsing any forraine forces, if at any time they should invade us by sea in Kent, or elsewhere."

Dudley, born in 1583, had studied at the University College at Oxford from 1598 till 1603, and afterwards busied himself with jurisprudence in London. He was knighted by James the First in 1607, and travelled on the Continent for his improvement. We have seen that he was one of the promoters of the five expeditions undertaken for the discovery of a North-West passage with the ship Discovery, from 1610 till 1616, successively commanded by Hudson, Button, Bileth (and Baffin). The unfortunate Hudson, as we have before stated, assigned Digges' name to an island in Hudson's Straits in his first voyage in 1610, as Bileth, in the case of Baffin, gave that name to a Cape in Baffin's Bay in 1616. This Cape Dudley Digges is, according to Ross' observation in 1818, situated in 76° 5′ of latitude, and south of Petovak, the settlement of Esquimaux in the Arctic Highlands, near Wolstenholme Sound, opposite to Wolstenholme Island, and north-west of Sovallick, the spot on the shore of Prince Regent's Bay where the meteoric iron, of which these Esquimaux make their knives, is found. Baffin fixed the latitude of Cape Dudley Digges at 76° 35′; Ross here saw a lofty chain inland, on account of which he names this region the Arctic Highlands. Esquimaux belonging to the Petovak settlement, came over the ice to his vessels in dog sledges; canoes they did not possess. Ross brought some of their knives with him to Great Britain. Not only Dr. Wollaston of London, but likewise Mr. Andrew Fyfe of Edinburgh, pointed out the nickel contained in the iron of which they are made, and thus renders their meteoric origin probable. The attention of the whalers visiting Baffin's Bay should be directed to this iron; and they should be requested, when accident leads them into the neigbourhood of Sovallick, and a landing there is practicable, to ascertain the situation and quantity of that metal existing there, and likewise to bring as much of it as possible with them. In the catalogue of the original Tradescant Museum and Garden, Sir Dudley's name stands amongst the patrons and benefactors of these establishments. He brought Charles the First a Narwal (Unicorn) horn, which the King ordered his physicians to examine. Parkinson the botanist has described it. Baffin, who in 1616 was with the North-West expedition equipped by Digges, Smith, and Wolstenholme, under Bileth's command, informed Wolstenholme, that near the places named after these gentlemen in the north of Buffin's Bay, they saw many narwals. In Tradescant's Museum there was a "Monoceros horne." Frobisher on his second voyage (1577) found a dead narwal with the "horne." At Windsor a "horne" seven feet in length is preserved. In 1581 Ivan Vassilovitch purchased for a great sum from the agent of a commercial house at Augsburg, a piece of a narwal's horn, three feet and a half long, and richly set with precious stones. This horn-stick (Possoch) was taken from the Kremlin by the Poles in 1611, together with many other treasures.

Sir Dudley Digges is known as the author of several works. In that first published long after his death (1655), "The Compleat Ambassador," Elizabeth's negotiations with reference to her marriage with the Duke of Anjou (1571), and with the Duke of Alençon (1581), are described. His first little work on the quality of war and soldiers ("Politique Discourses of the Worthinesse of Warre and Warriors"), appeared in 1604; and " The Defence of Trade, in a letter to Sir Thomas Smith, Governor of the East India Company," in 1615.

The voyage he made to Archangel in 1618, contemporaneously with Volünsky, we are already acquainted with. As soon as Michael Fedorovitch received intelligence of Digges' arrival there, he sent the Boyar, Fedor Vladimirovich, from Moscow, by way of Vologda and Ustjug, to meet and escort him to the metropolis.

The Poles were at that time making inroads into Russia in many directions, and Uvaroff in consequence received instructions, after manifold consultations with the Boyars, with regard to the course to be adopted with the embassy committed to his guidance, in the event of their falling in with any of these hostile parties. Digges, however, stood in such fear of the Poles, that even before Fedor Vladimirovitch reached him he turned back from Cholmogorü to Archangel, and embarked for England. The charge of the mission at Moscow he entrusted to Thomas Finch and Fabyan Smith who was then the agent there.

Sir Dudley's return from Cholmogorü without proceeding to Moscow in fulfilment of his mission, drew upon him the displeasure of King James the First, who banished him from the Court for some time. In a letter addressed to the Czar, Michael Fedorovitch, in 1619, there is the following passage:—" Notwithstanding the reasons which he (Digges) gave for his excuse, the kinge took this contempt of his retorne so distastefully, that (allbee the freinds he could make) hee was presently commanded from the Courte, and so remaineth in his Majestie's displeasure." In the same letter it is, however, mentioned that Digges' return did some service, for through him was received the intelligence of these hostile proceedings of the Poles against Russia; and this led to the refusal, by James the First, of the application just made to him by the King of Poland for auxiliary troops from England and Scotland. Sir Dudley Digges regained the favour of the king, and was sent to Holland in 1620 on a mission connected with East India affairs, and in 1621 to Ireland, when Member of Parliament, to inquire into its ecclesiastical and political condition. In 1626 he spoke very boldly in Parliament against the Duke of Buckingham, George Villiers, King Charles the First's great favourite, for which he was obliged to atone by imprisonment in the Tower, although but for a few days. Several of his later speeches have been preserved—one of them, in 1628, "on the right and privilege of the subject," was published in 1642. In 1630 the lucrative appointment of Master of the Rolls was promised to him, but he did not actually receive it until 1636. He died in 1639, and was buried in the church of Chilham, in Kent. We have a likeness of him engraved by H. R. Cooke, after a painting by Cornelius Jansen; and a smaller portrait of him in mezzotinto is by Woodburn. In the public documents drawn up at Archangel, he is mentioned as "Prince Thomyn Dudley Digges." I must yet observe that, in Rhymer's Fœdera, xvii., 257, the full power conferred on Sir Dudley Digges for his mission to Russia is incorrectly dated in 1620 instead of 1618.

Fédor Vladimirovich Uvaroff escorted Thomas Finch, Thomas Leak, the secretary, Richard James, the chaplain, and fourteen other persons from Vologda to Moscow, where this mission was received on the 19th of January, 1619, with all honours; and a suitable residence was allotted to them in the great ambassador's hotel at Kitaigorod.

Finch refused for a long time to give the Czar the explanations he desired. At an audience before the boyars, instead of the hundred thousand roubles which were expected, only forty thousand crowns (in weight 5335 pounds, 36 solotnik) were paid, which, according to the calculations of that time, amounted to somewhat more than sixteen thousand roubles. The princes Gregory Petrovitch Romodanovski (patrician of Bräusk), and Gregory Constantinovitch (patrician of Kaschira), carried on the negotiations. The sum offered was so insignificant, that they were on the point of declining to receive it, for at that time peace had already been concluded. The Fabyan Smith mentioned in the letter which Michael Fedorovitch wrote to James the First on this occasion, and who was employed as agent in the matter of the loan, was appointed to the chief post at the factory in Russia after Merrick. The Russian Government often obtained such articles as it needed from him. In 1614 he received payment for the iron guns and balls, 240 pistols, 320 pike-heads, and cloth for the soldiers at Jaroslavl, &c., which he had delivered. At the time of Sir Dudley Digges' arrival he was at Archangel. After Smith's decease Thomas Wyche became agent in Russia, and in 1634, Richard Swift in his stead. In the so-called Ashmolean Museum at Oxford I discovered the copy of a letter, dated the 31st of July, 1634, from Charles the First to Michael Federovitch relative to this person. Swift had been employed by King James the First in 1617, on a mission to Moscow. This appears from a letter of the Czar's of September, 1617, which is to be found in the same museum. Alexis Ivanovitch Sjusin, who had been employed in negotiating the peace with Sweden, was also sent to London at that time, with the secretary, Alexis Vitovtoff.

On the 16th of March (1619), Finch and his colleagues had their first audience from Michael Fedorovitch, and on the 15th of July a second one for leave-taking.

The Royal letter delivered by Finch, which contained Sir Dudley's credentials, was dated the 30th of May, 1618. Prince Volkonsky laid the ambassador's presents before the Czar, but unfortunately they are not specifically detailed. In his Imperial Majesty's armoury at Zarskoje-Sselo, there is a sword-blade with the date of 1618, and with the portraits of King James the First (fifty-three years old), his son, Prince Charles, Maurice, Prince of Orange, and of the Elector Palatine, Frederick the Fifth, who became the King's son-in-law in 1613.

On the 20th of August the English, escorted by Ivan Fomitch Ssütia, departed from Moscow for Archangel. In this journey they were accompanied by Isaac Massa, the Dutch ambassador, to whom we are indebted for that map of a part of our north coast of which we have said so much.

Dr. Richard James, the chaplain who accompanied the embassy, was a learned and diligent Oxonian. A number of his manuscripts, mostly of a theological nature, are extant in the Bodleian Library. He wrote an account of what he observed in Russia in 1618–1619, and which is described by Tanner in a list of these MSS. prepared after James's decease, as "An Account of his (James's) Travels into Russia, 8vo, in five sheets." As Dr. James's MSS. were obtained by purchase for the Bodleian Library, I naturally sought amongst them for the account of his Russian travels; but, notwithstanding all my trouble, I was unable to discover it, and think I may assert that this MS. does not now exist in the Bodleian

Library. Perhaps indeed it was never there, or was soon afterwards lost, for in the catalogue made in 1697 a note is inserted at No. 43 of James's papers, saying, "it is missing;" and it was precisely in this bundle that, according to a comparison with Tanner's catalogue, the account of his Russian travels ought to have been found. The loss is to be deplored, for James doubtless describes Philaret's entry into Moscow, and his introduction to the Patriarch. It is to be hoped that we shall still succeed in discovering this MS. somewhere in England, for it would be valuable for the knowledge it would give us of Moscow as it was at that period.

Some literary remains, however, brought by Dr. James from Russia, I discovered at Oxford. I shall first name some Russian songs of that time. One of them refers to Philaret's entry into Moscow; another is of the year 1605, and relates to Ksenia, the beautiful and accomplished daughter of the Czar Boriss Fedorovitch, subsequently known as the nun Olga, whom we have several times mentioned, and for whom, after the death of John the Danish prince, a bridegroom was sought in England (in the Hertford and Huntingdon families), Austria, and Schleswig-Holstein. The crime of which Rostuga was guilty towards this Princess, and through which he has deservedly become an object of abhorrence to all mankind, is sufficiently well known. A third relates to the youthful hero, Prince Michael Vassiljevitch Skopin Schuisky, commander-in-chief of the army, an ornament to his country and a pattern to his soldiers, through whose sudden death, late in the evening of the 23rd of April, 1610, the affairs of Russia, already so complicated, became still more so.

These Russian songs are of high value, and especially because they are altogether unchanged from what they were when copied for Dr. James: they were brought from Cholmogorü to England in the spring of 1610, and there they have hitherto lain unregarded. As respects the old Russian songs lately published in Russia, we neither know with certainty the period of their composition, nor the extent of the alterations which they have subsequently undergone.

I must observe that Dr. James remained in Russia longer than Finch and Lea. The embassy, indeed, quitted Moscow, as already stated, in August, 1619; but when it reached Archangel, the vessel which was to have conveyed it to England had already set sail, on account of the lateness of the season. As they now suffered shipwreck outside the bar in the last remaining merchant vessel, of whose departure they availed themselves for their voyage home, they returned to Archangel and Cholmogorü after the loss of most of their things. Finch and Lea, with two others, now departed by land; but James, with the remainder, stayed the whole winter at Cholmogorü, where this active Oxford scholar applied himself to the acquisition of the Russian language. I have likewise discovered a collection of Russian words, with an explanation of their meaning in English ("a Russian vocabulary"), which was brought to England by James. It appears from it that the English traders in Russia at that time had made themselves properly acquainted with the language of the country. Several animals, plants, utensils, implements, and other things, are not only named in English, but likewise specially described. This is the case, for example, with the word "Jitvouke," " A small bird, usually as large as larks, and also with claws of about the same length; back and belly of the same colour; but they have likewise on the side of the head two short horns of black feathers, and on the throat a black spot. The feet and bill are blackish, and on the head and throat are shades of a yellow colour. They taste like larks, and are very fat. On the 4th of October (viz. 1619), we ate at Cholmogorü eighteen of them, which were purchased for four copecks; and on the 6th, twelve of them were bought for three copecks." We likewise see from this description that here the snow (or mountain lark (alauda nivalis, s. alpestris) is meant; and we learn that it was then called Shitwonka, from shito (corn), their food. Opposite the word "Kinshal" is placed " a Persian dagger. The officer of the Customs at Archangel was wont to boast that he stabbed the Pretender, Demetrius, with one of the same description." This little book was stitched in leather at Cholmogorü, and a narrow strap is sewn to it, so as to be rolled round and thus to keep it together.

We have a sermon preached by Dr. James at Oxford in 1621, but not published until 1630, when it was dedicated to Sir Robert Cotton. It is surprising that Dr. James alludes in it to the two weeks before the great fast. He therein describes what he saw at

Moscow in 1619; and, amongst other things, says that a number of men ("scores of men") were murdered in a drunken state. In a poem, of which James was the author, a woman of Cholmogorü, named Maria, at whose house he must have lived, is depicted by him in a very unfriendly manner. This "heart's relief" he has entitled, "An execration on Marie of Cholmogorod, in whose house I should have binne lodged if my man had not tould me the condicion of the place." A few other lines are addressed by him to Anthony White, of Oxford, who, in consequence of his long absence, considered him to be dead, and had made an elegy on him.

In the same ship which conveyed Sir Dudley Digges, Tradescant, Dr. James, and the other persons already named, to Russia, was also David Gilbert, the Scotch captain. This Gilbert is the same who, as I have discovered in the Moscow archives, was induced to enter the Russian service under Boriss Fedorovitch at the same time as Captain Margeret, and who likewise served with the same person in the body-guard of the first Pretender, Demetrius, which was composed of foreigners. He was one of the fifty-two strangers whom the second Pretender, Demetrius, wished to drown in the Oka without any further examination, owing to an unfounded suspicion he entertained of them. These foreigners had already been driven from Koselsk towards Kaloga on the river just named, when Martin Beer, the chaplain, and Captain Gilbert, together with three others, Ensign Thomas Moritzen, and Reinhold von Engelhard and Johann von Reenen, two Livonian nobles, ventured to cross the Oka for the purpose of imploring Marian Morisckka, through the medium of the ladies who were with her, to intercede for them. She really became the preserver of these innocent and calumniated persons. Gilbert subsequently served in the Polish ranks, but was soon taken prisoner and brought to Moscow. Sir John Merrick, who returned to England in 1617, then induced King James to intercede for him with the Czar, Michael Federovitch. In the Tradescant (Ashmolean) Museum at Oxford, I discovered the original dispatch from Michael Fedorovitch, which contains a reply to James, wherein Gilbert's great crime is circumstantially represented. By this it appears that, on account of his desertion to the Poles, and the share he had taken in the many pillagings and blood-sheddings at Moscow, and in the empire generally, he had forfeited his life; but that at the king's request, he should be pardoned, and might return to his native country with Volunsky, the ambassador, who was dispatched to England in 1617. The above-named Russian dispatch (Gramota), discovered by me at Oxford, is much damaged. It is therein said, that in the letter from King James, delivered by Sir John Merrick, it was asserted that Gilbert was taken prisoner by Sholkevski's people, and obliged to enter the Polish service, but that he was again taken prisoner by the Russians without having anywhere lent his assistance in injuring them, and that he now had been in fetters three years. The King requested that he might be set at liberty, and permission given him either to return to his native country, or to enter the Russian service. Hereupon the reply given was, that Gilbert had engaged to serve the Czar Boriss Feodorovitch; but that, under Schuisky, he had gone over to the second usurper at Tuschino, and subsequently to the Poles. He then came to Moscow with Sholkevski, and was afterwards taken prisoner by the Russians whilst fighting against them. When, by permission of his Imperial Majesty, I examined the MS. of the archives of the Orusheinaja Palace, at Moscow, unrolled by me in 1836, I found, amongst other things, that David Gilbert, with Captains Jacob Margeret and Robert Dunbar, as well as Jacob Hock, an ensign, and Andrew Let (who had been recently baptized), were taken into the military service by Afanassy Ivanovitch Vlasseff, during his residence abroad in 1600 and 1601. Pay was given to each, according to his rank. At the same time (in 1836) I discovered the lists of the crowns, and other valuables, taken by the Poles from the Czar's treasury in the Kremlin in 1611. Amongst these, it may be incidentally remarked, were a crown which was intended for the Pretender, Demetrius, but the workmanship of which had not been completed; an hussar's saddle, ornamented with jewels of great value and gold; and, moreover, the richly-decorated "unicorn" stick, already alluded to, and three common narwal horns. In the documents found by me all the precious stones were separately enumerated, and their value affixed. From Masskevitch's Journal we find that these valuables, taken from the Kremlin, were distributed amongst the soldiers in Poland in 1614. The plain narwal horns were sawn in pieces, and delivered by weight, of which Masskevitch received two "Loth" (half ounces).

Captain Gilbert returned from England, in 1618, with his son Thomas, to make a fresh offer of his services to the Czar. On board the vessel he gave Tradescant an account, amongst other things, of the wonderful endurance of Tartar horses. Tradescant writes: "Ther Tartar horses be longe, much like to the Barbery horses, but of the best use of any in the knowne world, for as I have heard Captaine Gilbert report, that hathe long lived there, he had on whiche he hathe rod a wholl day together, and at night hathe give him a littille provender, and the next day hathe don the like, and so for many dayes, and yet he confessethe that he hathe not known seldom on of tire."

During his stay in England, Captain Gilbert gave some account of the first Pretender, Demetrius. According to him, Demetrius, a few days before his end, and consequently very soon after his nuptials (for between both events but nine days intervened), saw two apparitions in the night, which so much disturbed him that he first came to Gilbert in the ante-room, where his life-guards were, and then sent for Butschinsky his private secretary.

Gilbert likewise related in England, that he received from the second Pretender, Demetrius, a written invitation, in which the writing of the first usurper was imitated. When Gilbert approached him with his guards, he displayed so accurate a knowledge of all the affairs of the first Pretender, that as he, Gilbert, assures us, he should have believed in the identity of one with the other, owing to the correct allusions which the second impostor made to previous incidents, if he had not been personally so well acquainted with the first. The latter was, according to Gilbert, a man of very prepossessing exterior, but the second, "a very deformed wretch," as different from the first as day and night. It must be recollected that Gilbert stood in high favour with the first Demetrius, when officer of the guard; whereas the last one wished to have him thrown into the Oka. Gilbert farther stated that he had openly expressed this conviction to the Polish general (consequently to the Hetman Ruskinsky), who accompanied the second usurper, and asked him how it was that he took this Demetrius, who was so very different from the other, to be one and the same person; whereupon the reply was: " It is no matter, Captaine, this Demetrius shall serve our turne to be revenged of the . . . . Russe."

Besides Captain Gilbert and his son, another Scotch Captain, Robert Carr, accompanied Tradescant from England to Russia in 1618. Carr commanded one of the six companies of British Cavalry, which on the 24th of June, 1610, remained the longest in the field of battle, in the unfortunate affair at Kluschneff. From twelve to fourteen hundred men of these companies held their ground against eight thousand Poles, and thrice repelled their charges, but at the fourth were thrown into disorder, and dispersed. Carr, indeed, lost, like the other captains, his entire company, but was the only one of them who remained alive and unwounded. The names of the other captains were: Benson, Crale, Creyton (Crichton?), Kendrick, and York.

The young Gilbert (Thomas) and Captain Carr did not remain in Russia, but returned to England in 1619. Captain Gilbert, however, stayed there.

Jessy de Quester, who likewise came to Russia in Tradescant's company, must have been a son of Matthew De Quester, whom James the First named Foreign Post-master at the time of the first establishment of this department. De Quester resided in Philpot lane in the City.

I here conclude the explanatory addenda, which I have been induced to give in consequence of my discovery of Tradescant's journal of his travels. I think I have satisfactorily shown that researches into the English archives will furnish some not uninteresting supplements to the history of our country, if the documents discovered are compared with the contents of those preserved at Moscow.

APPENDIX.

A.

"Interea in Angliam et Scotiam missus Legatus, qua in legatione ita se gessit, ut jucundissima, gratissima, et gloriosissima sit ejus nominis memoria, et apud Anglos et Scotos, quos ipsos etiam eodem tempore, cum inter se maximum bellum gessissent et starent jam utrinque instructi exercitus infestis animis et signis, alter in alterius perniciem accincti, in concordiam dissidentes reconciliavit. Factum omnibus seculis memorandum. Tanti erat illius viri, apud peregrinos etiam homines, quædam vocis et vultus augusta magestas et gravissimis in rebus nominis autoritas."

B.

"Contra suos inimicos et hostem Swantonem Regni Swecie occupatorem gubernatorem. Et quum aliquis nostrum incipiet lites adversus Swantonem qui nunc gerit se pro gubernatore Regni Svecie, Ericum Sture capitaneum in Wiburg aliosque occupatores regni nostri Suetii infideles subditos atque rebelles tunc primus inter nos alter utri significabimus."

C.

"Annunciamus vobis plurimas et amicabiles salutationes, serenissime et carissime frater. Scribimus ad vestram celsitudinem quantum vestra misit celsitudo ad genitorem nostrum Johannem Imperatorem et Dominum tocius Russie et Magnum Ducem vestrum Oratorem Heraldum Magistrum David Kocken (Kocker?) Dei autem voluntas facta est quod genitor noster migravit in Dominum. Deinde a vobis ad nos venit vester nuncius Johannes Plagh, cum vestris credentialibus, literis et verbis, nam quid vir vester Magister David post obitum patris nostri a vobis retulit, vester nuncius Johannes Plagh nobis ex parte vestra ille idem retulit, quod si divina providentia genitor noster migrasset in Domino ut nos tunc vobiscum essemus simili modo, sicut vos cum genitore nostro in fraternitate et amicitia fuistis contra omnes inimicos, et nuncium quoque nostrum ad vos fratrem nostrum Johannem Regem cum hoc unacum vestris" (not nostris) " nunciis mitteremus. Nos autem vobiscum cum fratre nostro Johanne Dacie, Suecie, Norwagie, &c. Rege amicitiam et fraternitatem habere volumus, eodem modo sicuti vos cum nostro genitore habuistis. Et nunc ad vos nostrum nuntium Yschonia"(Ystoma) "cum hiis nostris litteris optamus quatenus vestras fortificatas literas de amicicia et fraternitate nomine vestro scribere mandaretur, qualiter apud genitorem nostrum vestre littere fuerint, et huiusmodi litteris vestris sigillum vestrum mandaretur appendi. Et super hiis litteris ad nos crucem in presencia nostri nuncii Ysconie (Ystoma) osculari veletis, istas quoque sic fortificatas litteras cum vestro nuncio una cum nostro nuncio Yscania" (Ystoma) " ad nos mittatis nobis hujusmodi tales vestras litteras obsignando. Et Deo favente cum idem noster nuncius

Yscania" (Ystoma) "una cum vestris nunciis cum huiusmodi vestris roboratis litteris ad nos redierit, quibus nobis visis nos vice versa de verbo ad verbum litteras nostras scribere, nec non sigillum appendi manderemus, et super talibus litteris nostris in presencia vestri nuncii crucem osculari volumus, et de post easdem nostras roboratas litteras ad vos una cum vestro nuncio remittamus. Et sic Deo auxiliante vobis volumus obsignare nuncium quoque nostrum Ysconiam" (Ystomam) " ad nos absque mora remittatis. Ex Muscovia, anno septimo millesimo decimo, quinto mensis Julii septuagesima die."

D.

"Johannes &c., Basilio tocius Russie Imperatori salutem et sincerem atque fraternalem in Domino dilectionem. Delectissime frater et confederate. Vestre Majestatis nuncius Yscania" (Ystoma) " tali die N. ad nos una cum David Heraldo nostro applicuit, atque venit nobis vestras litteras exhibens atque presentans. Ex quibus litteris clarius accepimus vos velle pie memorie domini Johannis Basilii vestigia in omnibus imitari, et precipue fraternalem amicitiam atque confederacionem nobiscum contrahere, ac insuper tali amicicia et confederacione litteras nostras conficere, et eos ad manus vestras una cum memorato nuncio nostra N. ac Yscania" (Ystoma) " in presentiarum dirigimus atque transmittimus, summopere desiderantes atque deprecantes ut similes litteras vestras eandem amiciciam et confederacionem continentes nobis remittere velitis. O Princeps, frater noster, socer ac parens."

E.

" Postquam regnum (nostrum Suecie) intravimus cum paulo populo ut voluerunt (ne regnicole nimium aggravarentur), opposuerunt se nobis in effectum faciendes nobiscum sicut Judei fecerunt contra Christum. Et tunc manus istorum Suecorum rebellium nostrorum sicut Deo placuit in persona evasimus. Et sic prefati Sucie rebelles adhuc totum nostrum regnum Suecie occupant et detenent contra Deum, contra justiciam, et juratam fidelitatem nobis prestitam. Unde ex corde monemur rogare fratrem et confederatum nostrum ut iniquitatem rebellium nostrorum menti sue habeat, &c."

F.

" Concessimus viro honorabili et forti Hugoni Wilibeo et aliis qui cum eo sunt servis nostris fidis et charis, ut pro suâ voluntate, in regiones eis prius incognitas eant, quæsituri ea quibus nos caremus, et adducant illis ex nostris terris id quod illi carent. Atque ita illis et nobis commodum inde accedat, sitque amicitia perpetua, et fœdus indissolubile inter illos et nos, dum permittent illi nos accipere de rebus quibus superabundant in regnis suis, et nos concedemus illis ex regnis nostris res, quibus destituuntur."

G.

" Accepimus literas vestras amoris et amicitie plenas

per dilectum Virum" (not, as has been copied for Alexander Turgenica, vestrum) " nuntium et Legatum Osiph Nepeam" (not, as in the copy quoted, epea) " ad nos delatas. Intelligimus—ex litteris vestris—vos de vestra liberalitate varia privilegia libertates et munitates mercatoribus nostris et aliis etiam nostri Anglie subditis qui in aliqua ditionis vestre parte mercaturam exercent dedisse et concessisse."

H.

"Fecimus ut quæ ab illo (Nepeja) vestro nomine proponebantur per certos nostros consiliarios, quibus negotium dedimus ut cum illo tractarent prolixe et diligenter perpenderentur."

I.

"Speramus hoc fundamentum mutue amicitie, hoc modo bene et feliciter jactum et stabilitum magnos et uberes fructus tum fraterni inter nos et successores nostros, amoris et amicitie firme tum perpetui inter subditos nostros commercii coniunctionem allaturum. Et in majorem spem adducimus fore ut sicut Deus, ex sua infinita bonitate et favore nostris temporibus, huic mari viam et navigationem, antea incognitam aperuit, sic etiam imposterum, in suum honorem et gloriam ad incrementum Christiane et Catholice Religionis, ad publicum commodum et utriusque partis subditorum et Regnorum bonum, sit eam conservaturus et prosperaturus." "Et quoniam vester legatus Ossiph Nepea, qui se hic apud nos in sua legatione prudenter et considerate gessit, jam ad vos redire instituit, qui optime exponere potest, et ut speramus prolixe vobis exponet quo animo sumus ergo hoc commercium nuper inter nostros vestrosque subditos et utriusque ditionis regna et urbes repertum."

K.

" Vi dirò brevemente siccome mi è venuto qualche occasione di andare a trattare in Moscovia un partito con quel Signore e per far questo primo mi è donato D (?) 400 contanti e di poi mezzo a participazione dello stesso negozio."

L.

" Non diciate che io sia andato se non in Svevia per qualche mio negozio che cosi hò scritto a ciascuno riservato a quelli di casa e questo acciò non ne fossi fatto una contramina al mio disegno. Partirò a Santo Giovanni."

M.

" Vestrum erga nos et nostros singulare studium facit ut libenter etiam hoc tempore Raphaelem Barberinum, virum quidem Italum, sed nobis, certis nominibus, valde charum, his nostris literis vestræ Maiestati commendemus. Petimus itaque, ut hic vir, vestra bona gratia atque voluntate et iussu etiam atque authoritate, si opus fuerit, beneque a Vestra Maiestate, humaniter a vestris subditis tractetur; utque sibi ac suis, cum bonis universis, tutum liberumque sit, per vestra regna atque provincias ire, transire, istic morari quamdiu placuerit, et inde abire atque recedere quandocunque illi ac suis libitum fuerit."

N.

" Avendo ottenuto per il paese del Moscovito franchigie e salvi condotti per me e mia gente, spero in futuro avervi a far del bene, perche, ho auto certe cognizioni di che pochi sono informati, ho di poi auto passaporti e salvi condotti dal Rè di Danimarca e dal Rè di Sueda, cose che le stimo e vagliono molto, e per non perdere l' occasione alli XI. del presente" (on the 11th of July, 1565) " ho spedito di quà una nave con X. M. (10,000) D (?) fra mercanzie e contanti che se a Dio piacerà vadia e torni a salvamento spero molto bene e così seguirò in futuro sperando che Dio per questa strada recompensi tutta la casa mia."

O.

" Non so che dirvi se non che stò semivivo aspettando che N. S. Iddio mi faccia grazia che la nave ch' io mandai venga a salvamento siccome in lui spero."

P.

" Perchè sò che doveti sapere che ho mandato una nave alle Nerve: vi dirò avere ricevuto lettere dal sopracarico" (he had passed the Sound). " Però se a Dio piaccia farmi la grazia che ritorni a salvamento sono molto certo di ristorarmi a doppio di ogni mio danno e da potermi contentare, perchè vi hò carico sale, che quindi primo costo mi costa D. 1500 la qual grazia di poterlo passare è stato gran favore che mi ha fatto il Rè di Danimarca a istanzia del Moscovito 'l quale mi fece lettere per detto Rè molto in mio favore e me ne fece ancora pel Rè di Sueda per aver passaporto franco dalle sue navi, dalle quali anzi mio ritorno hò tutto ottenuto."

Q.

"E detto Moscovito mi ha fatto privilegi e franchigie e esenzioni bellisime per me, mia nave, e miei uomini, sicche non pago di cosa alcuna uno soldo. E come l' paese chi vi va non ne può uscire, a me ha fatto, che mia gente sieno d'ogni cosa libere e franche. Però conchiudo che veggo la strada aperta da fare del bene e se io lo volessi andare a servire, come infinite volte mi fece dire da due Ferraresi prigioneri che vi sono, penserei starvi troppo bene, lasciato da parte la incommodità del paese; ma non me ne risolvo, se la necessità non me ne sforza, perche sò che mai piu potrei uscire di là."

R.

"Intelligimus Vestram Maiestatem eam etiam nostrarum literarum rationem habere, ut ad respectum earundem et plurimum semper nostris tribuat, et plus aliquando alienis etiam in nostram gratiam concedat, quam nos ipsæ pro illis postulamus. Id quod superiori anno, cuidam homini Italo, Raphaelo Barberino, accidit, quem nos, ut peregrinatorem non ut negociatorem, Vestræ Majestati commendavimus. Sed de hoc Italo homine, quomodo et nostrarum literarum commendatione et Vestræ Maiestatis bonitate ausit abuti et de aliis etiam rebus, quæ ad intercursum inter Nos ac Nostros institutum imprimis pertinent, Antonius Jenkinson, perdilectus noster famulus fusius, coram præsenti sui sermone, sed nostris verbis, animi nostri sententiam declarabit."

S.

" Quominus autem navigationem in Moscoviam permittere possimus, videt nos Serenitas Vestra gravissimis non solum nostris privatis, sed etiam religionis et reipublicæ totius Christianæ rationibus prohiberi. Instruitur eniam hostis, ut diximus, commeatu, instruitur, quod magis est, armis in illa Barbaria inusitatis, instruitur, quod quidem maxime ducendum esse existimamus, artificibus ipsis, ita, ut etiamsi ad illum nihil præterea importetur, tamen opera artificum ipsorum, qui illi, vigente ejusmodi navigatione, libere summittuntur, facile omnia simul et fabricentur in ipsa illius barbara ditione, quæ usus ipsi belli requirit, et quæ uti hactenus ipsi ignota fuerunt."

T.

" Cum enim hac navigatione recens admodum instituta, hostem non modo regni nostri temporarium sed etiam omnium nationum liberarum hæreditarium, Moscum, magnopere instrui et armari videamus, non solum armis, telis, commeatu, quæ, etsi magna sunt, tamen facilius profecto prohiberi possent, sed etiam aliis multo majoribus rebus, quæ neque satis ullo consilio provideri, et hostem ipsum magis etiam juvare possunt, artificibus inquam ipsis, qui arma, qui tela, qui cætera ejusmodi in illa Barbaria nec visa nec audita hosti fabricare non cessant ; ac præterea quod maxime attendendum est, cognitione omnium, etiam secretissimorum consiliorum nostrorum, quibus illi paulo post, ad interitum, quod absit, omnium nostrorum abutatur, sperandum profecto nobis esse non existimamus, ut hanc ejusmodi navigationem liberam esse patiamur."

U.

"Inter alia mandata hoc habet (Georgius Middleton) præcipuum ut sedulo agat cum Vestra Maiestate de apprehendendo, primo quoque tempore certos istic (at Narva) Anglos (Thomas Glover, Ralph Rutter, James Watson, Christopher Bennet) qui, ad apertum contemptum nostri, ad summam fraudem nostrorum, ad non levem injuriam etiam Vestræ Maiestatis, nimium infidos, injuriosos et iniquos, nobis omnibus esse gesserunt. Qui, uti accepimus, clam, insciis eorum dominis, qui hic in Anglia sunt, cum Polonis fœminis concubia contrahere, et propterea, si ratio apprehendendi eos non maturius, non tutius ineatur, pertimescendum est ne brevi in Poloniam confugiant."

W.

"Magnificis et illustribus Narvensis Emporii, sub potentissimo Imperatore Russiæ, e. c. supremis Gubernatoribus, amicis nostris charissimis. Magnifici, illustres amici charissimi. Misimus hoc anno duos nuncios,

Laurentium Manley et Georgium Middleton, utrumque nostrum perdilectum famulum, cum literis nostris ad Imperatoriam Maiestatem Russiæ—accepimus, facultatem transeundi per vestram Jurisdictionem ad Imperatorem vestrum nostro nuncio Georgio Middletono a vobis esse denegatum. Quæ res eo majorem nobis admirationem commovet, quo certiores nos sumus, vobis incertum esse non posse quæquam certa amicitiæ ratio, quæquam magna et multa mutuæ benevolentiæ officia, inter vestrum Principem et nos, inter nostros utrobique subditos, amice et humaniter hoc tempore intercedunt. Sed cum certæ jam res sunt momenti magni, quas communicandas habemus hoc tempore cum vestro Imperatore et quas intelligere imprimis intererit sua Maiestate, propterea a vobis primum pro vestra erga Principem vestrum obedientia, admodum requirimus, deinde pro vestra, uti speramus, erga nos quoque observantia etiam petimus, ut has nostras literas, quas cum his vestris conjunximus, primo quoque tempore, ad suam Maiestatem perferri curetis. Sic, ut nobis certo aliquando constet (id quod ut constare possit, diligenter procurabimus) vos fuisse in hoc officii parte et vestro principi obsequiosos Magistratus et nobis gratos et officiosos amicos. Quo officio vestro, vos nobis non minimam, et commendationem a vestro Principe, et gratiam a nobis etiam poteretis promereri. Id quod vobis, pro nostra quidem parte, exploratum erit, cum ulla vobis ad id idonea dabitur opportunitas. Fœliciter valeatis," &c.

X.

"Illustris Domine, Menstruum jam prope tempus aderit, quod servitium et operam meam, Regiæ Maiestati per tuam magnificentiam addicerem viamque ostenderem qua sine ulla sanguinis effusione hisce intestinis malis mederi posset. Verum quod tam opera quam inventum illud meum tuæ magnif. non arrideant temporis dilatio testatur. Cum igitur indies ad me legatus Ruthenicus (this is Ssavin) nuncios mittat meumque servitium non sine largo stipendio animo expectet, ego autem nihil omnino sine tuæ magnificentiæ licentia et consilio ea in re, sicut et in aliis, agere mecum constituerim, obnixe oro servo meo (he had first written, uxori meæ) in literis optime instituto, mentem tuam aperte indices prius quam legatus die solis proximo libellos meos supplices Reginæ exhibeat, causamque meæ detentionis in hisce squalidis carceribus ostendat, atque exitum liberum ex hac insula ad Russiam pro me impetret. Hoc gratius nihil mihi feceris meque in perpetuum ita tibi devincies ut si Regia hæc Maiestas mea opera uti volet, hic me at nutum semper paratum habiturus sis; si vero ut discedam hinc concesserit, non Moscovitarum et vicinorum tantum mores, temperamenta, cœli qualitatem, regionis situm, et res ibi memorandas ex literis meis inde ad te datis cognosces, sed et annuatim a me munuscula grati animi erga te significationes accipies quæ lata illa regio protulerit. Postremo, si Regiæ huic Maiestati arte mea prodesse non possum, obnixe oro tuam magnificentiam ut legato pro me apud serenis. suam nostram Reginam oranti Achates adstes, autorque sis Regiæ Maiest. ut me a vinculis hisce liberet. Quod te facturum pro solita tua humanitate atque innata in doctos . . . . non dubito. Valeat tua magnificentia. Bomelii quæso memor sis. Ex vinculis Regiis. Tuæ magnificentiæ addictissimus Eliseus Bomelius, medicus physicus."

Y.

"Ille (Jenkinson) verissime narrabit Serenitati Vestræ mercatores nullos statum et res nostras gubernare sed nosmet ipsos rebus gerendis invigilare ut virginem et reginam decet a Deo optimo maximo constitutam, nec usquam gentium cuiquam principi maiorem præberi obedientiam quam nobis a nostris populis, quod cum Dei optimi maximi munus sit eius numini gratias ob agimus humilissimas et maximas."

Z.

"Elizabetha, &c., Serenissimæ Orine Russiæ Imperatrici, &c., Serenissima et potentissima princeps amica et soror charissima. Singularis, quæ de insigni vestra prudentia virtutibus rarissimis et moribus tanta principe vere dignis fama circumfertur crebro etiam sermone præstantis viri Doctoris Jacobi medici nostri confirmata facit ut serenitatem vestram vero animi affectu amemus, eique fausta et fœlicia omnia ardenter optemus. Ideoque de valetudine et incolumitate vestra non sollicita esse non possimus. Itaque non solum (quod nobis amanter petiit) obstetricem expertam et peritam misimus, quæ partus dolores scientia leniat, sed medicum etiam nostrum qui nostram valetudinem curare solebat, prædictum Doctorem Jacobum una mandamus, hominem vobis antea cognitum fide plenum ut medica arte in qua eucellit, obstetricis actiones dirigat, et vestræ valetudini fideliter inserviat. Cupimus etiam vehementer, non in hiis solum sed in aliis etiam omnibus quæ serenitati vestræ placere possunt, sororio animo libentissime gratificari. Quam Deus optimus maximus, &c. Datum e Regia nostra Grinvici, die mensis Martii 24, anno Domini 1585 (that is, 1586), regni vero nostri 27."

THE END.

For Product Safety Concerns and Information please contact our EU representative GPSR@taylorandfrancis.com
Taylor & Francis Verlag GmbH, Kaufingerstraße 24, 80331 München, Germany

www.ingramcontent.com/pod-product-compliance
Lightning Source LLC
Chambersburg PA
CBHW051623230426
43669CB00013B/2158